After the Madness

AFTER THE MADNESS

A JUDGE'S OWN PRISON MEMOIR

SOL WACHTLER

RANDOM HOUSE   NEW YORK

Library of Congress Cataloging-in-Publication Data

Wachtler, Sol.
After the madness: a judge's own prison memoir / Sol Wachtler.
p.   cm.
Includes index.
ISBN 0-679-45653-8
1. Prisons—New York (State)   2. Wachtler, Sol—Diaries.
3. Prisoners—New York (State)—Diaries.   4. Judges—New York
(State)—Diaries.   I. Title.
HV9475.N7W33   1997   364.16'5'092—dc21   96-41079
[B]

Random House website address: http://www.randomhouse.com/
Printed in the United States of America on acid-free paper

9 8 7 6 5 4 3 2

To Those I Love

You, my family and friends, were the only barrier between me and the cold darkness of despair. Without your gift of love, understanding, and forgiveness I could not have survived.

So many of you visited me and reached out to me while I was hospitalized, in home confinement, and in prison. You brought your warmth of companionship and encouragement and were steadfast in your friendship, kindness, and affection. I shall be eternally grateful.

There is no man so good, who, were he to submit all his thoughts and actions to the laws, would not deserve hanging ten times in his life.

—MONTAIGNE

Do not judge a person until you have been in his position— you do not understand even yourself until the day of your death.

—HILLEL

Acknowledgments

Thank you Richard Curtis, my literary agent, for your confidence. And thank you, Harold Evans, publisher of Random House, for suggesting I write this book and for so quickly agreeing to publish it. I am also indebted to Random House and Harold for choosing Jonathan Karp as my editor and I am grateful to Jonathan for his remarkable intellect, diligence, and good judgment.

I thank my classmate Tom Wolfe and my Albany neighbor, William Kennedy—two remarkable writers and dear friends who spent so much of their valuable time instructing and encouraging me to "find my voice." And Nelson DeMille, a more recent friend and gifted author, for his helpful advice.

Butner Prison

Butner, North Carolina

Introduction

The facts of my case have been well publicized. I dwell on them in this journal not to excuse my wrongful conduct but to explain how I wound up in prison and how the abuse of drugs, even those legally prescribed, and untreated mental disorder, can destroy.

The decomposition of my life began slowly, almost imperceptibly. It began with my weakness in pursuing an affair with Joy Silverman, a married woman who was the stepdaughter of my wife's uncle. When Joy's stepfather died in 1984, I was named trustee of a trust established for her benefit.

It did not take long for our friendship to become an intimate relationship, with all the excitement of clandestine meetings and travel to romantic hideaways. The attention and adoration of this attractive woman, seventeen years my junior, made this—my only affair after thirty-eight years of marital fidelity—an excursion of breathless exhilaration.

My relationship with Joy and my ability to function appropriately ended with the onset of a major depression in the summer of 1990.

William Styron, in his book *Darkness Visible*, describes his depression as a "brain storm," literally, a storm in the brain, one that affects every part of your life and being. He was struck by a major depression when he was sixty. I was the same age when I too felt the first manifestations of this illness.

Styron also wrote of the indelible link between depression and preoccupation with serious imaginary illness: "Unwilling to accept its own gathering deterioration, the mind announces to its indwelling consciousness that it is the body with its correctable defects—not the precious and irreplaceable mind—that is going haywire."

The part of my body that I thought was going haywire was the brain itself. Persistent headaches and a weakness on my left side convinced me that I had a brain tumor. This misbelief was fostered by answers given me by doctors to hypothetical questions and my claustrophobic fear and consequent refusal to submit to a diagnostic magnetic imaging process (magnetic resonance imaging, or MRI), which requires the patient to be encased in a tunnel-like enclosure. Had I taken this diagnostic examination the true nature of my malady, an uncomplicated herniated disc, would have been revealed. The tumor that I was certain was growing in my brain was imaginary.

While suffering from this profound depression, and not wanting to bear the stigma of seeing a psychiatrist, I attempted to self-medicate. I was able to convince one doctor to prescribe Tenuate, an amphetaminelike drug that I used to elevate my energy level and thereby mask my depression (I took 1400 of them in a four-month period). And because I could not sleep, I was able to convince another doctor to prescribe a hypnotic called Halcion (I took 280 of them during the same four months). Still another doctor gave me a prescription for Pamelor, an antidepressant. And there were others. All of these drugs taken by themselves have dangerous side effects. Taken together the reaction can be devastating. In my case it contributed to and exacerbated a diagnosed manic-depressive (bipolar) disorder.

At first I thought my breakup with Joy, initiated by me, would be a positive step in my effort to combat depression. I would no longer have to lead a double life and continue to deceive my wife. That's what I thought. But I missed Joy. Her absence from my life started to take on a new dimension. In my despair, I began thinking of her as someone who could bring me solace. In my hopelessness, she came to symbolize hope. I felt a longing—not for Joy, but for the person whom I imagined Joy to be. I felt that if she would come back to me, I would be whole again.

For seven years I had been the one Joy turned to for advice on how to deal with her own problems and those involving her children. I wanted her to need me again. To accomplish this I embarked on a bizarre campaign of writing outrageous and harassing letters, letters that my mania convinced me would bring Joy back to me.

I went so far as to send a note containing a condom in an envelope addressed to Joy's fourteen-year-old daughter. I knew that her daughter would never receive it because I identified the envelope in such a way as to invite Joy's opening and intercepting it. As I anticipated, the letter was intercepted and never received by her daughter—but the fact that I did such a thing, calculated to distress Joy, was another of my unpardonable and shameful acts.

My behavior never brought Joy back to me for help. Instead it brought her to the F.B.I. and, ultimately, me to prison and ruin.

Shortly after my arrest on November 7, 1992, I was compelled to have the MRI scan that I had resisted for so long. It revealed UBOs (unidentified bright objects) "in the deep right parietal region" of my brain, where I thought my brain tumor was located. According to one study, an increased number of these UBOs "signal hyperintensities suggestive of abnormal tissue" found in bipolar patients.

The aberrational conduct exhibited by me prior to my arrest suggested mental illness, but diagnosis was necessary in order to determine treatment. For this purpose I was referred to Drs. William A.

Frosch and Frank T. Miller as the primary examining psychiatrists and to the Payne Whitney Psychiatric Clinic of the New York Hospital–Cornell Medical Center as the place for the examination.

Dr. Frosch, a professor of psychiatry at Cornell University Medical College, was the chairman of the Department of Psychiatry of the Payne Whitney Psychiatric Clinic and is considered one of the nation's foremost psychiatrists. Dr. Miller, the primary author of the report concerning my illness, was another psychiatrist of note. As a diplomate of the American Board of Psychiatry and Neurology, he practiced psychiatry under Dr. Frosch at Payne Whitney and was later named chairman of its Department of Affective Disorders.

On November 22, 1992, with the consent of the prosecutor, I was allowed to be taken to Payne Whitney for this examination. I was accompanied by an armed guard and was required to wear an electronic monitor strapped to my ankle. I was checked into the hospital under an assumed name in an effort to avoid the press.

My first day at Payne Whitney was absorbed by physical examinations and written and verbal psychiatric tests. My family members were also interviewed, which disclosed my family history of depression and the brutal suicide of my maternal grandmother.

I was then interviewed by Dr. Frank Miller. In our initial conversation, he asked me to tell him about my relationship with Joy and to describe the conduct that had led to my arrest.

I told him my story, complete with the details of how I assumed the guise of a fictitious lowlife whom I named David Purdy. It was the David Purdy character who was to harass Joy. My "plan" was to convince Joy that she needed my assistance, the assistance of her onetime protector, to rid her of the Purdy menace.

I remember thinking that my interview with Dr. Miller was very brief, lasting only a few minutes. I also remember thinking that I was particularly articulate in explaining my aberrational behavior. Apparently my memory of that session was flawed. The following is from Dr. Miller's notes of this initial interview:

On November 23, 1992, during my first interview of him at New York Hospital, Judge Wachtler's speech was pressured, loquacious, tangential, and circumstantial. It took approximately three hours to get from him information that typically takes 45 to 60 minutes. This occurred because he was unstoppable in his pressure of speech. His mood was expansive and grandiose. He did not understand the gravity of the situation. . . . For approximately 45 minutes, Judge Wachtler imitated the David Purdy character. When I realized that I was not able to interrupt this monologue I asked two other physicians to join us in the hope that their presence in the room would calm him.

To my dismay their presence only served to intensify his display and I asked them to leave. Although the situation of the interview was sobering and grim, he was not able to appreciate or grasp it. He had very limited insight and his judgement was poor, even though his higher intellectual functioning was intact.

Drs. Miller and Frosch continued their examination and testing, and after my three-week hospitalization, issued their diagnosis, called the Miller Report, which concluded with the finding: "Judge Wachtler's severe mental illness is best categorized as a drug induced and exacerbated bipolar disorder [manic depression]."

Less clinical were the observations made months earlier by my wife, Joan, a trained certified social worker, who dealt professionally with a patient population. Well aware of my depression, she was to make a diary entry in October 1991:

Something is terribly wrong. He's acting strangely. Very depressed, irritable, emotional. Moves his clothes in and out of our house. Spending little time at home. Came back from Florida after taking his mother down and told me it was the worst 3 days of his life—death, old people—he "feels he's dying." Doesn't understand what's happening to him. Feels "disassociated" with himself. Says a beautiful day is ugly. Hasn't slept in weeks even with pills—lost 15 pounds. Doesn't eat at all—drug related?

The Florida trip to which Joan referred was when I took my mother to her North Miami Beach apartment, something I had been doing for years. But this time I noticed that the residents of her building, who had been in their seventies when they moved in—like my mother—were now in their eighties and nineties. They were aging in place, and although death had thinned their numbers you had the sense of being among a great many very old and very frail people.

Men and women whom I remembered being parts of couples were now alone—widows and widowers. They sat around the pool, staring off into space, seeming to remember or trying to remember a different time—a less lonely time.

I remembered walking past a kitchen window. An old man sat motionless, reading a newspaper. There was a small fan atop a table, oscillations in a gentle arc causing his paper to riffle. When I walked past his window again, an hour later, nothing had changed. I'm certain that he was staring at the same page, his head held at the same angle. Was he dead? Did it matter?

I remember wondering what a person like that had to live for—and then I started wondering what I had to live for. I remembered a poem I read a long time ago, "Richard Cory." It told a story of a man who had all the blessings of family and wealth a person could wish for. Everyone envied him. And then one day he went home in his elegant carriage and put a bullet through his head.

I shared these ruminations with Joan at the time and she pleaded with me to see a psychiatrist. At first I rejected her suggestion out of hand. I could not compromise my reputation as a sound-thinking jurist by admitting the need for a psychiatrist. How would the public perceive—or trust—a jurist charged with the responsibility of deciding questions concerning their freedom or fortune if they knew that he was in need of psychiatric treatment? But the pain—and I mean that word in its literal sense—the pain of my depression was a torment that I could no longer endure. Although I would not see a psychiatrist, I did agree to see my physician, an internist.

I saw the doctor privately on Sunday mornings. I felt that too many questions would be invited if I were seen visiting the physician's office. I told the doctor only what I wanted to reveal. I did not speak of my recently ended affair with Joy, or the fact that I was taking the "upper" Tenuate on a regular basis to mask the agony and malaise of my depression. I was ashamed of both my adulterous affair and my growing drug dependency; both connoted weaknesses I was unwilling to confess. I told of my intense headaches and left-side debility, as well as my suspicions of a brain tumor.

She was quick to diagnose my clinical depression and urged me to consult a psychiatrist. I refused. I could not suffer the stigma that society imposes on someone who seeks to remedy a defect of the mind. A stigma which follows the taking of therapy, medication, and treatment. To seek such a remedy would be to publicly confess to such a defect, which my vanity and ambition would not permit.

The lesson of Thomas Eagleton, the U.S. senator from Missouri, was still on the minds of political leaders. He was dropped as a vice presidential candidate in 1972 when it was discovered that he was treated psychiatrically. Although psychiatric treatment given me probably would not be as dramatic as that which he received, would I be subject to the same negative political attitude if I saw a psychiatrist prior to seeking the Republican nomination for governor of New York?

She urged me to take an MRI, to learn more about my suspected tumor. I told her of my claustrophobia. I would only accept an X-ray. She argued that this was a poor substitute, and indeed it was. It did nothing to confirm the presence of the astrocytoma, the brain tumor that I believed, indeed was certain, had implanted itself inside my head.

Even without my telling her of the Tenuate, the doctor thought my ingestion of the various medications that I did tell her about—mostly over-the-counter—was dangerous. She ordered me to stop. When I told her that I would not be able to sleep without the Unisom, Percogesic, and codeine I had been taking, she prescribed Halcion as a substitute. The nortriptyline Pamelor was prescribed to help me overcome the acute melancholia that was plaguing me.

She continued to see me Sundays, monitoring my medication and my mood. I told her I had quit taking other medications. I lied. I was still taking the Tenuate, and all the other drugs that had taken a hold on my life. Between the spring of 1991 and the day of my arrest in 1992, I was to take some five thousand pills of one sort or another.

After my arrest, Dr. Donald F. Klein of the New York State Psychiatric Institute of Columbia University, perhaps this nation's leading psychopharmacologist, was one of those who examined me and studied my case. He concluded: "It was during the period of high, chronic consumption of Halcion and Tenuate that Judge Wachtler's judgment became gravely impaired. . . . Similarly, the chronic use of high-dose, high-potency benzodiazepines is associated with states of disinhibition [and] with impaired foresight and social judgment."

I have tried to describe my depression, the inner surface of the abyss I was living in. I can tell you about the physical manifestations—the loss of appetite, the constant weeping, the sleeplessness, the fluttering that seemed to fill my stomach. I can speak of the imagined brain tumor that became an inimicable part of my depression. I am convinced now that my "tumor" stemmed from my desire to accomplish an end—I believed it would kill me because some part of me did not want to live.

Certain aspects of depression can be delineated, but the horrors of depression defy description. When in full crisis, the suffering seems endless and unbearable. I was going so low, I felt I could touch those scary places of powerlessness and inadequacy.

And then came the episodes of mania, or what in my case was really hypomania, the opposite end of the mood swing.

I received a pamphlet in the mail the other day from the National Depressive and Manic-Depressive Association. In it there are poetic descriptions of both extremes of bipolar, or manic-depressive, disorder. On depression: "Slowly, slowly the shadow descends . . . all life, all color receding into darkness. I feel only grief and pain. . . . Where is my hope? Where is my life?" And on mania: "Screeching thoughts race on the road to oblivion." And on the combination of the two:

"The highest, biggest, quickest, can't keep up with it all, can do it all, from can't possibly fail to irritation to rage, and finally to the lowest, murky chamber of hell where the darkest mood slowly strangles every hope. . . . And, maybe, in-between, all is all right."

Manic behavior is characterized by a "high," a euphoric state that can be combined with irritability and sometimes paranoia. It is characterized by unrealistic overconfidence and grandiosity. You have a sense that you can do anything and do it exceedingly well.

Have a speech to deliver? "I don't have to prepare—my head is full of the world's greatest speeches—just give me a platform and watch the audience. I can make them laugh or cry—they will accept everything I say as if my words were spoken from Mount Sinai. They will be moved to follow me wherever I lead—they will adore me."

Have a problem? "I can resolve it. I have been endowed with a wisdom seldom bestowed on others. It is a kind of gift where solutions to problems seem to appear out of nowhere, fully formed and without obstacles."

You have something to say to me? "Say it. I may not listen, but you will think I'm listening and when you're finished you will be amazed at my ability to grasp the problem and arrive at a solution. Most amazing: My solution, no matter how preposterous it may seem to you, will be correct."

Get some sleep? "I find that I don't need any. For so many years I wasted all that time sleeping. I do my best thinking while lying awake, my mind racing, while others squander precious hours slumbering."

I'm talking too fast? "No I'm not—it's just that you're listening too slowly. Pay attention to me—you can learn a great deal."

You know how sometimes you have an idea while lying in bed at night, and when you get up in the morning the idea appears to be foolish? Well, in my case when I examined my nocturnal idea in the light of day, it seemed more brilliant than it had the night before.

> *The highest, biggest, quickest, can't keep up with it all, can do it all, from can't possibly fail to irritation to rage, and finally to the lowest, murky chamber of hell where the darkest mood slowly strangles every hope. . . . And, maybe, in-between, all is all right.*

If you should wonder how someone with such mood swings could function as Chief Judge of New York, I would refer you to Dr. John S. McIntyre, the president of the American Psychiatric Association, who wrote, commenting on my case:

> A patient may have severe mental illness which results in serious symptoms, including psychotic symptoms, in one area of his/her life and yet that person may function very effectively in a number of other spheres. This coexistence of excellent functioning in some areas and significantly disturbed thinking and behavior in one or more other areas is frequently true in bipolar disorder, especially the manic phase.

Dr. Miller noted that he had "treated numerous individuals who are manic depressive, and whose illness, though serious, had remained unrecognized to most co-workers, family and friends, until progressively bizarre behavior had become so pronounced as to make the illness obvious." And so it was in my case.

The manifestations of my bizarre behavior were noticed by my colleagues and staff, who in interviews after my arrest told of "instances where they discussed matters with him at length that he subsequently could not recall"; of speeches I delivered that they described as "disjointed, far too lengthy for the occasion, and noticeably agitated, which was very uncharacteristic for a man who was a known and an extremely polished speaker."

On one occasion I spoke to a group of high school teachers about some arcane legal doctrine. When a member of my staff suggested that it was the wrong speech for that audience, I told him that I knew better than anyone what my audiences would want to hear. I was terribly wrong about that speech and several others. On another occasion, I had all the members of the courthouse staff assemble in the courtroom in Albany for "an important message from the Chief Judge." I drove the three hours from Long Island to Albany to deliver "the message," which consisted of my telling the large gathering, through tears, that I "loved them very much."

The courthouse employees left wondering what I had in mind, as did my law clerks when—instead of the accustomed intense review of cases—I handled the discussion of them in summary fashion while driving in a car, or in a barbershop while I was getting a haircut. Speeches and matters that I once handled meticulously I now disposed of in an uncharacteristic grandiose and scattered manner.

Screeching thoughts racing on the road to oblivion . . .

An excerpt from Dr. Miller's report:

By June, the combination of prescription medications had initiated an increasingly intense pattern of manic behavior. Judge Wachtler continued to take Halcion and Tenuate on a daily basis. In June, while on a trip to Arizona, for the purpose of lecturing, he asked the sponsors of the conference to provide him with a room and a typewriter claiming he had a very important opinion to write. Instead, he wrote a letter to Ms. Silverman in which he gave his fictional creation David Purdy "a mission. . . ."

I was in Sedona, Arizona, to address the Nevada Bar Association. I couldn't sleep. I had taken two Halcion and two Unisom and still I couldn't sleep. Was it the three Tenuate I had taken that afternoon to keep me from depression? Maybe, but at the time I didn't think I really needed the sleep—what I needed was time to think.

And suddenly it came to me, a manically induced epiphany. Purdy would write a masterful letter outlining how much he knew of Joy's relationship with her new boyfriend, David Samson, and how it would be in her best interest to have Samson not build an incinerator in Linden, New Jersey. I had read in the paper that Samson was the lawyer for someone building that incinerator. "How clever of me," my racing mind told me. "This will surely move her to call me."

The next morning I was soaring mentally—I actually believed that I had devised an incredibly brilliant plan. It took me three hours to type this "definitive letter," which I remembered as consisting of several pages. After my arrest I saw the letter. It was in the possession of the prosecutor. It was typed on a single page, consisted of three paragraphs, and made absolutely no sense.

When I returned from Sedona, my continuing delusion told me that I had to do more than simply mail the Purdy letter to Joy. To do this right—to make it really work—I had to do it as Purdy would do it.

So as soon as I returned from Sedona, I went to Linden, New Jersey, where Purdy was supposed to have been sojourning. I went with my Stetson hat, string tie, and boots—because that is how Purdy would have dressed—and walked the streets of Linden in the small hours of the morning. Past the movie theater and the post office next door. I remember the sun, as it was rising, casting a shaft of light on a particular mailbox. I took this as a sign. I mailed the letter, certain that Joy would receive it and call her old and dear friend Sol for his assistance in thwarting the demon Purdy.

But Joy did not call. Inasmuch as I was still her trustee, I used this as a pretext to call her five days later. I wanted to see if I could discern whether the Purdy letter had had any effect on her. It was also important for me to know whether she suspected me of being her tormenter; if she did, my Purdy character had failed.

She answered the phone, but said she could not speak at the moment—she had to call back. The reason, as I found out after my arrest, was that she wanted to install a recording device to tape my conversation. During my conversation with her, the tape of which

Joy turned over to the prosecutor, she did not mention the Purdy letter. She said nothing to indicate that anything or anyone was bothering her. This was a sure sign to my mania-fed mind that she knew Purdy was a fiction. She knew that I, and not Purdy, was her nemesis.

After another bout of depression, and a sense of remorse for having harassed Joy, I returned to my delusional state of mind and the belief that I had to replace the harsh Purdy with a "person" of more gentility. While on another speaking engagement—this time in Oregon—I decided to replace Purdy with "Theresa O'Connor."

Theresa O'Connor's role in my bizarre scenario was to tell Joy that she, Theresa, had discovered the misdeeds of David Purdy, and that she had frightened him off. That Joy had nothing more to fear from him. My thought was that once Joy was made to realize that Purdy was no longer in her life, she would tell me about his existence and Theresa's intervention. Her telling me would be the sign I was looking for to indicate that Joy did not believe I was Purdy.

When I had written the letter using the name of David Purdy, I wanted to do everything possible to construct a character who had all the vestiges of a real person. I went so far as to call and learn all I could about the Y.M.C.A. in Houston, Texas, where my mind told me Purdy would live. I felt the same need with respect to developing a sense of Theresa O'Connor. I had to do this right. If I was going to write a letter over the signature of Theresa O'Connor, I had to know everything there was to know about her. My mania told me that Joy was not easily fooled. I had to think and act as Theresa O'Connor would think and act.

I imagined her as a devout Catholic—so I found a church in Linden, New Jersey, and called the pastor, ostensibly to get information and directions for a visit. And then I drove to Linden. The Church of the Holy Family was closed, but I was able to walk the neighborhood where Theresa would have lived. How did I find time for all of this with my busy schedule? Easy. When you are in a manic state you have boundless energy—you have to in order to be capable of doing all the wondrous things you were capable of doing.

I continued to call Joy on one pretext or another. The letters that Theresa O'Connor sent to her had no apparent effect. The only news that came to me, from Joy and others, was that she was happy and content in her new life with her new love. She neither wanted me, needed me, nor even missed me. I was now convinced, more than ever, that she knew I was both Purdy and O'Connor.

It was at the time of this mental upheaval that I became engaged in a duel with Mario Cuomo, the governor of New York State, concerning the court budget, which resulted in my bringing a lawsuit against him to preserve the integrity of the court system and the independence of the judiciary. Briefly, Cuomo wanted to cut the funds for the state courts, and I fought this attempt, which I thought would cripple our court system. In the middle of all of this—and far more disturbing to me—my mother-in-law, Elsie, whom I adored, was diagnosed as being terminally ill with cancer.

It wasn't only my imagined tumor, or the lawsuit with the governor, or the knowledge that Joy was now with another man, or Elsie's illness. It was depression. I felt a compelling need to be by myself, so much so that I found myself checking into hotels under aliases. When I awoke in those strange places, I could stay in bed in the mornings, and there was no one there to ask me, "What is the matter?" The fact is, I didn't know what was the matter but I knew I didn't want anyone asking. I just wanted to be left alone.

And then, after taking enough medication, the depression would suddenly lift, and there was the "high"—the mania.

Joy knew me so well. No matter what I wrote or what I did or how I disguised myself, she knew it was me. Her onetime protector, confidant, close friend, and lover had become a source of aggravated annoyance.

From Dr. Miller's report:

> At this point, his original goal of having Ms. Silverman call him for help and guidance was redefined by the compulsion to convince Ms. Silverman that Judge Wachtler was not involved with Purdy or O'Connor. All that followed was now motivated by this goal made pervasive by a manic state.

And in this state, I figured out a way to prove to her that I hadn't done anything, that there really was a David Purdy. I would find a day in August when she was at her summer home in Southampton, and actually have Purdy drop off a note at her apartment house in the city. And her doorman would say, "A fat old toothless gentleman calling himself David Purdy dropped off the note." Then she would know that I was not David Purdy. I thought myself so clever.

First I called Joy's Southampton home to be sure she was not in the city. She answered the phone. After a moment of silence she spoke: "You again," she said, "tsk-tsk-tsk, poor baby." I was right: She still thought—she knew—that I was her tormentor. She would be convinced otherwise, though, when David Purdy appeared *in person.*

And so I put on my cowboy boots, my Stetson hat, and a string tie—the same way I had dressed in Linden—and I walked down Park Avenue. I should say sauntered down Park Avenue, for eight blocks, until I came to her apartment house door. There I delivered the note to her doorman—a person who would have recognized Sol Wachtler in an instant. But he didn't recognize David Purdy. I thought myself perfect. Without even wearing a disguise, I was able to walk down Park Avenue and deliver a note to Joy's doorman and no one recognized me. I had made myself invisible. I was ecstatic. I believed: *I can do it all.*

Two weeks had gone by, and Joy still hadn't called. Could she still believe I was David Purdy? And then the awful truth dawned on me. She did know it was me! Every year before Evan, Joy's son, went off to college he discussed his course options with me. But this September he didn't call. Every year for the past several years I had delivered New York Mets souvenirs and Mets tickets to the son of Joy's best friend. The delivery of the souvenirs was always followed by a letter from him telling of his summer and expressing gratitude. This September, after I had the delivery made, he didn't write. And when my secretary called to see if he had received the gifts he said, "Yes," and abruptly hung up the phone. Obviously Joy had told her friend not to communicate with me. And Eleanor, Joy's and my friend and shared therapist, did not return my many phone calls.

They were all certain that I was David Purdy.

My distorted judgment told me that in order to prove them wrong, Purdy would have to make another visit. This time he would leave a note and ask for money as a price for his disappearance. How much should he ask for? $200,000? No, that's too much. It occurred to me that if Purdy asked for too much, and Joy didn't give it to him, then I wouldn't know whether her refusal was because she knew Purdy was me or because she just didn't want to spend that much money to get rid of him.

I decided to make it $20,000, to be left at the beauty parlor around the corner from her apartment, where I used to pick her up during our days of rendezvous. If Joy left the money it would prove to me and my skewed sense of reality that she believed that there really was a David Purdy and maybe—just maybe—she would call me. "Sol," she would say, "there is this awful man who has been harassing me. He has even called me on the phone. I feel so bad that I may have suspected you of being this fellow. And now he is demanding that I pay him to leave me alone. What should I do? Can you help me?" I thought myself so clever.

For more than a month before my arrest, my every move was being monitored by the F.B.I. The phone calls I was making to Joy were being received on a telephone that was installed and hardwired in Joy's apartment by the F.B.I. Of course, I never saw or picked up the money. I was followed by the F.B.I. on the day the money was to be left and I was arrested.

•   •   •

After my arrest, there followed a brief period of hospitalization. Then, for almost a year, because the prosecutor refused to consent to my being allowed out of my home on bail, I was subject to house arrest. During this period of hospitalization and house arrest, I withdrew from my drug abuse and was restored to normalcy with lithium and an antidepressant to control the diagnosed bipolar disorder. But as curative as the drugs were, even more so was my greater understanding of my malady, which I gained from an extremely well-written and well-researched book *Touched with Fire*, by a professor of psychiatry, Dr. Kay Redfield Jamison. It was sent to me by a journalist who took an interest in my case.

Dr. Jamison vividly describes the manifestations of bipolar disorder. She writes of the focused energy that can become an inspirational, compelling, and creative force. Perhaps I can trace some of my earlier accomplishments to the same driving force. Had my most recent manic focus been on positive goals rather than destructive aberration, I might be writing entries from the governor's mansion rather than a prison cell.

Please don't misunderstand. Being bipolar is not and should not be an excuse for criminal conduct. It should not even be a factor when assessing guilt or innocence. But the public and law enforcement should be aware of the manifestation of this disease so that someone who is afflicted can receive treatment as soon as possible. And if the mania or hypomania drives someone to commit acts that are antisocial or criminal in nature, that person should be stopped or arrested before the conduct escalates and causes more harm.

A month before my conduct reached serious criminal proportions, the prosecutor and scores of F.B.I. agents were observing and monitoring my every move. Proper law enforcement would have dictated that I be stopped or arrested sooner than I was—not only for my sake, but for the sake of Joy Silverman, who had to abide the prosecutor's nurturing of my criminal manic behavior.

Of course, the prosecutor was not interested in stopping me, through arrest or otherwise, until my criminal conduct increased to more serious, dramatic, and publicity-worthy proportions. When he was criticized for failing to recognize the implications of my mental illness, he responded that he did not consider me to be impaired mentally because I "was not walking around in a bathrobe and screaming like a banshee."

I went to prison on September 28, 1993, and was released to a halfway house on August 29, 1994. In prison I kept a journal, more for the purpose of preserving my own sanity than for the recording of experiences. I realized that such a record would be of interest to very few people. I would never have thought to open the pages of that journal again, except for a series of provocative events.

Shortly after I was released, there was an article in the November 1994 *Reader's Digest* entitled: "Must Our Prisons Be Resorts?" The author tells of his visits to certain prisons, which brought him to the unshakable conclusion that in most prisons, "Felons have access to a startling array of creature comforts" and that we "should require public officials to explain why prisons need to be resorts."

A few months later, I heard the author of this article being interviewed by a radio talk-show host. His article had been expanded into a book entitled *Criminal Justice?* His theme: "Today's correctional facility is an expensive, even enticing, hybrid of camp, clinic, and community college." He concludes that "American taxpayers are forced to provide programs and 'perks' without charge to those who rob, rape, or kill them."

While I was in prison I was able to buy a small portable radio. It had to be purchased at the prison commissary and cost me two months' salary from my prison work, doing orderly and other chores. With that perk I was able to listen to the radio at night in my cell. I listened, because there was little other choice, to radio talk shows where a host, often proud to boast of his political conservatism, speaks to callers. Usually the callers and the host agree with each other on all subjects, and proceed to massage each other's egos. It's as if their agreement on a conclusion makes the conclusion correct, even if neither knows what he is talking about.

I remember listening to one of these talk-show experts who was bemoaning the fact that prisoners enjoy the luxury of private rooms. I listened to this as I lay in one of the two double-decked bunks that filled my twelve-by-fourteen-foot cell at Rochester Prison, Minnesota. There were four of us in that cell. The only ventilation was a window that opened a few inches from the top. The four of us froze in the Minnesota winter; in the summer we were bathed in sweat, cramped on three-inch-thick oilcloth-covered mattresses that seemed to generate their own heat.

The talk-show host concluded that there is no reason why there shouldn't be *two* inmates in one double-decked bunk in each cell — to which I whispered, "Amen. To accomplish that they will have to move two of my cellmates."

Ordinarily I would say: So what? What difference does it make what is written on the subject of contemporary prison life or what talk-show hosts and their "guests" say?

But then I reflect on the fact that this kind of false information creates a political climate that invites repression and the call to make hard time harder. I remember the public approbation received by politicians who called for the removal of the free weights from the prison yard. (No one ever explained that the prisoners paid for those weights themselves out of the profits made from the commissary. And no one was there to explain that the prisoners who remained the most docile were those who set goals and were able to meet them by lifting weights.)

There seems to be no one there to tell the public that by restoring some degree of self-esteem to the prisoner incarcerated for a nonviolent crime, we can improve his reentry into society. And, whether we like it or not, almost all of them are coming out. If the prisoner is made to feel like garbage when he is in prison, he will for certain act like garbage when he is released. But the unanswered thrust of the political rhetoric, as well as much of talk radio, seems to be: because they acted like animals to get into prison, they should be treated like animals while they are in prison.

Then, of course, there is the constant political theme of new prison construction, using funds that are taken away from drug and mental-health treatment facilities, family and child-care services, vocational and employment training and placement, and the many other programs that lead to community stability.

Prisons for the incarceration of violent criminals are necessary. Predators who destroy our cities and communities, who cause our citizenry to live behind triple-locked doors, should be taken off the streets. But I am convinced that it is a wasteful, counterproductive distraction to use prisons for the nonviolent offender who is capable of redemption or rehabilitation.

To differ from the accepted verity that there should be more and harsher prisons, is to sound like a unrepentant liberal — but the rage to punish has become too intense in this country.

And so I open the pages of this journal with the hope that the reader will gain some greater knowledge of what our prisons and prisoners are really like. Perhaps there can be an acceptance of the fact that not everyone in prison is subhuman, that there should be a difference in the punishment meted out for nonviolent and violent crime, and that the goal of imprisonment should be to promote public safety instead of to punish sinners.

Aware of the caveat that you can't believe anything you hear in prison and only half of what you see, I have done my best to substantiate the facts and events that I have described. Because certain of the prisoners are or were in mental health units, this was not always a simple task. In most instances I was able to obtain presentence investigation reports prepared by probation departments, actual trial transcripts, and court records, proceedings, and decisions. In other instances I had to rely on what I was told.

In preparation of the manuscript, I took the liberty of rewriting portions of my original journal to make them more readable. All of the persons about whom I have written are real. I have changed a few names and have made a composite of some case histories, in order to protect individuals whose cases are still pending before the courts or other tribunals. For these reasons the following pseudonyms are used for actual persons: "Charley," the drug dealer; "Vinny," the cocaine dealer; "Max," the lawyer; "Jim McCrory and Dave Pistone," bank robbers; "Jim," counterfeiter; "Dan Deer," rapist; "Mike Kelly," armed bank robber; "Stan Bolle," drug dealer; "Reggie Johnson," drug dealer. Also pseudonyms are "Roger Gabel," prison official; and "Jack LaFarge" and "Betty McHugh," my schoolmates.

September 1993

September 27, 1993

It would have been a grand funeral. The governor and legislative leaders of New York State, not to mention the luminaries of the state and national judiciary, would have been there. My virtues as a judge, judicial reformer, and humanitarian would have been magnified and extolled from the pulpit and trumpeted on the editorial pages of *The New York Times*.

A few months later, one or more of the courthouses in this state would have borne my name. And people would tearfully say, "He could have been governor—maybe even vice president—or a member of the United States Supreme Court."

All this would have happened if I had died a year ago. But I didn't—and tomorrow I leave for federal prison.

The thought terrifies me.

How will the other prisoners relate to a former judge? The last person to whom they had turned for sympathy was a judge, and it was an unsympathetic judge who had had them dragged off to prison. How will they treat me? What will they do to me?

I fear the claustrophobic panic of being locked in a cell. The idea of losing my freedom, of being caged like an animal with other animals, of being stripped of my dignity—all of these images have made me genuinely afraid of going to prison.

The terror I felt watching those prison movies when I was much younger and the images of hopelessness that I witnessed during my more recent visits to penitentiaries are all that I think about.

I have had almost a year to prepare myself. A year spent mostly in electronically monitored home confinement, part of it with armed guards in my kitchen. That seemed intolerable, but it was not prison. How do you prepare yourself, psychologically, to go to prison—to enter a world that is so fearsome. Even now, as I write this entry, knowing that I leave tomorrow for prison, I cannot accept the fact that I'm going.

Does someone who is terminally ill really accept the fact that death is imminent, or is there always the hope of the miraculous cure, the last-minute reprieve?

I have spent most of the day with my wife, Joan, and my four children and their spouses. I have told them again how sorry I am to have brought such misery and sadness to our family. I have reviewed my will and our financial and other arrangements, and have completed whatever had to be done to allow life in my absence to continue in as orderly a fashion as possible.

There are lapses of silence—and tears.

Everyone makes an effort to be as upbeat as possible, but I have a sense of what each is feeling. I am certain they feel sorry for me. And although my children would neither admit nor give any indication of it, I am certain they feel a sense of shame that their father, of whom they were always so proud, is on his way to prison.

Tonight Joan and I will be alone. She will help me pack the few things that the probation officer said I can bring with me. Neither of us will sleep.

I get out of bed and go to an upstairs room that I used as an office during this period of home confinement. I open the file cabinet labeled THE UNITED STATES OF AMERICA V. SOL WACHTLER. It is filled with legal documents and court papers. Hundreds of papers, copies of motions, memoranda, written and filed during a time when we thought it possible to keep me from going to prison. The remnants of a lost battle.

Among these papers are copies of letters sent to Judge Anne Thompson, who sentenced me. And among those letters is one written to her by Joan. When I first read it, knowing of her enduring love despite the pain I had caused her, I wept. I read her prayer again, and again I weep.

August 29, 1993

Dear Judge Thompson:

. . . There hasn't been a day since Sol's arrest that I haven't cried—not for myself, not for the betrayal of our marriage, but for Sol. I am saddened when I think of what has happened to his life plan and of society's loss. I am unable to move on beyond the tragic consequences of his mental illness. I can only think about his unselfish lifetime of public service and good works. The tangible remains of this dedication are now housed in rented storage space. Cartons of plaques and awards. Fifteen hoods representing as many honorary degrees, the appreciation of law schools, universities, social service and policy organizations, and community groups. Memorabilia of dedication—all locked away in an anonymous crypt.

Sol Wachtler was never greedy, he never misused his office. He was sick. It is regrettable that those in law enforcement and others who watched what he was doing did not reach out to help him. Has our civilization so deteriorated that no one would exercise even that much compassion? I beg you with all my heart, not only to hear what I have tried to tell you, but please hear those others who know him—those who experienced the texture of this man's life. Through our testaments, please understand the person Sol Wachtler.

September 28, 1993

I keep thinking of the words of a folk song I once heard: "I wished I was dead—never knew there was worse things than dyin'."

With all of the debasement and humiliation that have become a part of my life during this past year since my arrest, I must now confront the added and ultimate disgrace not only of going to prison, but of being in prison.

As I was facing this apogee, or should I say nadir, of my shame, I was hoping that there would be no press to greet me, no pictures taken to feed the hungry maw of the tabloids. The judge who sentenced me had recommended that I serve my time at a federal camp in Pensacola, Florida. For some inexplicable reason, this was changed by the Bureau of Prisons three days before I was to begin my sentence. I was told later that the order came from high sources in Washington who wanted me to endure this high-security prison in Butner, North Carolina, rather than the less onerous demands of a federal prison camp.

Perhaps, because of the last-minute change in designation, the press would be waiting for me in Pensacola instead of here.

No such luck.

As the vehicle transporting me pulled up to the prison, the first thing I saw was the coiled, gleaming, and menacing razor-wire fence surrounding the squat gray buildings. The second was the inevitable cameras and microphones.

"Not nearly the number of reporters who were waiting for Jim Bakker, the evangelist," the warden later told me, "but then again, he was from around here."

I was greeted by four prison guards. They seemed to know me by sight so that, without introduction, I was searched and handcuffed. The duffel bag that Joan and I had packed so methodically the day before was taken from me, and I was led, hands manacled behind my back, down a long corridor to the prison receiving office.

After the routine of again being photographed and fingerprinted, I was introduced to the stunning invasion of privacy known as a "strip search." Of course I knew what a strip search was—I had written about this procedure in more than one of my court opinions. But knowing what it is—even knowing the necessity for it—does not prepare you for the experience of being stripped naked in front of strangers who then examine every crevice and orifice of your body.

For me as a judge there were many occasions when I engaged my colleagues in discussion and debate concerning the indignities inflicted upon prisoners. In recent years, many courts, mine included, have made the point that an individual does not forfeit all constitutional rights upon conviction of a crime. The right of freedom of speech, freedom of religion, protection against invidious discrimination, and even the protection of due process of law to prevent additional deprivation of life, liberty, or property all survive incarceration.

As should be expected, a sentence of imprisonment must and necessarily does carry with it certain deprivations, such things as liberty and, along with it, as one of our decisions put it, "the limitation of rights made necessary by the realities of confinement and the legitimate goals and policies of the correctional system."

When "strip-search cases" were being presented to our court, the government argued that these sorts of searches were necessary to be certain that illegal substances and weapons were not smuggled into prison. Prisoners' rights groups would argue that contraband is not brought into prisons in so obvious a way, and that the essential element of the strip search was to humiliate a detainee or the newly arrived prisoner.

I knew that a person subjected to this kind of public exposure must feel embarrassed, but I had come to believe that these searches were necessary and not simply another kind of punishment. Now I know what these searches are really like. I have been educated, not from reading a brief or from the words of a lawyer describing what a prisoner may have told him. I have learned by being commanded to strip, bend, spread, lift, and do a sort of naked and public pirouette that is beyond embarrassment.

If I were to discuss these cases with my colleagues again, I would be able to tell them of the humiliation which is visited by a strip search. My decision in the cases would be no different, but my discussion of the cases as well as the decisions relating to them would be more informed.

I believe these searches are necessary for prison security and to detect contraband that an inmate might attempt to smuggle into the prison vacuum. A strip search would fall within those permissive invasions "made necessary by the realities of confinement and the legitimate goals and policies of the correctional system." But if their secondary purpose is indeed to dehumanize, that too is accomplished.

As my handcuffed journey along the Butner corridors continued ("Stay to the left!"), I again began to wonder how I was going to survive a life behind bars. I kept telling myself that having endured military service and a rootless youth without friends, I should be able to survive, to get past these next fifteen months. But I was much younger then. Now I was close to sixty-five, more than twice the age of the guards and most of the other prisoners. And the last forty years of my life had been spent as a person given deference and comfort; the years had softened me.

I was now joined by other new prisoners and, again stripped naked, was shepherded cattle fashion in a straight line to be examined by a physician's assistant, an examination so perfunctory that it would have revealed only the grossest of abnormalities or illnesses. It was then, standing in line with the undressed, scarred, and tattooed bodies of my fellow miscreants, that I saw it. The red snake. I had never seen a red snake before.

This one glistened with the sweat of the inmate's back over which it appeared to slither. Its body was coiled and entwined through the eye of a skull—in one eye and out the other. At that moment the horror of my imprisonment became a crushing burden.

What was I doing here with these people, with this red snake? Where were my family, my friends, my court, my colleagues, my life? What had become of my honorary degrees and gold medals and plaques? All replaced by a red snake grotesquely tattooed on the back of a prisoner who would be my companion for the many months ahead. That red snake would be seared in my memory much like the mark of Cain—a reminder of my being cast out of civil society.

When the physical examination, and the endless finger, hand, and palm printing and photographing was over, I expected to be led to a cell. What I didn't expect was to be put in solitary confinement, which, at Butner, is the same as disciplinary segregation. But that's where they led me. Through the prison compound, in chains, past the gaze of curious inmates to that dimly lit corridor of cells known as "seclusion."

Ten years ago as a judge on the New York State Court of Appeals, seated in my lofty ceilinged, magnificent mahogany-paneled chambers, I wrote an opinion in the case *Wilkinson v. Skinner.* Wilkinson was a prisoner suing Skinner, who was a county sheriff. The prisoner was complaining that being put in segregation for a five-day period constituted cruel and unusual punishment, prohibited by the Constitution. Writing for the court, I observed: "Merely confining an inmate in a segregated cell does not constitute cruel and unusual punishment. There are, of course, some cells that are so subhuman as to constitute such punishment even for a very brief confinement. One day in some cells might be constitutionally intolerable." Of course, when I wrote that opinion, I never dreamed that one day I would be confined in segregation, not for five days but eventually for well over a month.

A judge should have the ability not only to make a decision but to fully appreciate the effect of that decision. A judicial opinion should never be handed down "to send a message"—that is not the constitutional job of judges—but a judge should be aware that there is a societal and individual effect with respect to every decision made from the bench.

When I was a judge, I tried my best to measure those effects. Most often I could relate the decision to everyday experiences. For example, I wrote the opinion that declared the New York State blue laws, the Sunday closing laws, unconstitutional. Those laws with their illogical and irrational exceptions made little sense. As one example, the legislature had provided that you could purchase certain publications on Sunday (magazines at a newsstand) but not others (Bibles at a bookstore).

The effect of these laws, and any decision relating to them, had to be measured against the impact Sunday store openings would have on the traditional observation of the Sabbath, on the workforce, and on shopping habits—things most people, including judges, could relate to.

But few judges can fully sense or relate to determinations concerning sentencing, or the inhumanity or cruelty of punishment. There was a time when I thought I was capable of measuring this kind of pain. The awesome responsibility of passing judgment on others, however, requires more than this kind of self-confidence or prideful conceit. My colleagues and I should have done more to learn just what being placed in solitary confinement really means. I am not saying that judges should have to suffer imprisonment to properly understand the dimension and effect of punishment, but they would all do well to make an effort to learn more about that which they are writing and deciding.

I believe that my analysis in the Wilkinson case was correct. My statement in that decision, "Confining someone in a segregation cell is not a minor punishment," was based on surmise, which is not always reliable. It was not based on experience or acquired knowledge. But in that case my surmise was correct.

Though the decision was not unanimous (4–3, with my opinion carrying by only a single vote), the majority of the judges on the court agreed with me, to wit: "Under certain circumstances, solitary confinement—even for a day—could constitute cruel and inhuman punishment."

I remember two members of my court, both former prosecutors for whom I had enormous respect, trying to convince the others of us during conference that solitary confinement was no more than a form of isolation necessary for discipline. They accepted the government's premise that solitary confinement provided privacy and solitude, which made this form of incarceration for short periods as acceptable as normal imprisonment. They argued that in most instances it was inaccurate and deceptive to conjure up images of "Devil's Island"–like confinement in connection with isolation cells. To call it "the hole," they said, was misleading.

They were wrong.

I was escorted to "seclusion," a row of ten-by-twelve-foot cells, each with its own steel sink and toilet. Against one wall there was a metal rack covered by a thin pad. This was the bed. The door was solid steel, with a small vertical slot that allowed for the guard to peer in. A small knee-high horizontal slot was used to deliver and return food trays.

The walls were of concrete block with a stuccolike graffiti-proof coating. Light came from one small barred window and a large fluorescent light that burned day and night. Etched into the window by some sharp object was the prophecy, "Yes, Jesus and God will help Ernest Shaw to come home now."

Before being locked in my cell, I was placed in a shower stall with a steel barred door and was again strip-searched. My clothes were placed in a locker, and I was issued a bright orange canvas jumpsuit with matching slipperlike sneakers. When I asked the guard why I could not wear my own clothes or something more like normal clothing, I was told that while I was in "seclusion" I had to wear the jumpsuit. When I asked how long I would be in seclusion, he said, "It depends."

"Depends on what?" I asked.

"On when and whether they release you," he replied, handing me a bedroll that consisted of two sheets, a pillow case, and a frayed, gray, burlaplike blanket.

I was again handcuffed and led to my cell. Once inside, I was told to pass my cuffed hands through the food slot so that the guard standing outside the door could unbind my wrists. I quickly went to the window to quell feelings of claustrophobia, which I've had ever since a deep-sea diving accident I suffered in my youth. Was it possible that I would remain in isolation for my entire prison term, in this cell with its slotted steel door and one-piece seatless steel toilet, with that breathless fear of being sealed alive in a coffin, unable to breathe? That's when I first learned why God and Jesus were concerned about what happened to Ernest Shaw.

And then I heard them. The occupants of the other "seclusion" cells. One, called "dogman" by the guards, howled like a wounded canine; another screamed, "Shut up!"; another sang a tuneless melody with words that spoke of "silver threads and golden needles." Several kept screaming, "Officer, officer" and all seemed preoccupied with a need for "smokes" and "matches." Many simply pounded on their doors. One shouted about the shortcomings of totalitarianism, and still another told the guards, in graphic terms, what they could expect if they didn't bring him some toilet paper—soon.

One of the guards told me that I could expect this clamor to continue unabated, since most of the inmates in the isolation cells either were mentally ill or had disciplinary problems, or both.

"When can I leave?" I asked.

"When the doctors are through with you and decide if it will be safe for you to join the general population," I was told.

Because my probation officer had sent me the list of things that I could bring to Butner, I assumed that the items in my duffel bag would be made available to me once I was assigned a cell. I soon discovered that all the items in the duffel—all the clothes I had brought, my pictures, my contact lenses, my radio, my books, pads, pencils—all would be sent home.

It was just yesterday—although it seems like months ago—that Joan and I so dutifully packed that bag. When we were informed that I could have a radio, to be listened to only with earphones, we thought that meant I could bring one with me. What they were really telling us was that I could have a radio but only if I bought one from the prison commissary.

And when they said I could have pictures of family members, what they meant was that photographs could be sent to me through the mail (except for Polaroid prints, because the double layer backing may conceal a prohibited substance). And you *can* have books, but they too must be sent to you. Friends and family can send paperbacks only, because they can easily be inspected; hardcover books must be sent directly from publishers or bookstores, because contraband is not likely to be concealed by those sources. And contact lenses are prohibited, because the liquid cleaners may be "spiked" and cannot readily be inspected. The pencils we packed are also prohibited in seclusion because they are potential weapons.

And so my duffel bag was sent home, unopened. I write this entry through eyes that can see blurredly, and with a two-inch-long pencil—sharpened at both ends—which a guard was good enough to give me.

Dinner has just been slipped through the door by a pair of disembodied hands in rubber gloves. There is no chair or table in my cell, so I eat sitting on the steel shelf which I will use for a bed, using my lap for a table. I feel aboriginal. The meal consists of two leathery meat patties, a portion of very oily fried potatoes, and what appears to be cabbage in a cream sauce. Everything is served cold, but I am hungry so I eat it all with my plastic spoon from the Styrofoam tray.

The cell to which I was originally assigned is located within the Mental Health Division of Butner. During this first day they gave me a choice: I could either sign an agreement to admit myself to the

Mental Health Division voluntarily, or, I was told, proceedings would be brought for an involuntary admission. While awaiting that determination, which could take awhile, I would be consigned to imprisonment in my "seclusion" cell. I consented to a voluntary admission.

Before going to sleep tonight, I asked for a pillow. I had a pillow case, but no pillow. My cell is filled with cigarette smoke from the adjoining cells, and I am told they have no pillow for me. As it grows later, the noise in the cell block increases. Another screamer has joined the pack with shouts of "No, no, no, no." Before I try to go to sleep—and it won't be easy with the noise, indigestion from my too quickly eaten meal, and the perpetual fluorescent light—I decided to read the only literature made available to me, the *Inmate Handbook*. But I have great difficulty without my lenses. Through squinting eyes I attempt to read a section entitled "The Living Will." It concludes with the sentence "This is the first and easiest step to ensure your death with dignity." I'll try to get to sleep so that I can dream of life with dignity.

September 29, 1993

I was wrong about the fluorescent light. Some thoughtful guard turned it off at midnight with a switch that, I learned, was located outside my cell. I was still awake. When the light was turned off, the security lights from the prison yard glowed through my window, casting the reminding shadow of the prison bars on my cell wall.

Despite the clamor from the other cells, I must have fallen asleep, because I was awakened at six this morning by the delivery of my breakfast tray. There were two large biscuits covering what appeared to be some sort of meat—probably corned beef hash. Fortunately, I was not hungry.

It suddenly occurred to me that I had no toothbrush, toothpaste, shaving cream, or razor. In fact, my spartan cell was without soap or even a towel. For someone who had gotten an "A" in hygiene at P.S.

130 and had learned to shower and brush with regularity, this was
no small matter.

As I was wondering how I was going to get through the day, a
guard's voice coming through the tray slot asked me if I wanted a
shower. When I answered "Yes, sir," he told me to put my hands
through the slot to be handcuffed. I was then escorted to the bar-
enclosed shower stall where I had been strip-searched the day before. An iron-bar gate was closed and my cuffs removed. I was then
given a toothbrush and toothpaste, soap, a disposable razor, a towel,
and clean underwear. Things once taken for granted can take on
the aura of heaven-sent miracles, even if delivered in a steel cage
and performed under the watchful gaze of a prison guard.

For the past several months, up until the time I pled guilty to my
crime, the U.S. attorney had insisted that I be denied bail, that I not
be permitted to walk the streets. The judge went along with the
prosecutor's recommendation, so for over six months I was kept in
confinement, part of the time under armed guards stationed in my
kitchen. I was compelled to wear an electronic device strapped to
my ankle and could not leave my home.

At the time it struck me as being perverse that accused rapists and
perpetrators of violent crimes were allowed out on bail, while I was
deprived of my freedom. It also struck me as more than strange that
as long as I was presumed innocent I was deprived of my freedom,
but the very day I entered my guilty plea the prosecutor recommended and the judge allowed that the ankle bracelet be removed.

But as difficult as the months of home confinement and the deprivation of freedom were, I was still able to retain certain, very important, vestiges of humanity: things like quietness and cleanliness
and privacy, and the ability to read and to be in touch with the outside world. Being in solitary confinement deprived me of all of these
things. It also deprived me of the ability to walk.

I can move four steps forward, two steps to the side (watch out for
the steel slab!), and back again. And again. And again. Like the animals in the zoo.

I remember as a child watching a polar bear traversing his caged habitat, which was built to resemble a fifty-foot-square chunk of the Arctic. He too walked back and forth, pacing his cell. When I told my father how I pitied this poor caged creature, he said not to feel sorry for the beast because that was the only life he knew. The answer satisfied me then — but it would not today.

While I was being taken back to my cell from the shower, again with my hands chained behind my back but now shaved, bathed, and with clean underwear, I asked the escorting guard if there would be any opportunity to leave my cell for some kind of recreation. I was told that I was to be locked down for twenty-three hours a day, but that I would be allowed out for the one remaining hour.

Later in the day — I don't recall the time because one hour seemed to fade into the next — I was shown the recreation cage. It was about twice the size of my cell. I was again reminded of the zoo, this time of the bird house in New York's Central Park.

"What do you do there?" I asked.

"Whatever you want to do — mostly just breathe." There was room for little else.

I was to learn later that the real recreation facilities were reserved for the general population, not for those in "seclusion." For us, recreation was a euphemism for fresh, albeit caged, air, one hour out of a twenty-four-hour day.

As the term "recreation" had its own meaning here, so did "seclusion." The word "seclusion" always had a special meaning for me. It evoked thoughts of a clearing in a verdant forest or a solitary house on a mountainside; or a lonely stretch of beach being licked by a gentle surf. The Bureau of Prisons has given the word a new meaning.

Every morning someone passes by my cell with reading material. Because without glasses I can't read for long periods, I spend most of my day lying on my bunk staring at the ceiling and thinking.

Not too long ago — less than a year ago — I could not find enough hours in the day to do what I had to do. I was charged with the executive responsibility of running the New York State court system, the largest unified court system in the country with thirteen thousand employees and a billion-dollar-a-year budget. I also presided over the New York State Court of Appeals, New York's seven-member court of last resort. My official duties, coupled with my speaking engagements and bar association and law school appearances left me with little spare time. And now I have so much time—to stare at the ceiling. And think.

I was just given another blanket, which I was able to fold and use as a pillow. Before I could fully appreciate this boon, a fish dinner was slipped through my door. The smell of the fish, long removed from both sea or freezer, caused me to gag.

I spent tonight like last night, sleeping fitfully and very little. The screams at night and the banging on the doors are more than disturbing; they are terrifying. One of the guards named, I swear, Mr. Cage, told me that this unit is called Disneyland.

September 30, 1993

This morning I was awakened by an overpowering stench. The stainless steel seatless toilet in the corner of my cell, which is equipped with an extraordinarily powerful flushing device, has backed up. Raw sewerage gushes from the other cells into mine. "Dante-esque" is the only word that comes to mind as I raise my feet and sit on my metal slab bed. I have been in prison for only two days and I cannot endure it. If death is my only way out, I want to die.

The guard tells me that I must vacate the cell. In order to do so I must walk across the fetid floor to the cell door so that I can place my hands through the slot to be manacled. This forces me to walk not two feet from the erupting toilet.

Once outside my cell, after being allowed to wash my feet, I receive official word that I will be leaving seclusion for a short period if I felt I could be comfortable in the general population.

A staff psychologist asked me if I had any fear for my safety. I told him the only inmates I would fear would be those whose appeals were unsuccessful in my court—a fear that one of them might take the loss, and consequential suffering, personally.

He assured me that this was highly unlikely because most of the inmates were from this part of the country and none were from or had dealings with the New York State correctional system. That turned out to be untrue. But at the time, oblivious to any such danger, I, along with two other inhabitants from seclusion, were led, in handcuffs and orange jumpsuits, into the general population.

It had been three days since I had seen and felt the warm sun. Like everything else I had always taken for granted—the smell of the fresh air, the sight of the blue sky, the quiet—all conspired to firm my resolve to survive this ordeal so that I could one day leave this alien world and appreciate, even more, what I had left behind. Not the power, prestige, and perquisites I once had, but the most precious of all my prior possessions: privacy and freedom.

I walked with our escort and my two companions into the prison compound. One turned to me and said, "I always wanted to sing in public, and when I did, everybody loved my sweet voice."

"What you talkin' about, nigger?" said my other chainmate, also black. "Who the fuck do you think you are?"

"I'm Sam Cooke," said the first, identifying himself as a deceased, once-popular singing star.

"Shee-it," snapped back the second, "if you Sam Cooke, you dead."

"No, people just think I'm dead, 'cause I been in 'seclusion.' But I'm alive. When I was young, people say I was too beautiful."

"Say what? You a ugly nigger. If Sam Cooke looked like you, no wonder he got himself killed." When he was finished taunting "Sam," he turned to me. "I know who you are. You're Saul, son of David, grandson of Solomon. I know the Old Testament—my mother kicked my ass every Sunday until I learned all the begats. Do you believe this fool, says he's Sam Cooke? Last month we had

Elvis here. Tha's right. White boy say he was Elvis Presley. Man
there are some sick motherfuckers in this place."

Our handcuffs were removed and I was told to walk around the
compound. I did so with some reluctance. Not only because my
bright orange jumpsuit made me feel as though I was dressed in a
neon announcement of my recent arrival, but also because I could
see by the curious expressions on the faces of my new companions
that they knew who and what I was "on the street."

I was immediately struck by the enormous size of most inmates—bulging biceps, bull necks. I marveled at them, wondering
whether they came into prison in that condition or got that way
working out on one of the seemingly endless number of free-weight
piles in the prison yard.

While I was pondering this enigma, one of the giants came over
to me and said, "Hello, judge, my name is Sanders. Name sound familiar?"

"I can't say that it does," I said thrusting my hands in my pockets
so he wouldn't see them tremble.

"Does *People versus Paul Sanders* ring a bell?"

"Should it?"

"I was before your court twelve years ago—I been here for eight.
I did the same thing you did. I kidnapped a lady."

I started to correct him about my crime, but thought better of it.

"You ruled in my favor," he said.

"Pleased to meet you," I said with a smile of relief.

He then proceeded to ask me a series of questions about detainers, writs of habeas corpus, speedy trial mandates, etc. As his question list grew, so too did a line behind him. I had been warned that
the population knew who I was and that there would be many who
would seek legal advice from me. I was also warned that if I gave advice to one, I couldn't refuse anyone else, and that I wouldn't have
a moment's peace.

"Hold on," I said. "You're talking about federal law—my field was
state law. If I knew anything about federal law, I wouldn't be here."

They seemed to accept this flawless logic and backed off.

Except for one.

A fellow named Alexander Anderson approached me with a court paper bearing my signature over my name as Chief Judge. It was a certificate denying him permission to appeal to the New York State Court of Appeals.

Pointing to my name at the top of the order he smiled broadly and said, "Do you know this fellow?" There was no anger or hostility in his voice, just pointed sarcasm.

I smiled weakly and said, "You must be Alexander Anderson."

He smiled back and sensing my discomfort said, "Hey man, you gotta do what you think is right."

When he was in my world, I had done something to him that he must have thought unfair. Now that I was in his world, he was willing to let the past stay there. Or so he led me to believe. I don't recall his case, but if I had still had the authority I probably would have granted him leave to appeal on the spot—not because of the merits of his case, but out of fear.

I thought there were no former New York inmates here! Were they lying to me? If I could meet two within five minutes, surely there are many more. Or could it be that they never even considered the danger of having a former New York judge put in the same prison with former New York defendants? Or could it just be that they just don't give a damn? That must be it.

While standing in the prison yard, surrounded by these citizens of my new world, I felt the need to call home—to speak to Joan.

I walked over to two guards who were having a conversation, and waited for an opportunity to speak. After several minutes of being ignored I said, "Excuse me, would it be possible for me to make a phone call?"

They answered simultaneously—or, rather, they both laughed at the same time—and then continued with their conversation, completely ignoring me. Leaving me to stand, once again, in silence and alone.

That was another thing I would have to get used to. When I was a judge, when I came into a room people would get to their feet, and when I spoke, people listened. When I wanted to amuse, even the feeblest attempt at humor would bring forth raucous laughter. And when I asked a question—even what must have often seemed an inane question—the answer was immediate. I was not accustomed to being so completely ignored.

But being ignored is better than being humiliated. I came to this conclusion when another guard, a very young one, came over to me and shouted an order that I heard but didn't understand.

"What?" I asked.

"Take the shit out of your ears and pay attention" was his answer.

When my companions and I were brought back to seclusion, I had a better sense of Butner's physical attributes. The grounds were beautifully maintained, and if you could forget the ominous guard tower that looked down on the general population, and the razor-wire fence that surrounded the whole facility like a giant slinky, you could convince yourself that you were on the site of a well-maintained industrial park or even in a schoolyard—a schoolyard monitored by bullies.

As I lay here on my steel-shelf bunk, trying to wish away the endless hours, I begin to remember the last time I had lived in North Carolina. Schoolyards and bullies were a part of my life even then.

They were good days but very lonely ones. My father was a traveling auctioneer.

How many children do you know who were able to travel all over the country, at least the eastern part of the country, without knowing what their next stop would be? It was one adventure after another. The car was my video monitor. Looking out of the car window unlocked for me a world not accessible to most young people of my generation. Their only lifeline to a wider world was the sightless radio or the make-believe scenes they saw at the movies. When other kids were learning about the cotton growing in the South, I saw it. And farm animals, and chain gangs, and Spanish moss draped over elegant trees.

I didn't think of myself as lonely—that's an adult's way of describing a child who has no friends or spends a lot of time by himself. That's how I spent my childhood, without friends. But a child with a raging imagination and new worlds to explore can never be lonely. He can be alone, but he is never without company.

When we moved from Brooklyn, New York, to Blowing Rock, North Carolina, my mother felt that it was important that my education should not be interrupted, and so I was quickly enrolled in the Blowing Rock Public School. In New York I was in the second grade, but in Blowing Rock, the equivalent was the third grade. So besides speaking with what my classmates considered a foreign accent, I was also one year younger than they. And I was Jewish.

But there was one thing that really set me apart. I was the only one in the class who wore shoes.

Jack LaFarge, and all the other kids in the schoolyard, could see that I was different. But Jack saw me through the eyes of a bully. He saw me as not only different, but weak and scared. I was both.

One day I came to school, shoes and all, and there was Jack surrounded by six or seven of his shoeless followers. They all looked as though they shared the same family tree. Three of them looked exactly like Edgar Bergen's Mortimer Snerd, and the others bore a resemblance to Disney's Goofy. One looked exactly like the banjo picker from the movie *Deliverance*.

"We gotta question for you, Solomon," Jack LaFarge said. "Do all Jews wear shoes to keep their money in?"

His followers gave him a big laugh, which sounded more like yuk-yuk-yuk.

"Yeah," said Goofy, "do you have Jew money in your shoes?" LaFarge shot him a dirty look—this was his Jew and Goofy had no business butting in. He was just there as part of an audience. This was Jack's show.

I started to tell LaFarge that besides being a way to hide money, shoes were a pretty good place to store your feet. I thought better of it, and said nothing. After all, this was Jack's show.

And Jack gave them his best. He struck a pose reminiscent of the great boxer John L. Sullivan—with fists clenched, bouncing on the balls of his barefeet, he danced around me jabbing the empty air. *Whap, whap, whap.* Meanwhile the surrounding crowd began chanting, "Jew, Jew, Jew," in cadence with his jabs.

Suddenly his right fist came at me. It was a direct hit and gave me a bloody nose. His claque roared its approval and I stood there holding my nose. He began circling again, and I started looking for an escape route. Now I was surrounded by what appeared to be a much larger crowd—there was nowhere for me to run.

I was reminded of that scene some years later when I was being trained as a member of the military police. They taught us that if you ever cornered an enemy without allowing him the opportunity to escape, be prepared for the fight of your life.

There I was, surrounded. I had to either fight or lie down. Before I could make up my mind, I saw his fist coming at me again. This time I struck my hand out to intercept his, but I missed. Instead of hitting his hand, I hit him in the throat. Right in the Adam's apple.

I heard a sharp intake of air and when I looked up LaFarge was standing there transfixed, his face frozen in fear. He looked like he was screaming, but nothing came out. His silent shriek was broken by a desperate attempt to get air into his lungs. And then he was crying. Jack LaFarge was crying. I was bleeding: the sign of a real man. He was crying: the sign of a girl.

Rather than enjoying this moment of triumph, I started to apologize—rather like David sending Goliath's family a condolence note. Fortunately, he couldn't hear me. His buddies were making too much noise. "The Jew whipped LaFarge's ass," they shouted. But they refused to acknowledge my pugilistic skills. They were too busy joining in the mass defection from their fallen hero. "Told you LaFarge was a candy-ass." "Couldn't even whup the pukey kike." "LaFarge is LaPussy."

Somehow, though I knew I had won, I also knew I would pay a price for the victory. More of a price than my bloody nose.

LaFarge fled from the field of battle, and his friends left too. I was there all alone. It was clear that my victory had served to disgrace him, but did nothing to elevate me in the eyes of the denizens of the Blowing Rock Public School.

Although Blowing Rock was a tourist mecca in the summer, the year-round population was rather small and the public school was attended by children who lived on adjacent farms. They were put to doing chores soon after they learned to walk, and aside from Daniel Boone, who was born in the next valley over, they had few heroes. Jack LaFarge had been one of them, and although he no longer was, they couldn't stand the thought of his being dethroned by an outsider.

I did not fully understand this as I woke up the next morning. But I did understand the social disadvantage I would suffer if I continued to wear shoes. I asked my mother if I could "please, please" go to school barefoot.

"I'd sooner see you go to school without pants," she said.

I would have welcomed this alternative if I had been convinced that if shoeless was good, pantless was better. Nevertheless, I decided I had better cut my losses, so I ran out of the house. But before I had left my frontyard, I took off both my shoes and socks and hid them under a bush. Now I would fit right in with my classmates— or so I thought.

The Great Smoky Mountains, where Blowing Rock is located, is part of the magnificent Blue Ridge. Both the "smoke" of the mountains and the "blue" of the ridge give that part of the world an almost mystical quality. It is little wonder that folktales of witches and Barbry Allen abound in these beautiful and majestic peaks and valleys.

I remember the walk that morning so well. I had never appreciated how great it is to let your barefeet feel the tender, moist grass. To have the wet mud ooze coldly between your toes. It was great. I didn't even mind the occasional cow flop that crossed my schoolbound odyssey. It felt no different from the mud between my toes. Life was good.

In fact, life couldn't be better. The day before, I had made the schoolyard bully cry. I was all ready to assume my role as the big man on the campus—and, most important of all, I was dressed for the role.

I looked down at my barefeet as I crossed the school's playing field. The scuffing of hundreds of barefeet—undoubtedly since the time of Daniel Boone—had left no grass on the hard-packed soil. My feet looked pale, almost white, against the red clay, and I suddenly realized that they looked as conspicuous as if I had been wearing shoes. I also realized that I was wearing what every other boy in Brooklyn wore when the weather was warm: shorts. Thin white legs and white feet sticking out of knee-length shorts didn't look nearly as appropriate as the denim overalls rolled over the tanned ankles of my classmates.

It was too late to do anything about that now. And besides, no one would dare criticize me after what I had done to LaFarge. In fact, I might even start a new fashion trend. I could picture my classmates wearing shorts just to be like me. But somehow I couldn't picture their wearing knickers when the weather turned cold.

While I was looking down at my feet I almost bumped into a person who was blocking my path. I looked up, and there she was. I don't know if it was her smile, or her very long hair, or the way she held her books, but just looking at her for that moment made me feel good. I tingled.

"Hi, Solomon," she said. "Want to walk me to school?"

"How did you know my name?" I asked.

"I saw you yesterday and someone told me your name—and besides, we once owned a nigger by the name of Solomon. He must have been Jewish too. My name is Betty, Betty McHugh, and I can yodel."

She had just said the word "nigger," which would have gotten me severely punished by my parents if I had said it. But the only thing that struck me was the "yodel" thing. I didn't know what to yodel was, but I figured it must be a very important thing to do because she seemed so proud of being able to do it. Still being in my "trying to impress mode," I wasn't about to be one-upped by a girl. "That's pretty good," I said, "but I can do yodel too."

"Let's hear," she said.

Hear? Did she say *hear?* I thought to yodel was some physical act—like playing stick ball or playing tennis. I couldn't do either of those things well, and so I was lying when I said I could yodel. Now here she was asking me to do it, and I didn't even know what it was that I was supposed to do.

"Why don't you go first," I said, getting ready to pay close attention so that I could imitate anything that she did.

"Okay," she said, and then erupted the strangest cacophony that I had ever heard.

"That was really great," I said, knowing that there was no way I could make sounds like that.

"So go ahead," she said.

Suddenly it occurred to me that maybe only girls yodel. That my yodeling, or even trying to yodel, right here in the middle of the schoolyard would be like trading in my shoes for high heels.

"In Brooklyn, boys don't yodel," I stated with a swagger, hoping that that would end the matter.

"What do they do?" she asked, putting me right back in the fire.

My mind was racing to catch up to a suitable answer. Unfortunately, the unsuitable answer sprang to my lips before I could call it back. "I dreidel," I replied, startling even myself.

"Oh!" She seemed both impressed and too embarrassed or polite to admit she didn't know what it meant.

"Yup," I said with a smirk as we started to walk to the school-house. "Nobody dreidels like me." As we walked, I wondered if my reputation would go up or down when the word spread that the Jewish kid dreidels. And what if they wanted a demonstration? I didn't have too much time to think about this problem. I had been so engrossed in my meeting with Betty that I hadn't noticed that the two of us were alone in the schoolyard.

It didn't take me long to figure out where the others were. In fact, they made their presence known in a very dramatic way. They came from behind the schoolhouse in single file and then deployed themselves in a skirmish line. They came at us as if they were prepared to do battle. I say "us" because Betty was at my side—at least I thought she was at my side. I turned around just in time to see her running in the opposite direction.

"Follow me," she shouted.

I just stood there frozen with a terror I had never before felt—glad, in a way, that Betty had left what I suspected would become for me a humiliating, if not fatal, field of battle. I wouldn't have wanted her to see me so frightened or hear how difficult it was for me to catch my breath.

The line of overalls came closer and I noticed they were dragging their feet to coax as much dust as possible from the red clay. I imagine this "redneck shuffle" was being done to make their approach even more portentous than it already was. If they were doing this to terrorize me more, their strategy, although primitive, was working remarkably well.

Behind them stood Jack LaFarge, his hands in his pockets, banished—deprived of joining his onetime followers in what promised to be a glorious and triumphant encounter.

And then I heard it. It sounded as if they were chanting some Buddhist incantation. At first I thought they were saying, "Fee, fie, foe, fum." But no, it was not the blood of an Englishmun that they were smelling. It was mine. And what they were saying was "Solomon Grundy, born on Monday, died on Tuesday, and that was the end of Solomon Grundy."

I took some solace in the fact that my last name was not Grundy, but somehow I knew the Solomon to whom they referred was the white-legged, long short–wearing outsider who was standing about twenty feet away from them shaking in his barefeet. And the subtlety of this being a Tuesday was not lost on me.

Before they could finish the closing lines of their "Solomon Grundy" mantra, they were on me. I had never seen so much denim or felt such pain. No one said a word—this was all business. They wanted to hurt me badly, and they did. I was on the ground in a fetal position, my hands covering my face. I thanked God that they weren't wearing shoes, because several of them started to kick me.

The smooth warm earth of the schoolyard had felt good on the bottoms of my feet, but having it pressed against my nose was something quite different. I came to this conclusion as someone forced my head into the ground. I couldn't breathe, my nostrils filled with red clay. And then suddenly, everything stopped, the grunting, the hitting, the kicking—everything except the pain.

I dared to raise my head and wipe the dirt from my face. I opened one eye. They were all running away. And then I heard the booming voice of my savior: "Y'all touch this boy again—so much as a hair on his head—an' I swan I gonna kill every damn one of you." He looked down at my huddled form. "You all right, son?"

"I think so—thanks to you," I said with both gratitude and dust on my tongue. But I hurt too much to get up. He grabbed me gently under my arms and lifted me to my feet. It was only then that I could see him. He looked to be seven feet tall, shod in boots reminiscent of those worn by Li'l Abner. In fact, he looked and was dressed very much like Li'l Abner.

"Mah name is Claude McHugh," said the giant, "and I know your name to be Solomon—mah baby sister Betty tol' me so. She come fetch me when she know'd those little bastards were goin' to beat up on you."

"Thank you, Mr. McHugh," I said. "I think you saved my life."

"Wanna pay me back?"

"Sure," I said, "anything."

"O.K., let's hear you dreidel."

Now how could I lie to someone who had just saved my life. I couldn't. I explained to the McHughs that my cousins in Brooklyn had taught me how to play with a dreidel, which was a small top used to play a game during Hanukkah.

"Durin' what?"

"Hanukkah—it's a Jewish holiday. You know, Dinah Shore is Jewish," I said irrelevantly, proud that I could give *my* people some credibility and celebrity by dropping the name of a blond Jewish singer with a Southern accent who was just starting to become a radio star.

"Does she dreidel too?"

"I guess," I said. "By the way, did you know her real name is Frances Rose?"

Claude gave me a puzzled look. Of course, I could have used Einstein or Disraeli to make my point, but the only Jewish celebrity I could come up with was Dinah Shore. It was just as well, because Claude was far more interested in dreideling.

Betty and I remained good friends and Claude became my full-time protector. Whether he was with me or not, his presence was always felt as a silent warning to the other kids. I even felt secure enough to wear shoes—but security doesn't always breed enough courage for death-defying acts.

Although Claude was a great deal older than I, he seemed to want to learn everything I could teach him. He had never been east of Asheville, nor west of the Tennessee border. He had never seen an ocean, and even more of a wonder to him was the image of a boardwalk, miles long, built on pilings along a beach.

I in turn learned a great deal from him. He taught me how to milk the McHugh cow, named, predictably, Bossie, and how at the same time to feed milk to an ugly, fuzzy-tailed tomcat seated three yards away by directing a stream of milk, fire-hose fashion, into its mouth.

One day, as the milk covered the bottom of the bucket, the sound changing from a tinny noise to a soft rumble, Claude looked at me and said, "Your turn. Now 'member, you give 't a pullin' squeeze or a squeezin' pull *down*. Not up or you'll be a hurtin' her. Go ahead now."

As I reached for Bossie's right front teat, she turned her head and stared at me with a look of displeasure. I froze. "I don't like the look she's giving me," I said. "I don't believe she wants me to milk her."

"Don' be a goofus," said Claude. "That's a love look—like the poem say: 'And when she give you an angry stare, that's when you know she care.' Milkin' a cow is like makin' love to a woman. A li'l slow at fust, and then to the squeezin' and then she's yourn fo-ever."

With this sage advice I again approached my task—this time with half-lidded eyes, trying to look like a romantic movie star. I grabbed and squeezed as I had been instructed. Suddenly Bossie wagged her tail like a golfer preparing to drive from a tee. After her warmups she swung it in a perfect arc, knocking me off my stool. Foamy milk poured all over the stall floor.

"Well, boy," said Claude, "I hope you do better with your love makin'."

October 1, 1993

When I was beginning to despair of ever getting out of my solitary cell, I was told that I was leaving seclusion. That did not mean that I was on my way to Pensacola. I was to be transferred to the Mental Health Division at Butner for further observation and the continuation of my medical treatment.

The Mental Health Division is located on a hill overlooking the buildings that house the rest of the prison population. The inmates in the general population referred to the inhabitants of the hill as the loonies, and the three buildings, named for three Eastern colleges (Maryland, Duke, and North Carolina), are referred to as the loony bins. I was to be housed in the Maryland bin, at least for a while.

The discharge from seclusion was without incident, and I was taken, again in handcuffs, to the entrance of Maryland. My shackles were removed and I was permitted to exchange my orange jumpsuit for my street clothes, the clothes I had been wearing when I came here, ages ago, it seemed.

I never thought that I would consider a ten-by-twelve-foot cell heaven, but after the hell of seclusion, my new one-man cell at Maryland seemed just that. There was a real cot and mattress, a small locker, a desk and chair. And, except for evening hours and certain periods of the day when steel corridor doors were locked shut, you could leave your cell at will. The doors had windows in them so that the guards could look in on an inmate at any time, but there are no locks on the individual cell doors. I was to regret that later, but at the time, this small reminder of freedom was most welcome.

My cell was located in a wing with several other single cells occupied by inmates who were diagnosed with various sorts and degrees of mental illness.

The room next to mine was occupied by a thirty-one-year-old confessed robber of nine banks named Tony. Tony's criminal career began in New York State when he was fifteen years old. I remember his case. He was the first juvenile tried as an adult, which permitted the juvenile to be incarcerated in an adult facility. Tony was sent to the prison in Elmira. The case was reviewed while I was on the Court of Appeals. I can remember discussing his case with my colleagues.

I was not at all troubled by Tony's plight at the time. None of us was concerned about treating this fifteen-year-old murderer as an adult. The early English common law had established the "presumption that an offender seven but under fourteen years old was incapable of distinguishing between right and wrong," but that any offender over fourteen years of age "was to be treated as an adult." That same yardstick was still being used. Our New York State legislature, which in 1825 had established the first reform school in the United States, was ready to concede that juveniles fifteen years and older were not only responsible for their serious criminal acts but that they should be put in prisons such as Elmira, which at that time housed inmates up to thirty years of age.

During the early seventies, when young offenders were considered predators instead of misguided or errant youth, reformatories all over the country were being closed. Juveniles like Tony who committed crimes of violence started to be consigned, without hesitation, to adult prisons.

The only debate at the time concerned the rehabilitation of these juvenile offenders. Indeed, shortly before this legislation had been enacted our court had observed that "a fifteen-year-old delinquent may well emerge from his incarceration with hardened adult criminals having had his juvenile criminal skills increased and intensified." I believe we were correct, but neither our understanding of the effect of this punishment nor our caution, in any way deterred the legislature or assisted Tony. Tony picked the wrong time to commit his felony.

But Tony's contact with crime had come before his arrest for murder at fifteen. He was raised in Little Italy. When he was nine years old he saw one of his uncles "whack" another of his uncles. "That's the way the wiseguys did it," Tony told me. "You had to be close to the guy you were going to kill."

What he couldn't understand was how or why the surviving uncle went to the funeral and wept for his victim. "I couldn't understand it then, but I understand it now," he said. I nodded, pretending that I too understood. I didn't.

When he was fifteen, a neighborhood bully punched him in the nose. He left the schoolyard only to return with a .38 pistol. Although he swore to me that he only intended to frighten his assailant and maybe hit him with the weapon, he ended up shooting him between the eyes. The bully died instantly.

As I said, Tony was tried as an adult. He was found guilty of manslaughter and sentenced to ten years in a New York State prison.

We have much to be proud of in New York State, but some of our prisons are a source of great shame. Tony saw them all: Elmira, Napanach, Auburn, Greenhaven, Comstock, Attica, and others.

He spent eight years fighting off aggressive homosexuals and others who referred to him as "Tony Kid." He told me of one such confrontation, when, on the advice of a more experienced inmate, he headed off the advances of a predator by smashing a mustard jar in his face.

But his greatest test came when he was in Auburn. He was twenty-one years old and became the target of Bala, a leader of the Latin Kings, one of the many prison gangs that inhabit prisons. In New York you have Puerto Rican, Cuban, Dominican, Colombian, African-American, and various other groupings all struggling for prison dominance and respect. Tony and this "Latin King" had a falling out at Napanach and so they were separated. Three years later they were inadvertently put together again at Auburn.

Tony had been warned that he was targeted and so gained possession of a handmade knife—a "shank"—for protection ("Everyone has steel in New York penitentiaries"). After a recreation period, he found himself isolated in a corner of the exercise yard. He was "called out," meaning that his nemesis "Bala" had challenged him to a fight. As he explains it: "When you are called out, you gotta do what you gotta do."

What he had to do was fight for his life. He did so successfully. Although he bears a scar on his back where his opponent stabbed him, causing a collapsed lung, he managed to stick Bala twelve times, putting him in a coma. For his victory Tony was rewarded with a sentence of ten years in solitary confinement. He was to do this time in Attica.

Because his victim did not die and an investigation of the battle showed that Tony had not been the initiator of the fight, his sentence in the hole was cut to thirty-seven months. His description of those thirty-seven months in solitary confinement was mind-numbing. Many of the prisoners threw feces and urine at the guards through the cell doors. For their protection, the guards installed Plexiglas shields over the cell door bars, which had the effect of stifling the air flow. He told me the smells would cause him to gag.

When he had served eight years of his ten-year sentence, three of them in the hole, "Tony Kid" was paroled. The sixteen-year-old was now twenty-four.

Determined to make a new life for himself, Tony went into the "escort" business. His two brothers already operated several of these agencies, which are in the business of arranging dates for lonely men. Most of his "girls" attended college and worked whenever they wanted to pick up some extra money. They had to be attractive and bright. There was no requirement that they have sex with their dates. As Tony put it, "I ain' no pimp."

It was a difficult job, because he not only arranged the date—he also provided, for a fee of course, limousine service, theater tickets, dinner reservations, etc.

The escort charged her date $500 for the first two hours (minimum) and $250 for each additional hour. Tony split fifty-fifty with the girls. Of course, he had the overhead expense of advertising on a local cable TV show and in certain magazines as well as the phone and beeper service. Any of the women who worked for him could beep him at "any place and any time."

By 1990, he was earning $280,000 a year from his business, which had grown from eleven to seventy working girls within a year.

But Tony was restless. His was a night business. He spent his days in New York City's Washington Square watching others enjoying the freedom that he had not yet learned to appreciate.

One afternoon he went to Astoria, Queens, looking for an apartment to house a branch office for his escort business in that borough. He remembers it as a hot summer day in 1991. As he walked along Ditmars Boulevard, he passed a Chase Manhattan Bank and he had the sudden, almost compulsive, urge to rob it.

He hastily wrote a note: "I have a gun, put the money in the bag," and passed it to a teller. The teller ducked under the counter; Tony panicked and he left empty-handed. He then remembered the lesson he learned in Napanach from Jim McCrory, one of New York's most illustrious bank robbers: You must plan bank robberies. They can't be spur-of-the-moment things.

The next February he successfully robbed his first bank. He again chose Chase Manhattan because, he said, "I wanted them to *chase* me—get it?"

This time he flashed a cap pistol while quietly ordering a teller to put fifties and hundreds in a bag that he handed her. She cooperatively deposited $19,000 in "Tony's bank"—as he referred to it—and he ducked into a subway where he was carried to safety.

During 1992 and up to August 1993 Tony robbed forty banks, all Chase Manhattan branches. His M.O. was always the same. He would enter the bank, put his cap pistol above his head, and tell everyone to remain still while he jumped over the counter and emptied each of the teller's drawers. He stole $480,000 in that fashion.

He recalled one incident, again in Queens, when instead of standing fast the bank customers all dropped to the floor. They had obviously seen too many bank robberies in the movies. Tony panicked, because the interior of the bank was visible from the street and he didn't want the passing crowd to see a bank full of prone customers. "Get up, for God's sake," he shouted. They all stood up with their hands behind their heads. "Put your hands down, for God's sake."

"It was like a friggin' game of 'Simon says,' " he told me.

He left that bank with $40,000.

"I never spent a cent of the bank's money. I had all the money I needed from the escort business," he said. "Once I robbed one bank two times in one day."

He was finally arrested in the summer of 1993.

Why did he rob banks when he didn't want, need, or spend the money? That's why he's in this Mental Health Division. The government is waiting for the completion of his mental examinations before charging him.

Charley is also waiting for a mental evaluation. He has already served two years in a Moroccan prison for smuggling hashish. He now faces twenty years to life for hijacking an airliner in San Francisco. He accomplished this feat by holding a fire ax to the pilot's throat. He felt the hijacking was necessary to escape an assassin who, he said, was determined to kill him.

My other wing mates are Ziggy, being held for a double homicide, Dominic, another bank robber ("used to dress as a priest"), Vinny, a major cocaine dealer from Atlanta, and Roger.

Roger went to the dedication of the Reagan Library for the purpose of shooting George Bush. He stands over six feet tall and weighs four hundred pounds—not what you would call inconspicuous. As Roger drew his weapon, Bush picked up a small child, so Roger, not wanting to hurt the child, put his gun back in his jacket.

A few days later, when the Secret Service was reviewing films of the library dedication, there was Roger, gun in hand, looking at the president. He is now looking at twenty years.

And then there's Max, a lawyer who took the fall for the head of a major crime family. And Vito, a capo in another crime family. There are rapists, arsonists, and murderers here. And me.

Alan Dershowitz, a Harvard Law professor, wrote an op-ed piece for *The New York Times* that was just sent me. He wrote: "Sol Wachtler was not a good judge—he was a great judge." That evaluation, in my present circumstance, is irrelevant. I am no longer any kind of judge.

I am a convict and I consider myself no better than my fellow convicts. I am no longer deputized by society to judge its members' crimes, and I do not. I measure them only by the way they treat me, and others. While we are here together we are the same, except that I'm older and will be here for a shorter period than most.

October 3, 1993

I no longer have to eat in my cell. Today I went with Tony to lunch. It is served in a commissary reminiscent of a military mess hall. Although we are quartered in the Mental Health Division, we eat with the general population.

With few exceptions, the inmates do not seem to resent me— some even treat me with deference, addressing me as "judge," but perhaps they do that more to anger the guards than to honor me. They are also quick to offer me assistance—this I attribute to their innate respect for my senior-citizen status. And some, also probably in deference to my age, are protective. Often when passing a hostile-looking clutch of inmates in the yard I'll hear some friendly and reassuring voice from another inmate saying, "Don't worry, judge, I've got your back."

When Tony and I were seated, we were joined at our table by two of New York's best-known bank robbers, Jim McCrory, whom I mentioned earlier, and his partner in crime, Dave Pistone. Tony had told me of this legendary pair, "who robbed banks like banks should be robbed."

"I would jump over the rail and empty the tellers' drawers, but these guys would empty the safes and everything—they're real pros," said Tony in awe. Their last robbery was for $350,000.

The next day Dave took me aside and told me that if anyone threatened or came near me, he would "take care of him."

Tony told me later that he was amazed that Dave offered me his protection. "That's not done too often," Tony said. "With Dave telling you he'll be there for you, you never have to worry. The word will spread that they have to go through Dave to get to you—ain' nobody gonna try." But Tony was talking about other rational inmates. I was later to learn that there was at least one inmate in the mental health unit who was not afraid of Dave.

October 4, 1993

The nights are lonely—as you would expect them to be. The light in my cell permits a certain amount of reading, but I still have no glasses and the dim bulb makes it even more difficult.

One of my college classmates and longtime friends, Tom Wolfe, the author of *The Right Stuff* and *Bonfire of the Vanities*, has encouraged me to write this journal. As an inspiration of style, he has urged me to read *Witness* by Whittaker Chambers. He sent it to me in a soft-cover edition and I am able to read a few pages at a time. It is an incredible book—so good that rather than being inspirational, I find it discouraging. It is a reminder of my own literary inadequacies.

Because my reading is sporadic, I spend most of my time lying in my bunk thinking. I think mostly about Albany, and my court, and the remarkable life I once had.

My career as a judge began in 1968.

Nelson Rockefeller, who was then governor of New York, had urged me during the previous year to enter a political race for the office of county executive of Nassau County, a municipality with a population of one and a half million people. I was then a relatively unknown town supervisor in North Hempstead, and the campaign was against a very popular incumbent named Eugene Nickerson, now a federal judge. It was a race I knew I would lose. I did.

It was a very long and brutal election campaign that, much to my and everyone else's amazement, I came within a few votes of winning.

The governor, in gratitude for my undertaking the race, offered me whatever governmental appointment I wished. I wanted to be a judge, and after some resistance from the local bar association, which was not amenable to the idea of having so young and inexperienced a jurist, I was appointed a justice of the New York State Supreme Court. In most states the Supreme Court is its highest court—the court of last resort; but in New York State, the state Supreme Court is the equivalent of what is called the Superior Court in most other states. It is a district trial court. I was then thirty-eight.

In 1972, when I was forty-two, Governor Rockefeller again summoned me, this time to run in a statewide election for a seat on the New York State Court of Appeals, New York's highest court. This, the court of Benjamin Cardozo, was the court that I as a law student revered as a beacon light of the common law. It was the most renowned state court in the country; its decisions were second in importance only to those of the United States Supreme Court. Becoming a judge on the New York State Court of Appeals was an honor to which I could never aspire, and which I felt I did not deserve.

The New York State Bar Association ultimately rated me qualified for the position, although it noted that if elected I would be the youngest judge ever to sit on that court.

I won the election and on January 1, 1973, was sworn in as one of seven judges who sit on the New York State Court of Appeals. From that date until the date of my arrest twenty years later I was given the opportunity to shape the jurisprudence of New York State and the lives of many of its citizens.

It was our court that decided that Grand Central Station should stand and the Sunday blue laws should fall; that Taiwan could not come to the Lake Placid Olympics and that environmental factors had to be weighed in the construction of an atomic power plant; that a man could be convicted of raping his wife; that a disabled newborn had a right to live and that an infirm adult had a right to die; that social club membership rules in New York could not discriminate against women; we even decided, because of a peculiar provision in the America's Cup trust, that San Diego beat New Zealand in the last America's Cup race.

Having the opportunity to be a judge went beyond deciding individual cases. It brought me to the realization that the accepted "truth" that ours is a nation "of laws and not of men" is not true at all. I believe that this thought gives us a false sense of security. It might be comforting to believe that past generations have separated right from wrong and good from evil, but if we just scratch the surface we find that the greatest responsibility for our national welfare does not rest with statutes carved in stone but with the principles, conscience, and morality of the individuals who constitute this generation. And that responsibility is discharged, in large measure, by judges.

One generation can never protect the rights of another, and although our greatest documents, the Declaration of Independence, the Constitution, and the Bill of Rights, are ideal reflections of our finest aspirations, they are not self-propelled chariots of justice. For all their beauty, they are only words, dependent on each generation to give them a meaning and content for its own time and place. And that's what judges are able to do.

I can't think of words less in need of annotation than the truth so proudly declared self-evident in our Declaration of Independence: "All men are created equal." Yet our Founders who wrote those words with hearts full of devotion to freedom and justice for mankind never once meant to include members of the black race, or women.

Decisions by judges in every generation have reflected different interpretations of the words "All men are created equal": From the 1857 *Dred Scott* decision, Supreme Court justices, interpreting the United States Constitution, held that a black person could be owned; to *Plessy v. Ferguson* in 1896, where the same Constitution was interpreted by a different set of Supreme Court justices to say that though there must be equal treatment for blacks, that equality could still be separate; to *Brown v. Board of Education* in 1954, where still different justices, interpreting the same Constitution, held that there must be true equality between the races. Recently, in a case out of Santa Clara, California, the court upheld affirmative action to achieve equality for women. All of these progressive interpretations of our Constitution have given the simple words "All men are created equal" a meaning and content consistent with and reflecting evolving principles, and a changing sense of morality and justice.

While privileged to serve as a judge I witnessed the same change and expansion of meaning occur with virtually all of our constitutional principles. As the pace of our lives quickened, so too did the pace of this change. I remember the arguments advanced by many critics of the courts. They contended, and still do, that the "original intent" of our Founders, established at our nation's birth and embraced by our Constitution, should not be tinkered with by judges. That argument never made much sense to me. We knew how our nation's Founders related to problems of their world and time, but we have no way of knowing how they would relate the Fourth

Amendment right against unlawful searches to electronic eaves-dropping, or the First Amendment's freedom of speech to the Internet or cyberspace. How would they have decided cases involving government regulation of Hudson River pollution, or the right of an unconscious patient to be removed from a life-support system, or of an assault victim to recover damages from a municipality that failed to respond to a 911 emergency call?

I never believed that our Founders intended for judges who came later to interpret the law consistent with some divined sense of *their* intent in the late eighteenth century, divorced somehow from the judge's contemporary understanding and morality. As a judge for twenty years—a generation—I had been given the responsibility of applying those contemporary standards in the explication of statutes and the definition of constitutional rights. It was more than a responsibility; it was a great privilege and honor.

On New Year's Eve in 1984, a telephone call from Governor Mario Cuomo enhanced that privilege and honor beyond measure.

Mario Cuomo and I had been friends for many years. When I was a relatively new judge on the Court of Appeals, he was serving as New York's secretary of state. Albany, like most state capitals, could boast of a social and recreational ambience available to those officials who were compelled to leave home and hearth to do the state's business. Because Mario and I were both committed to our official duties, neither of us became involved in those pastimes. We did, however, meet and dine together on occasion.

I recall one of those occasions after Mario had been elected to the office of lieutenant governor. The press had been speculating that one day the two of us would be running against each other for the governorship. Although we joked at the prospect, we both realized that it could happen.

When he graduated from law school, Mario had been hired as a law clerk for a Court of Appeals judge and always held the court in great esteem. He always told me that he could think of no greater honor—short of being governor—than being New York State's

Chief Judge. And so jokingly we struck an agreement: We would run against each other for governor and the one who was victorious would exercise the governor's power of appointment to make the other the Chief Judge. In that way, we would both win.

Mario did run for governor, and he won. During his first term in office there was a vacancy in the office of Chief Judge.

New York still elects its trial judges, but judges who sit on the New York Court of Appeals, including the Chief Judge of that court, are appointed by the governor from a list of candidates generated by a "merit" judicial screening panel. My name was on the panel's list submitted to the governor, but most people—myself included—thought that it would be politically difficult for Cuomo, a Democrat, to appoint Wachtler, a Republican, as the state's chief judicial officer.

The governor's appointee was to be informed on New Year's Eve, with the public announcement and swearing in of the new Chief Judge to be held in the state capital building the next day.

The evening of December 31 Joan and I were in my house in Albany, looking at the phone and waiting for it to ring. At eleven-thirty it did ring and I picked up the receiver instantly. It was Don Sheraw, the chief clerk of the court: "Judge, we just received word from the governor's office. He asked that all of the members of the court come to the executive chamber at ten A.M. tomorrow morning to congratulate the new Chief Judge and to be present at the swearing in."

"Who is . . . ?" I asked.

"Who is the new Chief Judge?" he asked, finishing my question.

"Who is the governor going to name?" I asked.

"I haven't been told," came the answer. "All I was told was to alert the judges of the court."

"Thank you, Don," I said. "I'll be there."

Joan, who was watching and listening to my end of the telephone conversation, sensed my disappointment.

"I didn't get it," I told her. "The governor wouldn't have set the time and place for the announcement without first telling the new Chief Judge."

It was now 11:55. I decided that it was time to end the vigil and take a shower. At the exact moment I stepped into the curtain-enclosed tub the phone rang. It was 11:58. I had told Joan that I wanted to answer the phone so she left it alone. I picked it up on the fourth ring.

"Sol, this is Mario."

"Hello, Mario," I answered, trying not to exhibit any emotion. Was he calling to tell me how sorry he was that political or other considerations made it impossible for him to appoint me?

"I'm going to do for you what I always wished someone would do for me," he said. "Tomorrow morning I will announce my appointment of you to serve as New York's Chief Judge."

I was so fortunate to have had so much. But the more you have, the greater your loss. All lost but the memories.

After my arrest, people tried to ease this loss by telling me that I should be grateful to have these wonderful memories—but those memories only sadden me and add to the depression that has plagued me for too many years.

Tonight a television movie is being shown in the unit. It can be seen in a small room but because of the terrible acoustics it can hardly be heard. A few of the inmates asked me to join them, and, rather than drown in memories and regret, I decided to do so. The movie is *Dead Bang*, starring Don Johnson.

The plot involved an L.A. policeman who teams up with an inept F.B.I. agent in order to combat a neofascist gang of terrorists. Sitting in a room with eight blacks and one other white, I wondered whom I should cheer for. Given my company, I couldn't applaud the gang of bigots. And because all my fellow viewers had been arrested by the F.B.I., I couldn't root for them either. I felt very uncomfortable.

Fortunately, the F.B.I. was made to look incompetent and Don Johnson did a single-handed job of routing the neo-Nazis. One of the inmates said, "Boy, are them F.B.I. agents stupid."

"They got *you*, nigger," said another.

"Tha's because I was stupider," said the first.

October 6, 1993

Many acts and functions should be done in privacy. In some instances this is dictated by our culture, in others by civility. There is very little of either in prison.

Witness the ritual of urine testing.

The national drug crisis brought with it the necessity of devising methods for detecting drug possession and drug use. Everything from sniffing dogs to breaking open school lockers was utilized as a means of uncovering drugs. Our court approved all of these methods under certain conditions. But when it came to determining whether random urine testing was within the bounds of a constitutional search, problems were created.

Of course, there was no problem when we considered the random testing of those engaged in occupations in which the public safety was involved. We held that bus drivers and airline pilots, for example, could be subjected to this kind of testing. But what about those involved in nonhazardous jobs, like schoolteachers?

In 1987, a local school board in Patchogue, New York, decided that its teachers should be subject to this random drug-testing ritual. The schoolteachers claimed it was a violation of their right against governmental intrusion. They felt that they should not be required to submit to this sort of involuntary testing, and brought an action to nullify the regulation. After highly publicized skirmishes in the lower courts, the case came to the Court of Appeals for a final determination. When the briefs arrived on my desk, my first reaction was "Why not? What is wrong with having a teacher urinate in a cup?" After all, we think nothing of it when we are asked to do so in a doctor's office.

But then I read the briefs and heard the oral arguments of counsel in court. I came away with the conviction that there was nothing at all routine about "routine urine testing." Indeed, we held that if there is no suspicion of the teacher's being a drug user, then he/she should not be subjected to the indignity of a urine test. In the opinion I wrote for the court I noted: "Requiring a person to urinate in the presence of a government official or agent, as is sometimes required in these cases, is at least as intrusive as a strip search."

Now, in prison, I once again found myself confronting a legal issue from a new and disconcerting angle.

It was four-thirty A.M. when a guard came into my cell and woke me with the beam of a flashlight.

"Get up and get dressed. You need to get to the lieutenant's office now. And don't piss."

It took me a few minutes to fully comprehend the orders. While I was getting dressed, the strangeness of the command "Don't piss" played over in my mind.

"Why not?" I asked as I pulled on my too-tight khaki pants.

"Why not, what?" he answered.

"Piss."

"I told you not to."

"I know, but why not?"

"You need to go to the lieutenant's office. Stop asking so damn many questions."

As we walked across the dark, cold, and quiet compound, I kept wondering what was going on. Why did the lieutenant "need" to see me?

I soon learned that what the lieutenant needed was not me, but rather my urine. I was subjected to my first of dozens of random urine tests.

The experience was as unpleasant as I had imagined it would be six years earlier, when I spared the Patchogue teachers a similar fate.

It was not like giving a specimen in the privacy of a bathroom in a doctor's office. Unless, of course, your doctor happened to dress himself as a prison guard and watch you—front and back with the use of mirrors—while you urinated in a small jar.

October 7, 1993

There is a law library here. Actually, I should say that there is a small room with some law books, which they call a law library. When it came time to assign me to a job, my first request was to the job of the law librarian, a job recently vacated. I was all but laughed at by the counselor assigned to me. I was told that my presence in the library would create too much of an attraction and disturbance; not only could I not be the librarian, but I should stay away from the library entirely.

Strange—after spending the last forty years of my life in and around law books, I am now not permitted to go near them. I don't recall that as being part of my sentence, and I know that if I protested the prohibition would be lifted, but I don't intend to challenge prison authority. Instead, I shall stay clear of law books and devote my full attention and intellect to the job assigned me, which is to pick up paper, cigarette butts, and other miscellaneous and nondescript debris from the athletic field. This must be done with a small broom and basket. A stick with a protruding nail, customarily used on the street for this chore, would be too much like a weapon.

The Maryland unit is for those of us who are in need of the most intense medical supervision and treatment. Some of the inmates/patients are here to be "studied": they are being evaluated to determine whether they are fit to stand trial or whether they were mentally impaired at the time they committed the crime they are charged with. Many of them have not yet been formally indicted.

Twice a day we line up for our medication, much like the inmates in the book *One Flew over the Cuckoo's Nest*. Some have become so dependent on this medication that they never leave the pill station. Others refuse the medication, claiming that the government is trying to rob them of their ability to function. More than one has whispered in my ear, as I awaited my daily medication, "Be careful man—they goin' to fuck up your brain."

Then there are those called zombies. They shuffle through the halls in silence, seemingly oblivious to everything and everybody— except when the time comes for their drugs. Then they dutifully fall in line.

There are also those who have been here for years, untried, still awaiting their return to sanity so that they can be placed in the dock to be found innocent or guilty.

Many hear voices. One is convinced that he has microchips in his brain that can be activated by some alien force. Another attempted suicide by jumping off a retaining wall in the compound. To prevent a recurrence they piled sand at the base of the wall to make any future attempt less lethal.

When I'm not in the mental health unit, in the dining room, or in the recreation area, I come in contact with the general population. Although many of these people's crimes were violent, they do not present themselves as violent men. Most are repeat offenders or parole violators who describe the other facilities they have been in as far different from Butner. As Tom, a convicted cocaine dealer doing ten years, put it: "The other prisons are like a miniature of the world outside—you got different social classes, different groups. This place—with the nuts 'on the hill' and the general population below—is not the same."

Interesting how Tom considered living with other prisoners, murderers, and thieves as being a "miniature of the world outside." Maybe he's right. Ordinary citizens, those who walk our streets every day, harbor many of the same sinful instincts as convicted felons. Fortunately they do not convert their thoughts to action.

Clarence Darrow put it well: "Everybody is a potential murderer. I've never killed anyone, but I frequently get satisfaction reading the obituary notices." And as for thieves, read G. K. Chesterton's *The Man Who Was Thursday*: "Thieves respect property. They merely wish the property to become their property that they may more perfectly respect it."

October 13, 1993

The long, dark, and cold shadow of my depression seems to be near me all the time. I can almost see it out of the corner of my eye and sometimes I feel it in the pit of my stomach. I have learned that the inmates in the Maryland section of the mental health unit are those with the most profound mental illness. They are referred to as patients, not inmates, and the unit is called the Maryland Mental Health Division, not Mental Disease.

The use of these euphemisms reminded me of the challenge I faced when I was an elected municipal official, a town supervisor in North Hempstead on Long Island. In order to start any urban renewal project involving federal funds it was necessary to form a commission for the purpose of reviewing proposals and disbursing funds. The thought of this wealthy North Shore township having an "urban renewal" project was anathema to the residents, yet federal law required that such a commission be in place before the projects could be funded. The solution was simple: I formed the commission, and instead of an "urban renewal commission," I called it the Suburban Preservation Commission. Words can be deceptive.

There is nothing healthy—mentally or otherwise—about the mental health unit at Butner. The spectrum of illnesses is similar to what you would find in any community—tuberculosis, AIDS, hepatitis—but there seem to be more cases. In addition, you have the mental diseases: bipolar disorder, schizophrenia, paranoia, and the most prevalent, depression.

• • •

At the time of my arrest, several renowned psychiatrists reported on my mental affliction, not to make excuses for my aberrant behavior but to provide an explanation of it. I was diagnosed as being severely depressed and suffering from bipolar or manic-depressive disorder.

I have now been evaluated by the psychiatric staff here at Butner. They are in diagnostic agreement with the several psychiatrists who examined me before I was sentenced. No one has to tell me that which now has been confirmed. I was mentally ill at the time I committed the crime for which I am being punished.

One would assume that now that my depression, manic behavior, and causal toxicity (caused by the drugs I was taking) have been evaluated and confirmed by the government's own medical experts here at Butner, there would be some understanding by the public — not forgiveness, but some understanding. That will not happen. There will always be those who will refuse to accept the fact that a person can function in what appears to be a normal fashion in his or her job, and still suffer from a mental disorder, that a person's judgment can be appropriate in most instances, but be terribly skewed in others. The Maryland unit is filled with examples. Jack is one.

He illustrated the observation made by Will Rogers in his autobiography: "This thing of being a hero, about the main thing to do is to know when to die. Prolonged life has ruined more men than it ever made."

You see, Jack was a genuine war hero. Now seventy years old, he was the most decorated soldier from the state of North Carolina, having won the Bronze Star and the Silver Star and the Purple Heart twice. He was given a battlefield commission in World War II and reenlisted during the Korean conflict. Because of wounds suffered in both wars, he received disability payments that, when combined with the social security and retirement benefits, were sufficient to allow him the financial security needed for a peaceful retirement.

But his retirement was not destined to be peaceful. For the past ten years he has been having bouts of depression. The symptoms were typical: inability to sleep, dramatic weight loss, difficulty in facing each day. Three years ago his wife convinced him to go to the Veterans Administration hospital for treatment. He was given the antidepressant fluoxetine hydrochloride (Prozac), and continued to take it for some six months. When he was gradually taken off this drug he began exhibiting strange behavior. At first, he told me, he started having bad dreams in which he relived the blood and gore of battles he had fought. He then imagined that he was celestially selected to stop all wars, that because of his wartime experiences he was more suited than anyone else to know of and tell of war's death and destruction.

After a while he slept very little. He stayed awake trying to devise the best way to fulfill his mission. One sleepless night it occurred to him that the only place for him to be effective in his quest for eternal peace was at the place where all nations convened, the United Nations Building in New York. During this period his family thought that his apparent mood elevation was a good sign that the depression had lifted. What they didn't realize was that he was in a manic state. He was off on a mission to end war for all time.

When he arrived in New York he donned a sheet, which gave him the appearance, or so he thought, of a "guru." In this "disguise," he delivered letters to the receptionist at the U.N. addressed to the heads of several nations, warning that their failure to pursue peace would result in physical harm being visited on them or their families.

He then returned to North Carolina to await the results of his handiwork. The only result he realized was his arrest and ultimate indictment for sending threatening letters to governmental officials. He faced up to ten years' imprisonment.

Fortunately for Jack, the U.S. attorney handling his case actively sought a way to avoid prosecuting this seventy-year-old man who had never before been in trouble. He thought it would be a travesty to send this man, who had done so much for his country, to prison.

Jack was sent to Butner for a "study." He was here for twelve months. Yesterday Jack was released. His diagnosis of mania after withdrawal from antidepressants was confirmed and the U.S. attorney moved for a dismissal of all charges against him. He told me this news as he wept.

This evening I moved into Jack's cell. Maybe it will improve my luck. But even if it doesn't, it is larger than mine and has a window. Of course, the window is barred and covered with opaque plastic. But it is an improvement.

October 14, 1993

Tony had been watching me write and asked me if I would help him do the same. I told him to write an account of one of his first bank robberies. Today he gave it to me. This is an unedited version:

> It was the control, the Power of the act itself that kept me going. Money was not the goal as it turned out to be more of a problems then it was worth. Jumping over the counters in one clair jump, not even haveing my feet touch the counters. Just my left hand on the counter. Like jumping a fence. When in a bank I could jump 10 feet high and across floors as if I was a bull frog. I was not afraid of being killed in fact I felt that not even bullets could stop me, it will go through me but can't stop me. I couldn't be stoped by an human forces. When I left the banks I would walk away never ran. I will have everything. From which way I will walk and what train I will catch, to what alternative streets will be taken in case of a beat cop comeing my way who may hear the 211 call over his radio. I have even returned to the same banks 3 times in a month. Even one time I returned the following day befor the F.B.I. showed up to interview the bank workers the day before. Nothing was impossible. I controled. Even when I knew the Chase Manhattan branch on Woodside Ave in Queens was staked out by a lone F.B.I. agent in shorts and Tee-shirt with a gym bag on the bench. he was sitting on across the street, I hanged a round, checked out what moves I will make if this or that happened or didn't happened and even sat 2 benches away, took off my shirt to catch the

sun and eat my hero. On the 3rd day while Mr. F.B.I. was trying to look as he was just another Joe blow I took Chase for the second time that month in and out within 45 seconds. Walked away with about $10,000. Walked a block to the number 7 train which ran above Woodside Ave and walked up the steps payed my $1.25 and befor the train came watched as Mr. F.B.I. ran across the street while dozens of police and agents cars flooded the streets. By then I was able to change my shirt and take my pants off as I had shorts on under my pants. Put my walkman on, smiled, did a little 2 step and when my train came went home to take a shower, eat and get ready for work.

October 15, 1993

Tony was transferred out of Maryland. Because he voiced strong objections to the move, he was thrown into the hole. That's why I was walking by myself in the yard this morning when I was approached by three large, black inmates. The largest towered over me and said, "You the judge?"

"Yes," I replied.

"You sentenced my daddy," he said with malice and a sneer.

"Wait a minute," I said, "I've been an appellate judge for twenty years . . ."

"Only kidding, Your Honor," he said, and all three doubled over with laughter.

October 16, 1993

The stories told by some of the inmates in the general population have a touch of romance. Jim was a counterfeiter. It seems that whenever I have a visitor, he too is visited by his very beautiful and well-dressed wife.

Jim was very good at what he did. He made his own plates, tracing the intricate engraving from a hundred-dollar bill projected and enlarged on a screen. As he traced the enlarged projected bill, a reduced-size engraving was made by a stylus that moved in tandem with the tracing. He mixed his own ink dye, and used dollar bills, bleached of their color, for paper. I'm told that the finished product would fool almost anyone.

Several years ago he started his one-man enterprise. He would take a stack of his hundreds, and visit a number of stores, where he would shop and pay—as you would suspect—cash for his purchases. He took his change in "real money." He was able to pass and consequently legitimize thousands of dollars in this fashion, until one day an astute vendor found that if he rubbed the bill hard enough, his finger would turn green.

Jim's arrest resulted in a conviction and a two-year sentence in a prison "camp," a facility which has no fences and from which escape is relatively easy. It was simple for Jim, being bored one afternoon and sensing a chill in the North Carolina air, to leave for a warmer climate.

He was able to catch a ride to Georgia, and while there rolled a drunk who resembled him in appearance, took his identification, and hitchhiked to Miami.

His boyish good looks and winsome smile were all he needed to get a job in a shopping mall as a salesman in a fashionable clothing store. As a salary advance, he was permitted to clothe himself in the kind of tailored suits that a man of substance would wear. Now all he had to do was become a man of substance.

It took him almost a year to outfit a new counterfeiting operation. During that time he met Nancy, an extremely attractive salesperson who worked in the mall. They first met while on their lunch break, and after several lunches and a dozen or so suppers, they became roommates—he moved into the house that her recently deceased mother had left her.

At first, Jim even thought about abandoning his life of crime. There he was, living in Florida with a stable job and a beautiful woman, contemplating marriage. Who could ask for more?

He could and did.

"Nancy, I've got something to tell you," he said one Sunday morning. He then proceeded to tell her his true identity as well as his life story. At first she thought he was joking, and then it dawned on her that he was telling the truth, that she was living with an escaped convict who intended to go back to the profession he knew best—making counterfeit, or "queer," as it is called on the street.

That explained the mysterious trunk he had stored in the garage; it was his counterfeiting paraphernalia. They were the tools of his trade.

She sat in stunned silence for at least ten minutes before she said, "Let's get married"—and then, with a smile, "You have to, now—so that I can't testify against you."

And so they were married. And Jim did go back into the business. They both used the "queer" at various stores in other malls, mostly for clothes. This explains why Nancy is so well dressed on visiting day. Jim tells me that at home he has several closets filled with clothes, most of which he has never worn and, given the sentence he is serving, will never be able to wear—unless styles are the same ten years from now.

This time he was not caught by an alert merchant. He made the mistake of falling in with some drug smugglers who were using his counterfeit money to pay off their Colombian drug suppliers. When an undercover agent of the Drug Enforcement Administration identified him as the counterfeiter, Jim had two choices. He could either identify all the players in the drug enterprise, and buy a fifteen-year sentence to include his escape charge; or he could be indicted for the escape, the counterfeiting, and a drug conspiracy charge and face life imprisonment. He has served four years of his fifteen-year sentence.

October 17, 1993

Paul Montclare, my son-in-law and initially my attorney, came to see me today. We discussed various aspects of my case, and I couldn't help reliving, once again, the incredible events in my life that were unfolding last year at this time.

It was last October, just one year ago. Joy was working with the F.B.I., actually nurturing my criminal conduct. I can't stop asking myself this question: Why, instead of leading me on and working with them, didn't she tell them to stop me, or arrest me?

Not that I blame her for what has happened to me—I did it to myself—it's just that I can't understand her obvious indifference while she was witness to my self-destruction. It was George Bernard Shaw who said, "The worst sin towards our fellow creatures is not to hate them, but to be indifferent to them: that's the essence of inhumanity."

October 21, 1993

"They call me the blue man."

Because he is always dressed in blue, I thought him aptly named.

"And that's not because I dress in blue—it's because I used to walk naked on the Syracuse University campus and that made me turn blue."

That's the kind of conversation you get from some of the patients in Maryland.

Then there's "Adolf Hitler," so named because he'll tell you that's his name. He does not walk around the compound, he goose-steps around the compound.

And, oh yes, I finally met Elvis Presley. He's four feet, eleven inches tall, shaves his head, and can't sing a note. But he really believes he's Elvis Presley.

With Elvis Presley, Sam Cooke, and Adolf Hitler all in the same unit, it is little wonder that my celebrity is diminished. I like it that way, but unfortunately, I am recognized more often than I would like.

Yesterday, in the dining room, an inmate shouted over several tables, "Hey, judge, how do you feel being in here?"

"How do you think I feel?" I answered.

My inquisitor thought for a moment and said, "Embarrassed."

He was right. In addition to the shame and the sense of loss I feel for the life I destroyed, there is the embarrassment. I have always put such a high priority on reputation and worked so hard to establish my credentials and integrity in the community. And now I'm a convict. I am embarrassed.

October 22, 1993

Several of my friends have been sentenced to prison, but all were sent to federal prison "camps," such as Allenwood, McKean, and Pensacola. They told me of their experiences, but none prepared me for the experiences that have become part of my life here at Butner.

This is a secure facility, an F.C.I., or federal correctional institution. Again, euphemism. Not a federal "prison" or a "penal institution," but a "correctional institution."

The main difference between this and a federal prison camp (F.P.C.) is the degree of security. Here at Butner you have the recently installed guard towers to accompany the razor-wire fences. At an F.P.C. your only constraint is the law, your conscience, and the fear of punishment, should you leave. This difference dictates the type of inmate.

At a low-security camp, you have the first offenders and white-collar criminals, the "short-timers." Here you have many repeat offenders; some are hardened criminals doing hard time. In a camp the inmates measure their sentences in weeks and months; at a prison like Butner, they measure their sentences in years and decades.

At a camp, many inmates tell you they feel themselves to be innocent; at an F.C.I. like Butner, for the most part, they curse the harshness of the system, the prosecutors, and the judges, but they freely admit their guilt.

The inmates at Butner have had a great deal of experience with prisons and the justice system, and all seem to agree that if you have to do time in prison, Butner is just about the best place to do it. The third and harshest category of federal prison is the United States Penitentiary (U.S.P.). Examples are Marion in Illinois, which was opened in 1963 to replace Alcatraz. The average sentence in Marion is forty years and half the inmates are serving their sentences for murder. Others, like Lewisberg and Leavenworth, have garnered reputations for their violent inmates and necessary high security. For that reason, once they get here from Marion or Lewisburg or some other penitentiary, they are eager to stay.

To stay here, you must behave. You avoid confrontation, you do what you are told, and you don't hesitate to advise the authorities about another inmate's misbehavior. In other words, as one of the guards told me, it's no disgrace at Butner to be a snitch. The units are full of them.

A snitch is being blamed for Dominic's disappearance from the unit. For some reason, it seems that inmates are put in the hole late at night or very early in the morning. That's what happened to Dominic. We said good night to him last night, and this morning he is gone. "In the hole," we are told.

The reason is none of our business, but the rumor is that he told someone that "Family Day was going to be a bloody day." Supposedly, this was taken as a threat that he was either going to hurt someone or repeat his attempt at suicide tomorrow, which is Family Day, a special visiting day. That was enough to warrant a one-way ticket, punched at two A.M., to the hole.

October 23, 1993

Today, Saturday, is visitors' day. More than that, it is Family Day. Supposedly, this is the only federal prison that sets aside a day for members of the inmate's family not only to visit but to go through the dining room and gym to see how we eat and play.

Joan and my oldest daughter, Lauren, came to visit and I was so pleased to see them. I regretted the wait and search that they had to endure before being allowed beyond the gate. It gave them more time to reflect on where I was and what I had become.

In *Don Quixote* the hero refers to absence as "the common cure of love," and that certainly is true of an absence enforced by the separation of imprisonment. Most marriages and families cannot survive this breach, and most states allow an automatic divorce for the spouse of someone condemned to serve a lengthy sentence.

But then there are those who seem completely devoted to each other, bound by history, children, or a shared vision of what it will be like when the time to be served is over. The vision, of course, was not connected to reality. The released prisoner would be subject to many of the same factors—poverty, drug addiction, ignorance, and sociopathic tendencies—that landed him in prison in the first place. Chances are, when he is back on the street, the vision, like the wife and family who waited for him, will leave him.

The family attachments of the prisoner reflect this duality of absence according to Rochefoucauld's maxim: "Absence diminishes mediocre passions and increases great ones, as the wind blows out candles and fans fire."

In some states, New York among them, there are so-called family reunion programs that allow inmates to spend a period of days with their spouses or various enumerated relatives in a private trailer located within the prison complex but outside the main prison buildings. The purpose of the program is to "preserve and strengthen family ties that have been disrupted as a result of incarceration, thereby enabling inmates to adjust to society more easily when released from prison."

One of the problems that arose in connection with the New York program when I was Chief Judge was a regulation promulgated by the corrections commissioner according to which a prisoner with AIDS could not participate in the arrangement.

The controversy was brought before the Court of Appeals, the prisoner contending that, inasmuch as other prisoners were allowed conjugal visits, he was being discriminated against because of his handicap. He also complained that his constitutional right to be free from the government's interference with his marriage were being impaired. Our court disagreed and, by divided opinion, held that the commissioner's rule was justified and legally enforceable.

When the case first came to our court, in 1987, I felt that, inasmuch as a prisoner had family-unit visits only as a matter of privilege and not as a matter of right, the commissioner could impose whatever conditions he wanted. However, that initial and visceral approach to a legal problem is often too simplistic and illustrates the difficulty of judicial decision making.

It is true that the commissioner was not required to establish the program, but having done so, and having accepted the prisoner as a member of the program, did he then have the power to decide that because the prisoner had AIDS he and his spouse could not have sexual relations? Or did the commissioner's AIDS regulation come close to being unconstitutional because it presupposed that if a husband and wife were in the trailer, the couple would engage in unsafe sexual relations? If so, the regulation could be read as an interference with a personal decision involving intimate marital relations, decisions which are constitutionally protected from governmental interference.

What if the commissioner felt that it would be socially undesirable and costly to the state's welfare system if impoverished prisoners were allowed to impregnate their wives. In that case, would he have been constitutionally permitted to promulgate a regulation mandating the use of contraceptives during conjugal visits? Of course not. Or what if he said that "prisoners shall have the privilege of family reunion program visits, except those who have no independent financial resources"?

Nevertheless I concurred in a separate opinion upholding the prohibition of conjugal visits for prisoners with AIDS because I felt that being charged with the "safety and security" of the community, the commissioner had the duty to protect "a visitor to the prison from the risk of being exposed to a concededly fatal infectious disease."

Not an easy decision and one that has caused me a great deal of reflection. I may have been wrong.

The federal prison system was never confronted with this problem, because federal prisons do not have family reunion programs or conjugal visits.

On her prior visits Joan had wept when she saw inmates and their families embrace. You could see the pain, regret, and sorrow that they shared. But today, she seemed to accept more readily the circumstances that these families had accepted long ago.

Mind you, these prisoners being visited had not been sentenced to short terms. For the most part they were here for five, ten, and twenty years. Prison was not an interlude in their lives—it *was* their lives.

I thought it would be very embarrassing to be with my wife and daughter at such a place. I was wrong. They both looked so beautiful, I found myself proud to be with them. Being with them made me feel loved, and that is so important.

At the same time, being with them brought back the sharp pain of regret and shame. Because of me they have traveled far from home, been searched and stared at, been lined up and crowded into this room, and been forced to spend a day in prison with these prisoners. Another chapter in this book of recent miseries, composed by me and dictated by my acts. I tried not to think of this as we exchanged light and meaningless conversation, but every now and again, tears came to my eyes and theirs.

When the family members left, the inmates were lined up and systematically strip-searched. What a humiliating way to end an otherwise elevating day. Fortunately our humiliation was not witnessed by family members. They had already left.

When I returned to my unit there was the customary count and then the mail call. Every day I receive dozens of letters, many from people I have never met. Surprisingly, they are all very supportive, and many exhibit unique wisdom. Today—by coincidence, the very day Joan visited me—I received a letter from a man named Max Wise. He wrote:

> With that woman, Joy, it was new infatuation. Something new for you, the new romance, the candlelight dinners and the newness of any romance. Then as quick as it started it was over. All the caring, the words of love, the giving you gave was like it meant nothing. Judge, what you had with that woman was not love. Love is what you had with the woman who is with you thirty-nine years and who is waiting for you when you get out. What you had with this other woman was only sex. These kinds of relationships don't last long.

Maybe Max is right. Before my sentencing, the prosecutor's psychiatrist made the observation, "Sol Wachtler was brilliant and sophisticated in affairs of the mind, but was exceedingly naive in the realm of emotions." He, too, was probably right.

To many members of my generation, sex was both alien and powerful. Joy's generation had come to deal with sex in a much different way. To me, sex was not a source of gratification or biological function; it was an extraordinary force that bound two people together. I remember my first exposure to this phenomenon when, at age ten, I returned to Brooklyn from Blowing Rock, North Carolina.

Brooklyn was a world of hard flat surfaces where every boy's world seemed to relate to a bouncing ball. There seemed to be at least a hundred different games that filled the summer schedule: stoop ball, box ball, punch ball, stick ball, handball, Chinese handball. I was bad at all of them, not only because I had such poor eye-hand coordination, but because I couldn't learn the rules. There were two kinds of balls, the red solid sponge type, which seemed to me to make the most sense since it remained solid, and the pumped-up gray shell, which resembled a shaved tennis ball. The gray shell was preferred by everyone but me. To this day I can't figure out why they liked those gray ones, which would go flabby if they were hit too hard.

In fact, it seemed that my likes and dislikes were always different from those of the rest of the boys. They convinced me that my judgment was pretty bad because I didn't go to Public School 130 like the rest of them, and my accent seemed rather strange. The accent I blame on my Southern forays; I'm still trying to figure out the source of my poor judgment.

There was one thing I did learn about that summer. Sex. In fact, it seems that all of us were totally preoccupied by only two things, sex and sports, not realizing at the time that the two could be combined. When I say we were preoccupied with sex, I don't mean having sex; I mean thinking about sex, talking about sex, and fantasizing about sex.

To me and the others, sex was like science fiction—a mysterious, exciting, make-believe world, filled with wondrous and sometimes dangerous treasures and adventures. Sort of like Mars. Were there really Martians on Mars? Were those canals part of a great civilization? Much later when *Explorer IV* finally visited that forbidding and foreboding planet, I would find that there were no Martians, the canals were merely dried-up riverbeds, and Mars seemed no more exciting than the quotidian existence on earth, albeit a little hotter.

But at the age of ten I had no way of gaining any reliable information about sex. I had to glean what information I could from what were referred to as "health" classes. Therefore, I grew up believing that if you just brushed your teeth right and your fingernails were clean everything from sex to the worldwide food shortage would somehow work itself out.

My children really learned the facts of life in school. They told me that their schools showed films explaining reproduction. The only movie I remember seeing in "health" was about the importance of covering your nose with a handkerchief when you sneezed. To illustrate the point, a cartoon character sneezed without benefit of even a tissue, and five hundred angry Vikings came pouring out of his nose carrying huge swords and slashing everyone within a five-hundred-foot radius. To this day when someone sneezes nearby, a small voice within me warns, "Watch out, here come the Vikings!"

I could have gone to my brother, Morty, to find out the true answer to at least some of the many questions about sex that were bothering me. He was only three years older, but at that age three years is a big difference, and I considered him to be very smart. But Morty was preparing for his Bar Mitzvah, and besides, why learn from a knowledgeable source when you can pick up misinformation in the gutter? Naturally, I learned all about sex from the neighborhood's sex expert, Kenny.

The first thing Kenny taught us was that a woman could not get pregnant unless you had sex twice in the same night. So if you just waited until past twelve o'clock for the second time, you had nothing to worry about. For years I thought that the rhythm method referred to having the self-restraint to wait until after midnight to do "it" again. I also figured that people's forgetfulness in not changing their clocks at the start of daylight savings time probably resulted in numerous unwanted pregnancies.

Incidentally, Kenny's expertise was not limited to sexual matters. He was also the one that told us that if you sneezed while you were making yourself cross-eyed, your eyes snapped and spun around and you ended up staring at your brain the rest of your life—a very boring prospect in Kenny's case.

The remainder of my knowledge about sex came from dog-eared "dirty" books. I particularly remember one day when Kenny excitedly showed me two passages from a dirty book he had taken from his father, John O'Hara's *From the Terrace*. One passage had the male hero staring at his lover and saying something to the effect of "He knew every inch of her body." At the time, I could not understand why that was supposed to be "sexy." He knew every inch of her body—I envisioned him saying "Hello, heart, how is the stomach today?"

The other dog-eared part of the book Kenny showed me described the sex act, known to the lexicographers in my neighborhood as "it." But all the book said was "He kissed her and the next thing he knew it was morning." This led me to believe that you blacked out when you did "it"; not too great for enjoyment but probably made it easier to comply with the not-twice-before-midnight rule. I understand that the little girls in the neighborhood were being told that you heard bells ringing, while I was learning that you felt nothing.

I remember one of those hot summer days. Too hot to play punch, stoop, hand, or stick ball, a perfect day for the beach. My cousins, my brother, and a group of neighborhood kids all walked to the BMT subway, which for five cents apiece took us to Brighton Beach, right next to Coney Island. I was one of the younger of this group of incipient virilists but they allowed me to join them in the taking of a sex test. The results would determine your position in the macho pecking order. The score was based on how much you had "gotten off of" a girl.

The test listed sex acts from one to twenty, encompassing everything from holding hands (one) to getting your hand inside a blouse (seven) until you finally arrived at number twenty, called "all the way." All the way was like the Holy Grail—we all knew we'd spend our lives pursuing it, but we were equally certain we would die before obtaining it.

In any event, when it came time for me to take the test, I checked off one through six, and seeing I hadn't gotten to seven with a girl yet, I stopped there. Six was not bad for a ten-year-old, I thought. It wasn't about to make Clark Gable fear for his crown, but I thought it about average for a boy my age. But then, almost by accident, my eye wandered down to number nineteen.

Number nineteen described an oral sex act in the vernacular. I had never seen or heard the term before; however, before I left North Carolina, Betty and I had gotten into a really heavy necking session. She introduced me to what she called a "Blowing Rock kiss," which consisted of softly blowing in my ear. I remember the pleasant sensation and tingle it caused.

Anyway, I assumed that nineteen was the same thing as a "Blowing Rock kiss" so I blithely checked it off. Well, much to my shock a hush fell over the crowd. Then all hell broke loose. For the life of me, I could not discern what all the excitement was about. But for the rest of the day I had to answer a steady stream of questions:

"What did it feel like?" "Oh, you really can't describe it." (Grabbing me by the throat.) "Describe or die." "How often did she do it to you?"

"Oh, about four times my last night there."

(Chorus.) "Four times in one night! Unbelievable."

"The first time she did it, she did it about ten times to me." (Shouts, fistfuls of sand thrown in the air, friends prostrating at my feet, suspicious looks from Morty.)

I could not understand my newfound fame. I had not lied, I was just ignorant. It never occurred to me or my friends that the odds of getting number nineteen when you had only checked off to number six previous to that were infinitesimal. It was like winning a Gold Medal in swimming in the Olympics before you passed your deep-end test.

October 28, 1993

One month has passed. Everyone tells me how quickly the time goes, but this has seemed a very long month.

I have learned a great deal about prison life, and although here on "the hill" they try to convince you that you are a patient rather than an inmate, there are constant reminders that you are in a prison: besides being surrounded by steel, the most persistent are the many guards who walk around with dozens of keys jingling—or is it jangling?—on their belts.

Then there are the patients themselves. Some who sit against the wall, rocking back and forth. Others who constantly talk or laugh to themselves, or to some invisible companion. And those who say nothing at all. And then there's the devil.

The devil seems to be ever present here on the hill. Some patients scream at him during the night, and others avoid him by not venturing into certain parts of the compound. Some swear he lurks in the laundry room, or other rooms they feel should be avoided. There was one bizarre sighting last month.

As I mentioned, each of the units bears the name of an Eastern college or university, and each of the units has its college logo painted on the wall. One of the mental health units is Duke University, which has as its college logo a blue devil, and Duke's wall had a large picture of a winking devil painted in bright blue. I say "had" because this visage sent one of the patients into a fit of hysteria and had to be painted over.

October 31, 1993

Conventional wisdom tells us that most convicts claim to be innocent. That is not true. Of the some six hundred prisoners in the general prison population, I have yet to meet one who professes innocence. Sometimes they minimize the nature of their crime, sometimes claiming that a statute was too broadly read by the prosecutor or the court or protesting the use or misapplication of the sentencing guidelines. But most often they claim entrapment.

Recently the government has used informers who appear to be causing the commission of a crime rather than merely monitoring it for future prosecution. This raises the question as to whether the accused was an unsuspecting innocent, urged and coached by the government informer or agent into committing a crime, or an unsuspecting felon predisposed to commit the crime when afforded an opportunity to do so.

Julio is serving twenty years for selling narcotics, and he swears that he was entrapped. Drugs were plentiful in his Queens, New York, neighborhood, and as a well-known community leader he could get all he wanted. But he was careful never to use or deal—

the penalties were too severe and his family and freedom too precious. Like most of Butner's inmates, he had a record and wasn't about to jeopardize his status.

One afternoon five years ago, a longtime friend came to him with a proposition. If Julio could tell him where he could get a quantity of cocaine, he and Julio could make a small fortune. Julio told him to "get lost." "I told him straight up and down—frankly, I don' deal in that shit."

But the friend pressed him. "Look, you don' have to deal—just steer me to the right man." Julio still refused.

The next day another friend, who happened to be working for the F.B.I. to reduce his own sentence, told Julio he had three kilos of cocaine and was looking to sell. Julio gave in. He contacted his first friend to tell him that his second friend had some "blow." Julio wanted no part of the proceeds; he was just helping "two friends get together." Julio was arrested for conspiracy to sell and as of 1993 had more than a dozen years left to serve.

"Entrapment, right, judge?" Julio asked me, nodding his head in the affirmative. It was almost as if my agreeing with him would be all he needed to go home to his wife and family.

"Well, entrapment is usually a question for the jury," I said not wanting to disappoint him entirely.

"But the jury convicted me—they was wrong, right?"

I proceeded to tell Julio that if the jury found him to be "behaviorally predisposed" to commit an offense, and the police merely afforded him the opportunity, that is not entrapment. The perfect example was in the Abscam trials of a decade ago. There the F.B.I. created an operation "to test the faith of those in high echelons of government." It chose public officials who, the F.B.I. claimed, had previously indicated a receptivity to bribes.

The F.B.I. agents posed as representatives of wealthy Arab sheikhs offering bribes for various favors. Every official who succumbed to the bribe temptation was found guilty, and not one jury accepted the "entrapment" defense.

I personally do not believe that in their zeal to catch criminals, the police should encourage criminal activity. You shouldn't inseminate a criminal intention in order to abort the criminal act. But I did not share this insight with Julio. He was not interested in my philosophical approach to law enforcement. His sole concern was the possibility of being back home with his wife and children.

"So what do you think, judge, if I get a new trial do you think I can prove it was entrapment?" Julio asked me again, as if he hadn't heard a word of my explanation.

"Whatever you say, Julio," I answered in exasperation.

It made him happy to hear me say that. Sometimes people ask for advice when they already know the answer but wish they didn't. But who knows? Maybe the defense will work for him if there is a second chance. It did for de Lorean.

One final and personal note on entrapment. I don't believe that the law should ever punish a person for criminal predisposition as opposed to criminal acts. I believe almost anyone can be "predisposed" to do something wrong if a prosecutor is able to push the right buttons. Whenever a defendant claims entrapment, the prosecutor is entitled to prove predisposition in order to overcome the defense. Predisposition is shown by demonstrating a defendant's previous criminal acts or even bad reputation.

There is a rule of evidence that prohibits prosecutors from proving guilt on the basis of past acts, but the courts have created an exception to this rule that allows prosecutors to show past acts and bad reputation to prove "predisposition," where entrapment is a defense. This exception troubles me because juries, considering the past acts and bad reputation of a defendant, will sometimes convict for reasons totally unrelated to the crime for which the defendant is being tried.

November 1993

November 3, 1993

My son Philip said something to me tonight that struck me as more than interesting. He said that some people who know of the kind of prison I'm in have remarked how strong I am to endure confinement, not in a federal camp—jokingly referred to as a Club Fed—but in a real prison. The first thought that leapt to mind was that it was not a sign of strength—I had no choice.

Awhile ago Dr. Viktor Frankl wrote a book concerning the prison experience. He concluded that "everything can be taken from a man but one thing: the last of the human freedoms—to choose one's attitude in any given set of circumstances, to choose one's own way." That thought has sustained me during this terrible time. He made the point that the sort of person the prisoner becomes is the result of this inner decision, and not the result of prison influences alone.

November 6, 1993

When I was Chief Judge, I promulgated a regulation that required all judges who presided over criminal trials to visit state prisons. I felt that a judge should have some understanding of the penal system, which is part of the continuum of the justice system.

The term for prisons in the old Western movies was "hoosegow." It was a term born of the belief on the part of Mexicans in the Old West that "justice" (*jusgado* in Spanish, pronounced "hoosgado"), was the same as "prison." In other words, when a Mexican was before the *jusgado* system he could count on going to the "hoosegow"— they were one and the same.

In 1962 the American Law Institute endorsed a Model Penal Code. The most significant portion of that code is Section 7.01, which provides that punishment other than prisons should be used unless imprisonment is necessary for the protection of the public. Public safety rather than punishment was proclaimed to be the goal of sentencing.

But there was and is no constituency for pursuing this goal. Other than prisoners and their families and a few reformers, no one cares about reducing the prison population. Lawyers are concerned more with procedure and due process, access to courts, rights of appeal, rules of evidence; they are not concerned with such overarching principles as who should be populating our prisons. No law has ever been developed implementing the use of prisons solely for the protection of the public.

Congress is now debating changes in the Crime Bill that will have the effect of repeating and exacerbating failed policies. More jails will be built, mandatory sentences will be increased without drawing a distinction between violent and nonviolent crimes, states will be induced to keep prisoners locked up longer, and the public will be put to enormous expense to redeem political pledges for jail construction and a bloated prison bureaucracy.

This is not to say that there aren't many crimes that should be punished by imprisonment and many criminals who belong in prison. I remember my last visit as a judge to Attica, where I was expressing sympathy for some inmates to a guard. "They didn't get here by being good people," the guard reminded me.

There are many people here in Butner who don't belong here. A fellow named Bobby who walks the halls seeing his "dead buddy" has been found incompetent to stand trial for five years. He should be in a mental hospital, as should Ziggy, who has been here for a decade doing what they call the "Thorazine shuffle."

But others do belong here. There is the sex offender who, with his female companion, abducted small children, molested, and then murdered them. Because the state where he was prosecuted could not protect him from a hostile prison population, he will be spending several life sentences in federal prisons. He is now at Butner in a special sex offender unit unique to this prison.

And then there is the fellow with whom I had lunch last week. I remember coming into the mess hall, standing with my tray, and looking for an empty seat. Most of the tables seat four, and although the room is always crowded, the quick consumption of meals contributes to a rapid turnover so that you're not left standing waiting for a table for very long. On this afternoon I was surprised to find a four-man table with only a single occupant. I quickly sat down.

My dining companion was a refined-looking gentleman who greeted me with a warm smile. "You're the judge, aren't you?"

His question was friendly, and it struck me that if I encountered this distinguished-looking fellow in a board room, or if he came before my court to argue a case, he would look very much at home.

"I once was," I answered, wanting very much to know what his occupation was before he did whatever he did to end up at Butner. I would not ask, however, and he did not satisfy my curiosity by volunteering the information.

"How do you get along with these misfits?" he inquired.

"So far so good," I said.

"Best thing to do is not socialize with them — have as little to do with them as possible," he advised. "Take me, for instance, you notice how no one comes near me? That's because I let them know that I don't want to have anything to do with them. They stay out of my face, and I stay out of theirs."

What he said about his isolation was obviously true. I noticed that not only were the seats at his table empty, but the other inmates seemed to look at him as if he were a piece of offal. They obviously had as little regard for him as he had for them.

"Look at them," he said, "thieves and worse."

When you are seated with a stranger at a meal, you seldom make conversation. Eating is for avoiding hunger, not making friends. It is done as quickly and as painlessly as possible. After you have finished eating, and before you leave, you rap twice on the table with the knuckle of a closed fist as a symbolic good-bye. That's what my companion did as he left the table.

Shortly after, when I left the table, I was approached by another inmate.

"Judge," he said, "that fellow you had lunch with—he's from the sex unit. I don't think you should have anything to do with him."

I thought that was unfair. So what if he was from the sex offender unit? He, like all of us, had committed a criminal act and, also like the rest of us, was being punished. As sinners ourselves, who are we to sit in judgment on other sinners? Who are we to say that a fellow rogue should be doubly punished by being ostracized while imprisoned because his crime may have been one of sexual perversion rather than a more commonly accepted criminal act?

It wasn't until the next day that I was told that he was ordered confined to the sex offender unit after being convicted of murder and necrophilia—that is, the day after murdering a woman, he dug up the body of his victim for the purpose of having sex with her.

I will not eat with him again.

Of course, not all sex offenders are housed in the sex offender unit, just those who have committed deviant sexual crimes, usually violent and always with an unconsenting partner, most beyond perversion and many involving children. They are pariahs among the prisoner population and are always in danger from the rest. In the general population are several rapists—for some reason, the law does not consider rape a deviant sexual act. It surprised me that rapists would be in a federal prison because rape is generally thought of as a state crime with prosecution and incarceration under state auspices. But when the rape occurs on an Indian reservation, it comes within the jurisdiction of the federal courts. That's why Dan Deer is here. He's one of those who deserves to be in prison, but the question is, for how long?

He is a remarkable athlete who looks much older than his forty-one years, and is fiercely proud of his Cherokee ancestry. I can remember, when I was a boy, visiting Cherokee, North Carolina. It was not far from Blowing Rock, the place where I spent a small portion of my youth. In addition to the tourist attractions endemic to all "Indian villages" was the habitat of much of what is left of the Cherokee nation east of the Mississippi.

Dan was born in Cherokee and had lived his entire life there. I can remember, when I was young and innocent, not being able to understand how these people who had once owned this country had been reduced to such poverty. And they did seem to be very poor. Dan's house, for example, was without plumbing or electricity. It was heated by a wood-burning stove in the kitchen. He was one of seven children, all of whom lived in two rooms with dirt floors.

Because of his athletic prowess, the tribal leaders as well as his Native American age peers marked him for greatness. He ran faster, jumped higher, and hit and kicked a ball farther than anyone else on the reservation. For that matter, he was a better athlete than any competitors from the neighboring towns. He was going to be for Cherokee what Jim Thorpe was for Carlyle.

The most important football game of the year was when Cherokee played Hendersonville. The afternoon before the game Dan, the team captain, was offered a full scholarship to attend and play football at Duke University. Cherokee gained an upset victory over Hendersonville, and that day the captain of the Cherokee team—soon to be a student at Duke University—felt himself to be the luckiest person alive.

After the game, Dan and his teammates, having heard the Hendersonville players talking about a party in nearby Boone, North

Carolina, decided that it would be a good place to celebrate. It was a party given by Clariesse Jessup, the daughter of Rod Jessup, one of Boone's leading citizens.

The party was being held in the family's backyard, which was illuminated by colorful Chinese lanterns. A three-piece band was playing the Beatles tune "I Wanna Hold Your Hand" when Dan and his teammates pulled up in their red pickup truck. Dan had a vivid recollection of everything that happened that day.

When the Cherokees got out of the truck, a strange silence fell over the party. The band stopped playing.

"What the hell is this all about?" asked Clariesse. "This the Boston Tea Party or somethin'?"

"Weren't you expectin' us?" asked Dan.

"Sooner have the niggers from 'cross town," said Clariesse.

Dan's day had been too perfect to have it spoiled this way. After a moment's silence, he said, "We didn't come to party, we came to piss."

Whereupon the entire team—the heart of the eastern Cherokee nation—began to urinate in full formation and in full view of Clariesse Jessup and the offspring of Boone's finest families.

"Now that we're empty, let's fill up, men," said Dan. The team then made a dash to the punch bowl, a large crystal vessel filled with two parts grape juice and one part gin. The punch was called "purple passion."

Dan remembers having four drinks, dancing in a large circle, falling down, and blacking out. He woke up in the Swain County jail. It was four A.M., and he called to his jailer. "What the hell am I doing here?" he asked.

"What the hell were you doing banging that Jessup girl out on the reservation?" was the answer.

That all happened in 1971, twenty-two years ago. Dan Deer was sentenced to twenty years for raping Clariesse Jessup. He swears he doesn't remember, but the evidence of his having taken the Jessup girl back to the reservation and raping her in his pickup truck before passing out was overwhelming. He has served time in three federal prisons. Every time he is released on parole, he violates the terms of his probation by being drunk in a public place. He is now scheduled for release in 1995.

Dan is over forty years old. He can still recall every play of the Cherokee-Hendersonville game.

November 7, 1993

I was arrested one year ago today. I think about that day—the day of my arrest, the beginning of my demise—constantly. It comes back to me as a nightmare, one that I relive asleep and awake.

When I was a member of the military police at Camp Gordon, Georgia, forty years ago, I was in charge of "line-of-duty" investigations. We had to determine whether a soldier's death on the army post was sufficiently related to his military duties to qualify his heirs for certain government benefits. The initial stage of the investigation was to view the body—preferably at the scene of death.

I can remember looking at the corpses of those young men. Some had been mangled in automobile accidents; others lay as if in sleep, having consumed too much alcohol or drugs. I would notice how neatly their shoes were tied, their belts buckled, their shirts buttoned, and I would wonder: When they were getting dressed this morning, could they ever imagine that their day would end like this?

When I left Albany on November 7, 1992, I too was neatly dressed. I had met with the board of the New York State Bar Association the night before and I wore the same navy blue suit the next day. I was neatly dressed, never imagining that my day would end the way it did.

I had left New York City earlier than anticipated, still enjoying the euphoria given me by a medication called Tenuate, an amphetaminelike drug that I had been taking regularly to keep up my energy level. Actually, it was more than the Tenuate that gave me the high. I was to learn later, too late, as it turned out, that I was in a manic state—in the grip of the madness that impairs a person's judgment, makes risk taking seem appropriate, and leads to a distorted sense of one's abilities. I believed I could do anything, and I was certain that I could do it better than anyone else.

I was traveling along the Long Island Expressway, five miles from my home, when a van pulled alongside on my right and slowed to my speed. Glancing over, I noticed the driver pointing to his own door. I figured that was his way of indicating my door was open, so I formed a silent "thank you" with my lips and reached over to check. But the door was firmly shut. The van stayed alongside, the driver continuing to point. I smiled and shrugged, trying to let him know that I couldn't understand what he was trying to tell me, but that I appreciated his effort.

Suddenly the van accelerated, swerved directly in front of me, and stopped short, forcing me to jam on the brakes to avoid a collision. What the hell was he doing? Before I could figure out the answer to that question or decide on what I should do next, two other vehicles screeched to a halt on either side, neatly boxing me in. Immediately from the three vehicles, six men—I was struck by how disheveled they were—leapt out and clustered around my car windows. My heart pounded uncontrollably. An abduction! I was being taken by terrorists! I had been warned about this possibility by court security personnel: as Chief Judge I was a likely target. And here it was—it was happening!

I knew the correct procedure was to stay in the car with the doors locked. But as I reached for the lock switch, a badge was pressed against the windshield in front of my face: "Federal Bureau of Investigation." At that moment the six men together, sounding like a well-rehearsed chorus, shouted: "F.B.I.! You're under arrest!"

Before I knew what was happening my door was opened and I was hauled from the car, ordered to put my hands behind my back, and roughly handcuffed and searched. By this time other cars had stopped and a crowd of onlookers was staring at my humiliation. I pleaded with the agent who had cuffed me to let me get back into my car, which seemed my only available shelter from the curious stares of the growing crowd.

"Not until I read you your rights," he said, and then proceeded, slowly and painstakingly, to recite to the handcuffed judge constitutional rights that I had been defining and explicating in judicial opinions, articles, and speeches for more than a generation.

I could not believe any of this was real; it was like the worst bad dream imaginable. But I felt less the vague sense of dread in a bad dream than the overt fear, incipient panic, and helpless anger any man must feel when handcuffed, searched, and read his rights before a crowd of strangers in the middle of an otherwise placid afternoon, particularly a man who in his confusion did not realize that he had done anything wrong. The instinctive menace I always experienced when stopped by a police officer was intensified a thousandfold—no, beyond calculation—by the staggering plunge from the dignity of my office, where the law in all its majesty was expounded and applied, to the status of publicly apprehended criminal, under physical restraint and at the mercy of nameless enforcers.

How could my situation be described? "Kafkaesque"? In a single stroke on this afternoon of the worst day of my life, I had become a different creature, no less so, psychologically, than Gregor Samsa, who in *Metamorphosis* awakens one morning to find himself transformed into a large insect.

After being forced to stand in front of that gawking crowd for what seemed an eternity, I was finally allowed to get into one of the F.B.I. vehicles. I could not find a comfortable way to sit with my hands tightly manacled behind me. When I asked one of the agents if he could please release or loosen the handcuffs, he curtly refused.

"What is this all about?" I asked. "Is this some kind of an exercise? What am I being arrested for?"

The three agents in the car looked at each other. "Extortion," answered one.

Extortion! That meant threatening someone with the intent of extracting money. Strangely enough, I felt relieved by this revelation—it confirmed the fact that my arrest was some terrible mistake. Any claim that I had been willing to sell my vote in a case was utterly unsustainable. In twenty-five years on the bench, I had never thought of doing such a thing. Someone was setting me up.

"What was the name of the case?" I asked the unshaven agent seated next to me.

"I can't answer any more questions, but believe me, we've got a ton of evidence against you. We've been following you for weeks."

"All I'm asking is the name of the case," I pled.

The agent demonstratively stroked his several days' growth of beard. "Look at this!" he snarled. "I was up all night watching your house in Albany!"

So, I was to blame for his beard as well as his discomfort. Now I understood why the pain and discomfort the handcuffs were causing me seemed to be giving him some degree of pleasure.

Perhaps the implausible charge of extortion was only meant to torment me, and my crime was altogether different? A pedestrian struck on the Thruway during drug-caused distraction? No, if it were anything like that they wouldn't have been following me. What was it the agent had said? "For weeks." But given the fact that my captors were from the F.B.I. it was perhaps something that happened out of state during the past week when I had taken my mother to Florida. Or perhaps when I was in Kentucky, where I had gone during that same week to speak at the Louisville Law School.

They were as uninterested in my repeated requests for the facts behind my arrest as by my physical distress. As we continued westward toward lower Manhattan, ironically following in reverse the same route I had lightheartedly taken less than an hour before, the full realization of what was happening slowly sank into my gut: I, the Chief Judge of New York State, arrested and handcuffed by the

F.B.I., was being taken "downtown," presumably to arraignment, publicity, and—whatever the resolution of the episode—irreparable humiliation. But why?

We finally arrived at the F.B.I. New York office, located in the federal courthouse in lower Manhattan. Because this was a Saturday, when the courthouse was closed, I anticipated the building would be empty. I was wrong. The office was filled with at least a hundred people, all of them F.B.I. agents, one of my captors assured me.

"I didn't know the office was open on Saturday," I said, amazed to see so large a crowd standing among the sea of desks in the huge room.

"It's not," he said. "They're here because of you." And in fact the casual chatter and occasional laughter stopped abruptly as I entered. One and all, they fell silent, staring at me.

I was taken to a conference room, where the handcuffs were at last removed. Then I was informed that a criminal complaint had been filed in New Jersey, charging me with conspiracy to commit extortion, interstate racketeering, blackmail, threats to kidnap, and a myriad of other crimes all tied to various conspiracies. The person making the complaint—the victim—was one J.S. Even in my confused state, I now knew exactly what this was all about: The extortion charge had been brought against me by Joy Silverman, my former—or, as the press was later to refer to her, my "erstwhile"—lover.

My first thought was that our secret liaison, which I had concealed so well (or so I thought at the time) was about to become public knowledge. My second was what a terrible scandal this would visit on Joy.

And then I asked myself the question that haunts me to this day. Why didn't Joy call *me* instead of the F.B.I.? That's all I really wanted—for her to call me, to need me, as she had for so many years. All she had to do was call me to stop whoever it was from harassing her—wouldn't that have been preferable to filing a criminal complaint? Joy knew it was me all along: Why didn't she just call and ask me to stop? Wouldn't that have been preferable to precipitating the cataclysmic publicity that would bring ruination to me and unhappiness to her?

And Joan, my wife, what would she think? During these last few years I had been uncaring, insensitive. My official duties, and the vanity that drove me to accept almost every speaking engagement offered anywhere in the country, had kept me away from home for weeks at a time. Throughout our long married life she had always been understanding, but how could she, how could anyone, possibly understand this?

The handcuffs seemed to be alive, increasing the pain which they inflicted, reminding me where I was. Arrested. A prisoner.

My children! What will they think of their father? My children. I had always told them that I would never be rich, but would leave them an inheritance more precious than riches: a family name to be ever proud of. And indeed they had always been proud of me. Nothing meant more to me than their adoration, a special delight when I was watching them from some dais where I was about to receive an award, and I knew they thrived on my adoration and praise for their accomplishments. How would they react now that I had deprived them of their promised inheritance?

And my mother and brother, who had also been so proud of me. Often, when my mother and I were dining at a restaurant, she would engage a total stranger at the next table in conversation just to let slip the fact that her son, the man sitting with her, was the Chief Judge of New York State.

I was jarred out of these despairing ruminations by an agent asking me to sign consents to searches of my homes in Albany and Long Island and my Manhattan apartment. I mechanically complied and explained where the keys could be found. After he left, I asked if I could call my wife, only to be told that an agent would make the call for me to tell her what had happened. I shrank from imagining how the news, terrible in itself, would shock her when delivered in this fashion.

Several minutes later, Michael Chertoff and Otto Obermaier, United States attorneys for New Jersey and the Southern District of New York, respectively, came into the conference room along with Jim Fox, New York F.B.I. director. I thought ruefully of how not long ago Obermaier had been my guest at a federal-state judicial conference in Florida.

Fox and I had met as guests on a mutual friend's yacht the prior summer. In a magazine article, Fox has described that moment when he saw me in handcuffs. After admitting the perverse pleasure he felt during the excitement of the events surrounding my arrest, he noted the surprised look on my face—that also seemed to pleasure him.

I asked if I could call my attorney, Paul Montclare, who also happened to be my son-in-law. An agent took me to a phone in a corner and placed the call. He handed me the receiver and my daughter, Lauren, answered. "Lauren," I said, trying to control my urgency, "stay on the line, have Paul pick up another phone." I explained that I wanted to speak to them both at once, and then spent awful moments waiting to tell them what had happened to me—or, to be more painfully accurate, what I had done.

Lauren, our first child, had become a lawyer. In law school and practicing before the state courts, it had always been a matter of great pride to her that I was her father.

Sitting there, holding the receiver as if it were a lash about to scourge me, my soul cried out for this to be not real, only a ghastly nightmare. I had momentarily dozed at the wheel of my car and was about to exit the Long Island Expressway. Then the familiar trip to Fairway Drive, where Joan would be waiting at the door and I would be given another chance to be a good, responsible, and loving husband.

Paul was now on the phone. I spoke slowly and deliberately: "Paul, Lauren, I have been arrested." I could only imagine their utter disbelief.

A few weeks earlier I had told them that Joy was being harassed and that I had gotten word that she suspected me as her harasser.

"Remember I told you that Joy suspected I was the one harassing her? She was right" — and suddenly the phone went dead.

We later learned that, as Paul supposed at the time, the call was being illegally monitored by the F.B.I. and the wiretap had disrupted the connection. He was able to call right back to say that he and Lauren were on their way to Manhattan, and that I should not discuss the case any further at present.

I was then handcuffed again and taken to the booking room to be photographed and fingerprinted. The process was endless, at least it felt so — everything and everyone, myself included, seemed to be moving in slow motion. The sense of being trapped in a paralyzing bad dream was stronger than ever. . . . Could it possibly be that I was holding under my chin a small plastic placard bearing my name and a serial number?

As for the fingerprinting, not just fingers get printed, but palms, fists, and entire hands too. A humiliating business, after which the handcuffs were refastened, and they were left on even after I was brought back to the conference room, where Paul and Lauren were waiting for me.

Paul, I learned, had already met with Chertoff and had seen some of the evidence that had led to my arrest. It was, he later told me, conclusive — my guilt could not be denied. (I have, as it happens, never denied it.) Paul told me that apparently the F.B.I. had known for weeks that I was the one harassing Joy.

He was shown the letters I had written and investigative reports that verified the threats I had made to Joy over the past weeks.

"So why did they wait so long to arrest me?" I asked.

"Because they wanted you to keep going — they wanted you to go further, further than you had gone. They wanted you to hang yourself."

"And during these last several weeks," I hesitated before finishing the question, "did Joy work with them?"

Paul looked at me blankly. "What difference does that make?" he answered.

• • •

The next step was to have bail set by a federal magistrate. Lauren overheard Chertoff telling the agents in attendance "not to bring him down until after the press arrives." I soon learned that press presence was the metronome that timed all of Chertoff's actions. Only when the press was in full attendance was I escorted to the courtroom, there to stand as a defendant in the very type of setting where for a quarter of a century I had presided as a judge.

The proceeding before the magistrate was brief. Only the highlights registered on my consciousness, numbed by the unremitting intensity of the previous two hours. I do recall noting the faces of the journalists whom for years I had known personally as well as in their professional capacities. They were gaping at me in disbelief.

And I clearly remember that shortly after the magistrate entered the courtroom, Chertoff, in an excited, high-pitched voice that was to become all too familiar, asked that I be locked up, incarcerated in the Metropolitan Correctional Center over the weekend. The magistrate, who was in the process of discharging me on my own recognizance, wanted to know why.

"Because this man is a danger to a woman and her child!" exclaimed Chertoff. "They are in dread fear of him. You have to protect them."

Paul was on his feet indicating he would be agreeable to my transfer to a hospital for observation. After a brief exchange between him and Chertoff, it was agreed that I would be removed to the psychiatric unit of Long Island Jewish Hospital.

Federal marshals then took me — still in handcuffs — to a veritable caravan waiting to escort me to the hospital. In contrast to the TV-like curtness of the F.B.I. agents who arrested me, the federal marshals who were now assigned to me were extremely considerate and even apologized for the use of the handcuffs. "Regulations," they explained.

They also apologized for the uncontrolled media crush. They expressed displeasure that Chertoff's public relations director was dictating the timetable for my appearance in court, as well as for the entire security operation.

The caravan left the courthouse. As we drove, the car radio kept repeating the sensational news of "Chief Judge Sol Wachtler's arrest." We heard Chertoff's broadcast lamentation "that someone of such prominence had fallen so far so fast." But when he feigned distress at seeing a "brilliant career go down in flames," one of the marshals reacted with visible skepticism. In response to my quizzical look, he and the others shared with me stories of their experiences with various prosecutors, especially Chertoff.

It seems that in the process of learning the art of "prosecuting for publicity" while he was in the Southern District of New York, Chertoff would participate in a pastime enjoyed by assistants in that office. They would bet on whether a particular sensational arrest or indictment would make the front page of *The New York Times*. Odds were higher if one of them bet on its being printed above the centerfold.

When our journey ended, the marshals led me from the van to a basement door. I had entered the Long Island Jewish Hospital hundreds of times in the past, but never through the basement. Conference rooms and the boardroom were the places for a distinguished judge who had served on the board of trustees of that hospital for a quarter of a century. When I approached those rooms, I always did so through the lobby, past a plaque proclaiming my honored status. But not today. Instead of exchanging easy greetings with fellow trustees, members of the medical staff, and respectful hospital personnel, I was being hustled in handcuffs through bare basement corridors. The marshals had chosen this route to avoid throngs of reporters, for which I would have been grateful had not my shame and humiliation overwhelmed all other thoughts.

Most of the events of this endless day blur numbingly together in my memory, but a few stand out in stark clarity. One was that walk down the corridor, surrounded by armed men, with chained wrists hidden under a coat draped so awkwardly that it must have attracted rather than deflected attention. Certainly no one seemed inhibited from staring at this broken man and his vaguely ominous retinue.

Another moment forever etched in my mind is the way my wife and two of my children—the others were on their way—greeted me when I entered the room in which I would be confined. Joan's unqualified and unquestioning declaration is as clear now as the moment she spoke it: "I love you very much" was uttered with an infinite tenderness painfully enhanced by the tears she tried to hide.

Philip, my youngest, gave me a strong hug and said, "It's going to be okay, Pop!" Twenty years earlier, Philip, a lovely boy of ten, had watched as I was sworn in as a judge of the Court of Appeals. Immediately afterward he smiled up at me, saying, "I'm proud of you, Pop!" The congratulatory letter from the president of the United States ran a distant second to my sheer delight from those sparkling words.

And my older brother, Morty, who had always been so proud and protective of me, in tears, stood beside me with the rest of my family.

Before more could be said, two of the marshals, guns visible at their hips, asked "the family members" to "please step out of the room for a moment." The direction sounded like the one given by a funeral director before preparing a corpse for viewing. Alone with me, they removed the handcuffs but then started to manacle me to my bed.

"Is this really necessary?" I asked.

"I'm afraid so," said one. "Instructions from the U.S. attorney."

At that moment, as if on cue, Paul and Lauren arrived. I asked Paul what sense there could be in chaining me to my bed in view of the fact that I was being guarded by two armed marshals. Paul knew that nothing in the court proceedings called for it, and went to call Chertoff. He came back after a few minutes with no better news than that Chertoff, reached at home, insisted I must remain "guarded and shackled" for the duration of my stay at the hospital. This information threw yet a further pall, if such were possible, over the visit. When my family was leaving, it was barely possible for any of us to make even a pretense of hopefulness.

Once alone, except for the guards, I experienced a sense of separation from the world more frightening than anything in my entire life. In the space of less than a day, all the patterns and prospects of my life had been destroyed. It was worse than dying, which at least leaves accomplishments and reputation intact, whereas I, still living, was faced with the horror of leaving nothing save a squalid episode that would thrust into obscurity any good I had ever done.

In thinking of those people who had come to depend upon me directly or indirectly, I suddenly felt deep concern for my staff. My two administrative assistants, Carol and Frank, who were planning a life together, would be instantly jobless. Same with my security officer, Neil, recently a father and homeowner. Jane, my secretary, and Cathy, Kevin, and Michael, my three law clerks—Michael had been with me for twenty years and had just lost his young wife to cancer—all would be unemployed, their futures perhaps tainted because of their association with me. I could do nothing for any of them. Shackled to a hospital bed, armed guards at the door, I was in a state of physical and psychic helplessness below that of the feeblest child.

It was now two o'clock in the morning. One day of the nightmare was over, and a new one had begun. The marshals agreed to keep the chains off until I fell asleep. This gave me an incentive not to sleep, and enabled me to be examined by a number of doctors.

My own physician and friend, Geraldine Lanman, introduced me to Dr. Sanford Solomon, the psychiatrist who, over the next few months and years, would bring me out of my disturbed mental state. "Sandy," who had never met me and had not heard the news of my arrest, was roused from his sleep to come to the hospital. He met briefly in the waiting room with Joan and the children, then came up to my room, expecting to find me in a state of paranoid anxiety. Instead, he later recounted, he saw "what appeared to be a very old and frail man, cowering and weeping in the corner of a chair, repeating, between sobs, how sorry he was to have brought shame on his family and his court."

Sandy and Geraldine spoke to me at great length that night, but my exhausted mind failed to register much of what was said. When they left, the marshals came from their posts at the door to chain my ankle to the bed. There I remained shackled for three days and nights, except when going to the bathroom or shower. On those occasions, I was accompanied by the armed guards, who freely expressed amazement at the degree of security imposed upon me by the United States attorney.

It is difficult to convey the intensity and inflexibility of the deliberate humiliations visited upon me on the orders of that one person. The very form of the arrest could not have been contrived with any other purpose in mind. Why, otherwise, would I have been melodramatically surrounded on a crowded public highway, literally dragged from my car, and frisked and handcuffed for all to see? I had thought this sort of urgent apprehension was reserved for desperate and armed felons fleeing from or headed toward a criminal enterprise; even heads of crime families, charged with murder, were usually allowed "to surrender themselves to authorities," as opposed to being arrested by a platoon of F.B.I. agents. In my case, tailed as I was by three vehicles of armed men, there was obviously not the slightest risk in delaying the arrest until I reached a secluded neighborhood or even my home, which was five minutes away.

But that public humiliation was more than equaled by the degrading humiliations I was then forced to undergo in private, chained like a dangerous animal, ceaselessly watched by armed guards. When Joan, our children, and their spouses came to my hospital room the next day, I covered my chains with a blanket in a pathetic effort to lessen my shame and their embarrassment.

The visit is etched in my memory like a medieval woodcut. Joan, seated in the only chair, Marjorie, holding my hand and kneeling beside the bed, Alison, just arrived from Boston, standing with folded arms, trying to look cheerful and, professional actress that she was, almost bringing it off. And Philip and Lauren, after spending most of the night with Joan in the waiting room, eyes visibly swollen as much from crying as from lack of sleep. And my children-in-law, completing the links to this revivifying circle of love.

Even as they showered me with words of comfort and every evidence of loving concern, it was difficult for me to believe that this family—my family—could see me as anything but repulsive. It was more than their patience I would have to ask for: I, who had always prided myself on being a source of strength that could never fail them now was in desperate need of *their* strength. I was also in need of their forgiveness.

The nightmare of that first night in captivity will never go away—never.

November 11, 1993

Butner was mentioned in *The New York Times* this morning. I should say that Jonathan Pollard, who is incarcerated here at Butner, was mentioned in *The New York Times.*

Jonathan is our most prominent inmate, having been arrested eight years ago for espionage. He pled guilty to the crime of passing government secrets to Israel, secrets that he accessed while a civilian employee of naval intelligence. Mind you, he is not a traitor—traitors deal with hostile nations. Jonathan gave our government's secrets to Israel, a friendly nation.

I say "gave" our secrets, although he admits to receiving fifty thousand dollars from Israel. His defenders, and there are many, will tell you that the money was to reimburse him for travel and other expenses during the period he was a spy. Those same supporters will tell you that he gave no information to Israel that it was not already entitled to as our ally.

Those who are antagonistic to Pollard will tell you that when he delivered those suitcases filled with secrets to Israel, he was selling out America—that Israel could well have traded those secrets off to Russia, or some other nation hostile to America, so that his espionage could have been traitorous.

The interesting part of the Pollard case is the change in the attitude of American Jews. When he was sentenced to life imprisonment, most mainstream Jewish groups were reluctant to take up his cause. They were afraid that to do so could indicate a lack of patriotism. But with the end of the Cold War that attitude has changed. Even the Israeli government, which at first was indifferent to Pollard's fate, has now come to his aid; a plea was made yesterday by Israel's Prime Minister Yitzhak Rabin for presidential clemency.

On December 24, 1992, George Bush pardoned former Secretary of Defense Caspar Weinberger, who had been indicted on five felony counts including perjury and obstruction of justice. There are those who say that he did so to protect himself from jeopardy in the Iran-Contra matter. Since that time, there has been renewed interest in the power of the president with respect to sentences and pardons.

There are five specific varieties of leniency that a president can grant under Article II of the Constitution: pardon, amnesty, commutation of sentence, remission of fines, and reprieve.

A pardon is a complete remission of the consequences that come with the violation of law. The slate is wiped clean, as if the offender had never been charged or convicted. Thus President Nixon was pardoned by President Ford.

Amnesty means the crime will be overlooked because punishment would not benefit the public welfare.

Commutation, which is what Pollard seeks, is a limited form of clemency that substitutes milder punishment for the one imposed by the court. Commutations ordinarily shorten an offender's sentence to time already served. The most limited form of clemency is reprieve, which simply postpones the imposition of a sentence.

The American Zionist movement, and scores of influential members of the Jewish community, have placed full-page ads in *The New York Times* urging commutation of Pollard's sentence. President Clinton is considering what course to take.

The Talmud, a collection of Jewish law and tradition, is the subject of constant debate and discussion among Jewish scholars.

When I had the opportunity to speak to Jonathan, most often as he walked to and from his prison job as a tailor, we had long and engaging conversations almost Talmudic in nature. Strange, two prisoners in Butner, North Carolina, discussing matters of faith and Hebraic philosophy.

He is a man of profound faith, who told me that he did not want to be cast in the role of martyr. He felt that the faithful should be motivated by ideals, and not by individuals or their deeds. I reminded him that it is the conduct of individuals that exemplified ideals, and therefore the exaltation of those individuals was both natural and appropriate. His Talmudic response was that if the ideal becomes so much identified with a person, and that person should be corrupted or exhibit some human failing, then the ideal would be similarly diminished. That, he said, would be unfair to the individual and the ideal.

He does not come across as a rabid spy, and yet he concedes his guilt in passing secrets to Israel. He makes the point that his eight years in solitary confinement at the penitentiary at Marion has been punishment enough, and his supporters note that no one convicted of espionage in this country has ever served more than ten years. Furthermore, Pollard's guilty plea was in the context of a plea agreement whereby the prosecutor stipulated that a five-year sentence would be sufficient. Nevertheless the judge ignored the plea agreement and sentenced Pollard to a life term in prison.

It is impossible to be in the presence of this soft-spoken and gentle man without feeling that eight years in solitary confinement is, indeed, punishment enough for him.

A month after Rabin's request was heard by President Clinton, Pollard's plea for commutation of his sentence was rejected. At that time I was back in solitary under "protection" after I was stabbed. As I was walking through the compound, in handcuffs, I walked past Jonathan. I told him how sorry I was that his commutation had been denied. His answer was "Never mind that. How are you being treated?"

November 15, 1993

Today, "Beetlejuice" cut his throat. Don't ask me the origin of his name. I couldn't tell you that anymore than I can tell you where the razor blade he used came from. He didn't kill himself, though.

He is one of those seemingly lifeless patients who would walk stiff-legged through the unit, his joints and psyche affected by the powerful antipsychotic drug Haldol.

Beetlejuice is here on a study. Some federal judge in Tennessee is waiting to learn, from the doctors here at Butner, whether Beetlejuice is competent to stand trial. That is, can he understand the nature of the charges against him, and is he able to assist in his own defense. The judge has been waiting, the doctors have been studying, and Beetlejuice has been doing the "Haldol strut" for six years. His trial will not be held until he is declared competent.

His case illustrates the difficulty the justice system has had for centuries in dealing with mental illness. When and if he is found competent to stand trial, and if he pleads insanity as a defense, the finder of fact, be it judge or jury, will have to determine not his current mental state, but whether he was insane at the time the crime was committed, many years ago.

There is an incompatibility between the law and psychiatry. The law says that a person should be punished for his unlawful acts. Psychiatry assumes that behavior is caused by forces within the person or by the environment acting on the person; if a person is unable to control his or her conduct it would be uncivilized to punish that person. In other words, the law simply asks the question, "Did he do the wrongful act?" and the behavioral sciences ask the question, "Why did he do the wrongful act?"

A psychiatrist or psychologist will not use the term "insanity." Both the word and the definition belong in the lexicon of lawyers, and lawyers have been trying for centuries to establish standards and criteria that can be used to determine whether a person can be held legally responsible for his crime.

The touchstone of all definitions for insanity came from an English case decided in 1843. It involved a man named David Mc-Naughton, who suffered from what a psychiatrist in this century would describe as paranoia. He believed that the prime minister of England, Robert Peel, was part of a plot to destroy him. After dodging shadows and imaginary assassins all over Europe, he decided that the only way to rid himself of his tormentor was to kill him. He shot the person whom he believed to be the prime minister, in front of Number 10 Downing Street. Unfortunately for the private secretary of Mr. Peel, and Mr. McNaughton, he shot the wrong man.

The McNaughton trial captured the public's imagination. For two days, medical experts convinced a jury that McNaughton was indeed delusional and therefore not responsible for his crime. He was committed in an "insane asylum," where he eventually died.

Despite the fact that he was never allowed to go free, the public and Queen Victoria thought it a travesty of justice that someone so guilty should be allowed to escape the gallows. And so the high court judges were instructed to devise a definition of insanity that would assure that a civilized perspective be maintained without impeding justice. Thus, long before psychiatry was considered a science the so-called McNaughton rule was formulated. It held that before a person can be successful in proving an insanity defense it must be shown that "at the time of committing the act, the accused was laboring under such a defect of reason, from a disease of the mind, as not to know the nature and quality of the act he was doing, or, if he did know it, that he did not know that what he was doing was wrong."

After 150 years, the McNaughton rule is still the law in almost half the states. The remainder of the states have adopted variations of the Model Penal Code developed by the American Law Institute, a standard that softened the McNaughton rule insofar as it requires a defendant only to lack "substantial capacity" to "appreciate" the nature of the act, not to "not know the nature . . . of the act he was doing," as required by *McNaughton*.

This liberalized test was the standard for the federal courts when John W. Hinkley, Jr., gunned down President Reagan on March 30, 1981. At his trial fifteen months later, Hinkley's lawyers managed to persuade a jury that Hinkley was responding to the forces of a diseased mind and that he did not "appreciate" what he was doing. Hinkley enjoyed the additional advantage of having the trial judge place the burden on the prosecution to prove Hinkley's sanity, rather than placing the burden on Hinkley to prove his insanity.

Hinkley was found "not guilty by reason of insanity" and was initially incarcerated here in Butner. He is now committed to St. Elizabeth's Hospital in Washington, D.C.

In 1984, partially as a result of the Hinkley verdict, Congress passed and President Reagan signed into law the Comprehensive Crime Control Act, which revived the "right versus wrong" criterion of the McNaughton rule back into the insanity defense and placed the burden of proving an insanity defense on the defendant.

At the time I committed my criminal acts, I may not have appreciated the extent of my wrongdoing, and my judgment while I was in a manic state may have been dreadfully impaired—but I was not legally insane. My capacity was diminished, but I knew that what I was doing was wrong, and therefore, under the applicable federal standard, I was responsible for my conduct.

There were many who urged me to use insanity as a defense. I felt that would be wrong, that I should take responsibility for my wrongful conduct. But there is a provision of law that allows sentencing judges to deviate from the sentencing guidelines where there is proof of "diminished capacity."

Despite the affidavits of six eminent psychiatrists, all of whom concurred in the diagnosis of my manic-depressive state, the prosecutor insisted that no reduction be considered in my case. The judge said she accepted the fact that I was mentally ill, but said that she didn't "understand" the nature or extent of my mental condition. She disregarded this factor entirely in determining my sentence of fifteen months' incarceration and two years of supervised release.

As I noted, the government had agreed that I should serve my sentence at a low-security "camp." However, after listening to the government vehemently insist for several months that I had no significant mental problem, it suddenly discovered that I indeed had a problem that was so significant it could only be treated at a mental health facility such as the one at F.C.I. Butner. So I was sentenced on the assumption that I was without any mitigating mental problems or "diminished capacity"—and then more severely incarcerated precisely because I had serious mental problems.

My own case aside, I do not envy the medical staff here at Butner or any other penal institute, or the judges for that matter. They must dispassionately weigh the mental stability of those awaiting trial and, in many instances, assess the state of a person's sanity as it was months and even years ago. Not an easy job, but necessary if we are to maintain our faith in a system of laws that punishes those guilty of criminal conduct but seeks to treat rather than punish those who are not responsible for that conduct because of mental disease.

November 18, 1993

Every now and again the inmates here at Butner are treated to an "art appreciation" lecture by the head of the art therapy department of the mental health unit. This evening after dinner I went with Tony and Jonathan Pollard to a slide show illustrating the work of the French artist Gauguin. When it was over, the instructor asked if there were any questions.

"Yes," said one of the inmates. "Can you point to any specific nuance or deviation in style that can be credited to van Gogh's influence on Gauguin?"

I was not surprised at the inept answers given by the instructor, but I marveled at the astuteness of the question.

"That fellow knows his art," I whispered to Tony.

"He should," Tony replied, "he's one of the country's biggest art thieves."

November 21, 1993

What is it they say about the dawn following the darkness? For me, this year, the darkness has been followed by more darkness.

Today started like every other Sunday. Normally we are expected to be out of bed before seven A.M., but those of us in the mental health unit are permitted to sleep a bit later. Because of an intense headache, which kept me up most of last night, I took advantage of this Sunday respite.

After lunch, and during the recreation period, Tony and I took a few turns around the track and then sat with Dave Pistone and Jim McCrory, watching a slow and dull game of bocci being played on this unseasonably warm afternoon.

Bocci is a game I have always associated with Little Italy in New York. When I was town supervisor, I built a bocci court in one of our town parks to accommodate transplanted Italian-Americans who love this game. The court occupies a very small space and was inexpensive to build—a perfect recreational implant for a prison. The game resembles lawn bowling but is played on a hard-packed clay surface. *Bocci* in Italian means "kiss," and the object of the game is for the participants to roll duckpin-size balls as close as they can to the "bellini," a tennis ball–size target. If your ball comes so close as to touch, to kiss, the bellini, that's a "bocci" and earns extra points.

As I sat with my three bank-robber friends, they each reminisced about Italian neighborhoods in New York City where the old Italian men, "mustached Petes" they called them, would go day after day to sip their homemade vino and play bocci. Watching the game being played in a prison yard seemed incongruous.

Later that afternoon all the prisoners returned to their units for the four o'clock count. This ritual takes place every day and requires the inmates to stand by their beds to make certain that all are ac-counted for.

Our evening meal followed shortly after the count—in all re-spects it was like every other Sunday at Butner. Only this Sunday, I was very tired because of both the prior sleepless night and the day's warm sun. I took my turn on the pill line, called Joan, and at about seven-thirty went to my cell. I had intended to listen to my radio with the earplug, and then go to sleep. Someone else had other plans for my evening.

At about 8:05, I was stabbed twice in the back.

I was lying on my left side. I don't know whether I had dozed off or was simply lingering on the edge of sleep, when my pillow was folded over my face and I felt two strong punches in the right center of my back. I got to my feet in time to see my cell door close behind someone bolting from my cell. Cell doors are not locked in the mental health unit.

As I turned on my light, I felt my undershirt sticking to my back. I knew instantly that I was bleeding. I opened my door but saw no one in the hall.

I shouted for help to an inmate walking by my cell. I told him to have anyone seen leaving the area stopped and to get the guard. Within seconds the guard was in my cell looking at my back.

"There's blood back there," he said, "but it is hard to tell how much damage was done."

He helped me on with my robe and escorted me to the room next to the unit entrance, where the guard maintains an office.

"Did you see anyone run by here?" I asked him.

"No," he answered, "but I was watching the pill line, and some-one could have slipped around the other way."

The guard was calm and, quite appropriately, thought first of the medical aspects of the situation. I was certain I would be ambu-lanced off to Duke Medical Center; instead, I was walked across the unit courtyard to the prison hospital. It was a cold night, and I was clothed only in a short-sleeved bathrobe over my bloody underwear.

As soon as I was in the hospital I was examined not by a doctor but a physician's assistant. He told me that the wounds were superficial, that they had not penetrated the chest cavity, and that it did not appear that any internal organs had been damaged. The P.A. then put stitches in the wounds—no anesthetic (I was reminded of the scene where Rambo sewed up his wound with a needle and thread). I was then X-rayed and consigned to protective custody.

"Protective custody" is another euphemism for "seclusion," which is a euphemism for the hole, which is an aphorism for hell.

When I left seclusion almost two months ago, I swore that I would never return. But, then, when I was a young man I also swore I would never go to prison. During this past year, I have had little to say about my destiny and nothing to say about the way I have been treated.

"What are these for?" I asked the guard who was handcuffing me.

"We have to cuff all inmates going into seclusion."

I write this entry from the hole. Soon the light will go out, and I will hear the banging on the doors and the cries for help. Because the dogman is still here, the barking has already begun.

November 22, 1993

That makes it two nights in a row without sleep. Every bad thing I remember about this place seems magnified, especially the hardness of the metal shelf on which I sleep. The thin mattress pad does little to protect the stab wounds, which gave me a good deal of pain last night. When I asked for something to ease the pain or aid my sleep, I was told that I could not be given a painkiller other than Tylenol or Motrin, two over-the-counter analgesics that do me no good at all.

This morning, when I thought that things could not get worse, they did. I was handcuffed and brought to a small room in the seclusion wing. A uniformed person was there; after introducing himself as Lieutenant Briggs from security, he proceeded to ask me to tell him once again what happened last night. I told him the details as best as I could remember.

"Sol," he said, "you did a lousy job. We all know you did it to yourself."

I looked at him in silence and disbelief. "Are you saying I stabbed myself?" I finally managed.

"I'm saying that we know who did it, and I'm looking at him."

"But why would I stab myself?"

"Because you want to get out of Butner, and you figured that this would be the quickest way to do it."

He was wrong about my wanting to get out of Butner. I had just been assigned to a decent-sized cell and was starting to feel comfortable in the general population. And I had no way of knowing where the Bureau of Prisons would send me if I were forced to leave this place.

"But I want to stay in Butner—if I wanted to leave, I would have requested a transfer. Why in the world would I want to stab myself to be transferred?"

"I don't know," said the lieutenant. "You tell me. Are you writing a book?"

"Well, I'm keeping a journal," I answered.

He looked at me and with a half smile said, "This would make a juicy chapter wouldn't it?"

"Are you suggesting that I stabbed myself to get material for my journal?"

"I'm suggesting that you did it for whatever reason you may have."

"What makes you so sure I did it to myself?" I asked.

"For one thing," he said, "you were too cool last night. If someone had just stabbed me, I'd be mad as hell. You were Mr. Cool."

I couldn't tell him that I was Mr. Cool because I was numb with fear, so I gave him an answer with which he could deal.

"First of all," I said, "I don't know how I could stab myself in the middle of my own back. It would be mechanically impossible. Second, I would suggest that if you really believe what you're saying, you give me a lie detector test."

"You'd take a lie detector test?"

"I just suggested it, didn't I?"

"And if I asked you, did you stab yourself, what would you say?"

"I would say no."

"Did you ask an officer for a phone last night to call your wife to alert the media about the stabbing?" He asked this question with a now-I've-got-you tone.

"No, I asked the officer for a phone so I could tell my wife what happened for fear that she would hear it through the media," I answered. But they never allowed me to call.

He stared at me for a full minute. "O.K.," he said, "let's call your wife."

After a few tries, I was able to find Joan, and I told her as best I could that I was well, and that I'd received two superficial wounds in an accident. I assiduously avoided using the verb "stabbed." Joan, with questioning far more appropriate than the lieutenant's, was able to piece the incident together in a few short minutes.

This afternoon Lieutenant Briggs returned, this time with an F.B.I. agent. There is an old police interrogation device known as the "Mutt and Jeff," sometimes called the "good cop, bad cop" routine. It's used to break a suspect down. One interrogator poses as friendly and easy going "Mutt," the other as irascible and tenacious. I may be wrong, but I had the feeling that the friendly F.B.I. agent sounded a lot like Mutt.

I found this encounter even more humiliating. I imagine the cause for my humiliation was being questioned while dressed in a terry robe, underwear, slippers, and handcuffs.

It took me awhile, but tonight, because of the compassion of one of the guards, I was able to use a phone, by way of a long extension cord which reached the food slot in the door, to speak to Joan. The apparent strength which she exhibited this afternoon was dissolved in tears this evening. She broke my heart telling me, between sobs, that I should not be in Butner—she told me that I should apply for an immediate transfer. I tried to convince her otherwise but she wasn't listening.

I believe Joan feels my pain more than I do. I will not be able to sleep tonight thinking of her and how my misconduct has subjected her to a punishment that she doesn't deserve.

Before I began my last year of law school, in 1952, I wanted more than anything to marry Joan. I thought of her constantly. After being with her, I found separation almost painful. She was my first love, and I adored her.

I realized that after law school I would have to serve at least two years in the army. Then there was the awesome prospect of earning a living. I knew how difficult it was to break into the practice of law, and I had no family or other connections to ease my entry into this competitive profession. Nevertheless, with the irresponsibility of youth, I asked Joan to marry me.

She said yes. Her mother, Elsie, recently widowed, said, "Are you serious?"

Although I believe she liked me, Elsie could not envision her only daughter married to this young man who had such limited prospects. Joan and I finally wore her down and she gave her consent, most reluctantly.

The marriage was to be in the spring of 1952. It was to be held at the Plaza Hotel in New York City.

On the night of February 23, 1952, Joan, Elsie, and I were together trying to devise a wedding list. The process was tedious and difficult. One of the difficulties, unspoken but very much with us, was the fact that Joan's father had died a very young man, at forty-seven years of age, and the prospect of having the wedding ceremony in his absence was difficult to accept.

Elopement was a tradition in my family. My father had eloped with my mother, and my brother, Morty, had eloped with my sister-in-law (he was seventeen at the time and she was fifteen). So why shouldn't Joan and I do the same? That evening, with guest lists strewn about, together with sample menus and suggested formats for wedding invitations, Joan and I decided to elope. One of her uncles knew a rabbi who would accommodate us, so just before midnight Joan and I went to the rabbi's apartment—with Elsie—and were married. Probably one of the few elopements where the bride's mother was brought along.

Our honeymoon was a night spent at a New York hotel and the next morning we both returned to our respective schools, Joan to Sarah Lawrence in New York, and I to Washington and Lee in Virginia.

We rented a small apartment in Lexington, Virginia. It was in a prefabricated complex built for married students. The rental was thirty-five dollars per month, furnished. If you didn't mind being separated from your neighbor's unit by little more than beaverboard and had no aversion to bringing in fifty-pound blocks of ice for the ice box, it was ideal.

Joan came down to be with me as often as she could. She graduated from Sarah Lawrence and I from law school at the end of that school year in 1952.

After graduation, we decided to start our life together in Hollywood, Florida, where my parents lived. Because they were in New York that summer, we moved into their empty Florida house. Those were the years before houses were air conditioned and before mosquito control had been perfected. It didn't take us long to figure out why so few people spent summers in Florida.

The Korean War was raging in the Far East, and we knew that it was only a matter of time before I would be drafted into the military. While we waited for my draft notice to arrive, I clerked in a law office in Hollywood and Joan taught a kindergarten class. We felt that we really couldn't start a career or family until I completed my military service.

With the impatience of youth, and wanting to get on with my life, I went to Atlanta, Georgia, the headquarters for the 3rd Army, and volunteered for an early draft. I was sworn in the next day in Chamblee, Georgia.

As I stood waiting for my physical examination, I looked at my fellow draftees. They all bore a striking resemblance to the young people with whom I had gone to public school in the rural South. The only difference was that these, my new companions, were wearing shoes. Many had no teeth, and all were at least five years younger than I. I was two months away from my twenty-fourth birthday.

I was assigned to the military police and stationed at Camp Gordon, Georgia, where I was put in charge of the Courts and Boards Section and became an instructor in military law at the Provost Marshal General School. We found a small house, which we rented, and in May 1954 we had our first child, Lauren.

November 23, 1993

Still in the hole. Another night without sleep. One of the screamers sounds so violent that I am thankful for the tight security.

I wasn't able to shower this morning; in the hole there is no shower, shave, or toothbrushing on Tuesdays. Fortunately, a member of the medical staff interceded on my behalf so that I could be presentable at a conference convened to "evaluate" me. Most of the evaluation was consumed by my agitated exchange with another lieutenant:

"Wachtler, do you know *why* you're in seclusion?"

"I'm told it's for my security, until the investigation of the stabbing is concluded."

"That's right—it's for your safety. Why then do you seem so agitated?"

"Because I can't understand why, if this is for my safety, I have to be handcuffed like this."

"That's procedure. I'm surprised that you don't understand procedure."

I understood procedure, I also understood bureaucratic non-sense that masquerades as "procedure." What possible reason could there be for my being shackled?

"I can understand why I'm being held in a safe place, but I can't understand why I'm being held here like more of a prisoner than I already am."

Before the lieutenant would answer, I said, "I know, procedure." And that was the end of my "interview."

But it was not the end of my ordeal. After eating the lunch passed to me through the slotted door—again with rubber-gloved hands—I was told to put my hands through the same slot to be cuffed. I was to be taken to the security lieutenant and the F.B.I. for further questioning.

After being led down the hall, still in my underwear and robe, I was escorted into the interrogation room. This time, in addition to the lieutenant and the F.B.I. agent, there were two young women. My escorting guard reminded me to keep my robe closed. "Women present," he cautioned.

I was again asked to tell the story of my stabbing. When, during my narrative, I said that I wasn't certain whether I was asleep or just dozing, the lieutenant pounced.

"You told me yesterday that you may have fallen asleep."

"I'm telling you the same thing today," I told him.

"No you're not—today you're saying that you may have been *awake*."

"That's right," I said, "and if I wasn't awake, I was dozing. Haven't you ever looked at your watch and then what appears to be a few minutes later, you look again only to find that an hour has passed? You would have sworn you were awake—but you must have slept."

"Yes, but—" The lieutenant was stilled by a sharp glance from the F.B.I. agent.

"Please continue, judge," he said. It felt good to be called "judge" by someone other than an inmate—even if I knew it came from a "good cop."

After I finished my account, the lieutenant could not contain himself. "When you felt that first blow, the first stab, why didn't you turn around and hit your attacker?"

I again explained that the two blows came so close together, they seemed instantaneous. That by the time I turned to face the door, the assailant had left my cell. That by the time I got to the door, the hall was empty. The only thing I could remember was the strong body odor and cigarette smell left by the stabber.

"How's the book coming?" asked the lieutenant.

"He thinks I stabbed myself to get a good chapter in my journal," I told the agent, and then, to the lieutenant, "I've already written part of the entry."

"I haven't given up on that theory," shot back the lieutenant. He then stared at me through narrowed eyes. "What seems to be bothering you, Sol?"

"Frankly, lieutenant, I find this to be a degrading experience. To be here in my underwear and robe with the four of you—in handcuffs."

"I know," said the lieutenant, "last year at this time you were with the big mucky-mucks in New York."

"No," I said, "last year about this time, I was a person with some degree of dignity. And now I sit here with you making me feel like a piece of garbage."

"No comment," said the lieutenant with a grin that was comment enough.

"Isn't it plausible that you were doing this to leave Butner?" asked the F.B.I. agent.

"No, I've told you I want to stay here."

"Then maybe you stabbed yourself in order to stay here," the agent countered.

"Agent," I said, "I've been associated, in one way or another, with law enforcement for forty years. If you want to stay in a place like this, you do what I had been doing, and want to continue doing. You keep a low profile. You don't attract mass media by stabbing yourself or having someone do it for you."

"Did you?" asked one of the women present, to whom no one had bothered to introduce me.

"Did I what?" I asked.

"Did you get someone to stab you?"

"No, I did not. Think about that for a moment. Do you think I would go up to an inmate and say, 'Hey, fellow, would you do me a favor and stab me twice some evening? I know you'll probably do twenty years in Springfield if they catch you, but I sure would be appreciative.' "

The agent quickly changed the subject. "Tell us about this fellow Dave whose brief you typed."

"I never typed anyone's brief," I said. "Dave Pistone did ask me to look at a brief he had written and I told him it was awful. I told him not to quote Shakespeare, and to cut his sixty pages down to four."

"Someone said they saw him in the unit with you."

"That's untrue. As far as I know, Dave has never been in the unit—certainly never with me."

"What is he here for?"

"Bank robbery."

"A lot of people have come forward and told us that there are some bikers here, Hell's Angels, who were out to get you because you handed out some tough sentences to them for making methadone. Do you think there's anything to that?"

"In my twenty-five years on the bench, I've never sentenced anyone. I may have been on the court when one of their convictions was affirmed, or I may have denied leave to appeal to one, but I would have no way of knowing that."

On that note my four inquisitors left, but I'm certain I'll see them again.

When I returned to my cell, I was again able to use a phone, which was passed to me through the food slot. I called Joan, who after inquiring about my condition told me that news of the stabbing had reached the press. She also told me that a New York *Daily News* reporter had received word, attributed to a Butner source, that my wounds were self-inflicted. I was furious, first, that the story of the stabbing had gotten out, and second, that someone from Butner was tossing the "self-inflicted" red herring on the table.

I immediately requested a guard to allow me to speak to Dr. Sally Johnson, the assistant warden. When I was unable to make contact with her, I called Paul and Joan instructing them to tell the facts surrounding the stabbing to the media so that friends and family would not imagine me writhing in agony after some act of self-impaling.

November 24, 1993

Last night a physician's assistant—I have yet to see a doctor—gave me Benadryl, an antihistamine, to help me sleep. It didn't work. My new next-door cell neighbor not only demanded a cigarette and light every fifteen minutes, he also insisted on bouncing some object against the wall that separates the cells. When you're in the hole, the way in which you demand a cigarette is to hammer on your cell's metal door with your shoe while shouting as loudly as you can, "Officer! Officer! Officer! GIVE ME A SMOKE!"

After five A.M. pill time, and six A.M. breakfast, I was summoned, once again in underwear, bathrobe, and handcuffs, to the interrogation room. This time Mr. Meko, the assistant warden in charge of public relations, was waiting for me.

"Well," he began, "the media has the story."

I couldn't hide my anger: "I understand they have a story, attributable to Butner, that my wounds were self-inflicted."

"No," he said, "they have the straight story—that you were stabbed, by someone unknown, and that we are investigating."

Apparently his appraisal of the way the story was being carried was accurate; however, one television station did quote a "source close to the situation" as saying that "there is a suspicion that the stabbing was self-inflicted." The New York Daily News carried the same story, quoting the F.B.I. as the source.

Mr. Meko was quick to tell me that Butner was not permitted to make any statement to the media concerning the incident, unless I gave my permission. I told him that he would be permitted to tell the media of the occurrence, and to confirm the ongoing investigation, but, I cautioned, the outside world was not to be told of Lieutenant Briggs's outrageous hypothesis of my self-stabbing. He assured me that I had no reason for concern.

This afternoon, Paul and Lauren came from New York, primarily to see whether I was "really all right," and to inquire about my being held in solitary confinement. They found me in good health, but were told that the confinement, the handcuffs, the solitude, and the lack of fresh air which were endemic to my life in "seclusion" would continue to be a part of my life at least until next week.

One guard told me that I would be in the hole until the investigation of my stabbing was concluded. That could mean weeks or months.

November 25, 1993

A day for giving thanks. Last Thanksgiving, Joan and I shared a turkey dinner on a paper plate behind locked and guarded doors at the Payne Whitney Psychiatric Clinic in New York. It was probably the most depressing day in both of our lives.

Three days after my arrest, on November 10, 1992, I was unchained from my hospital bed and allowed access to a telephone. I called the senior associate judge of the Court of Appeals, and while we both wept, I told him that he was to consider my call as my official resignation as Chief Judge and as my resignation as a member of the Court of Appeals. In an instant, my career and the ambition of my lifetime vanished—dissolved with a single phone call.

The federal marshals then escorted me to my home, where I was turned over to two other armed guards who were assigned to keep me in custody.

The U.S. attorney allowed me to go home only on the condition that these guards remain in my home around the clock, that all visitors who came to see me be required to sign a registry, and that my home confinement be monitored by an ankle bracelet along with a stationary monitoring device linked to my telephone system. If I were to attempt to leave my home, assuming I could escape the watchful eyes of my guards, the electric monitoring alarm would alert a central listening post, which would arrange for my immediate apprehension.

The U.S. attorney let it be known that unless I agreed to these terms of home confinement, he would seek a court order for my incarceration at the Metropolitan Correctional Center, one of the more horrendous of the federal facilities. Rather than risk this internment, I agreed to his conditions.

During the next two weeks, the U.S. attorney continued holding press conferences. I could not turn on the radio or watch television without hearing of his brilliance or my eclipse. This drumbeat, coupled with my home confinement, exacerbated my already depressed state.

On November 22, I was taken to the Payne Whitney Psychiatric Clinic at New York Hospital for observation, where I was confined for the next three weeks. I say "confined," because in addition to the locked and guarded door to my ward, the U.S. attorney insisted that the electronic monitor remain strapped to my ankle. Since the stationary monitoring device was set up in the clinic's nursing station, I could not leave my room, not even to go to the dining or recreation area. All meals were brought to me.

And that is why, last Thanksgiving, Joan and I were in that confined hospital room, imagining that no Thanksgiving celebration could be more dismal. I was wrong.

I have just finished eating the Thanksgiving meal that was passed through the food slot in my solitary-cell door. They provided all the fixings, except one. They had the sweet potatoes, cranberry sauce, stuffing, even the pumpkin pie. The only thing missing was the turkey. Instead we had ham—at least I think it was ham. They have a way of spicing and pressing various mystery meats to simulate ham. A true wonder of science.

November 26, 1993

Days have a way of running together when you're in solitary confinement. It has been five days since I was stabbed.

They have not yet recovered the weapon and although they have apprehended a suspect who was seen running from my cell soon after the incident, I have the sense that they're not convinced they have the right man. They're certainly not convinced enough to let me return to my unit. It would appear that I'm here for the duration of this Thanksgiving weekend.

I've just been told that Joan and my son Philip will soon be here to see me.

In order to see a visitor when you are in seclusion, you must first take off your orange jumpsuit and dress in khakis. You are then handcuffed and taken, in my case with two guards, across the compound to a small room in another building. Before you enter the room the handcuffs are removed, but the visit is conducted with a guard present at all times.

November 27–28, 1993

I seem to spend most of my time staring at the ceiling. I have a radio that I can listen to with an earphone. The reception is very poor, and I can only tune in to one station, but it really doesn't matter because I can't seem to concentrate on either the talk or the music. I try to read, but I find myself reading the same sentence over and over again and I can't seem to remember what I was reading just yesterday.

I don't know today's date. I know it's Monday, but I can't for the life of me figure out the date. I can remember Joan's visits—she was here on a Friday and Saturday, but it seems she was here yesterday, which means today must be Sunday, but I know it's Monday.

Such are the thoughts that plague me. In addition to not knowing what date it is, I sometimes forget—only momentarily—where I am. I imagine this is what has been referred to as being "stir crazy."

And now another day has passed, so it must be Tuesday. I have never been swept away in such an incredible time warp. I called Joan tonight, thinking that I was with her yesterday; it has actually been two days since I saw her.

November 29–30, 1993

"Pack up, Weshler, you're moving." I knew better than to ask where. All I know is that when it comes to the hole, moving is better than staying. A nurse has just removed the stitches from my stab wounds, so perhaps they're thinking of taking me out of the hole.

No need to rejoice, I'm just being moved to another and smaller cell—still in seclusion. I suspect that they needed my former cell for two inmates and could no longer afford to maintain it as a single.

I tried in my first journal entries to describe what kind of agony being in solitary confinement is. I found then, as I now find, that describing it is beyond my ability. You are surrounded by disembodied voices. The dogman has become the duckman—instead of barking all night, he quacks all night. Please don't laugh. You can't help but feel sorry for some of these tormented souls who would probably be imprisoned by their own afflicted minds even if allowed to be physically free.

And they pray a great deal. I don't know whether their prayers are born of religious conviction or because there's nothing else to do.

Perhaps they have discovered that this is where God is—where there is nothing else.

Coincidentally, I just received a letter from Joe Bellacosa, my dear friend and former judicial colleague. He told me that he was a lector at last Sunday's Mass. He read from Matthew 25:31–46, wherein Jesus speaks of dividing all of the nations before him. Those on his right would have his Father's blessing, and inherit the kingdom prepared for them from the creation of the world. Those on the left would be condemned to hell's fire. Why? Because those on his right comforted him in illness, and "in prison you came to visit me," whereas the ones on his left "did not come to comfort me when I was ill and in prison."

Of course, Jesus was not speaking of himself in other than allegorical terms. He says, "I assure you, as often as you did it for one of my least brothers, you did it for me."

Joe sent me a photostat of his airline ticket. He's taking time from his very busy court schedule to visit me on December 6. Either he misses me and wants to see me as much as I want to see him—or the reading from the Holy Gospel according to Saint Matthew scared the hell out of him.

December 1993

December 6, 1993

My daughter Alison and her husband, Barry, spent two visiting days with me this week. Lauren, Joan, and Paul did the same. Philip, Marjorie, and Morty have also come down here during these past weeks.

I've come to think of their love as the only important thing in my life. It is the wall between me and utter despair. When I think of some of the other prisoners who are deprived of that shared love, I can understand how meaningless life must seem to them. I can understand why so many weep and curse the darkness—why, for so many, the burden of solitude is too much to bear.

Joe Bellacosa, my friend of forty years, who had sat with me as a judge on New York State's highest court for eight years, came to visit me today. He flew down from Albany this morning to, as he put it, give me "a hug." He did more than that. He gave me reassurance of the affection and concern of my former colleagues and delivered a warm note from Judith Kaye, the Chief Judge.

As we spoke of the court schedule, the dynamics of the conferences where the consensus of judicial decisions are molded, and the
personalities of the various judges, both those who have been sitting
and those newly appointed, I felt a sadness come over me. This was a
life I would never again share. I will never again be given the privilege
of putting my hand to the molding of New York State's jurisprudence,
a pursuit to which I dedicated twenty-five years of my life.

"Bernhard Goetz is back in the news," Joe informed me. He was
referring to the so-called "subway gunman."

"What did he do now?" I asked.

"He's being sued by one of the fellows he gunned down," Joe
told me.

His reference to the case of *People v. Bernhard Goetz* reminded
me of one of those occasions when I was given an opportunity of
contributing to the law.

A grand jury had indicted Bernhard Goetz on attempted murder
and assault charges. The facts of the case became the subject of international headlines. To this day one cannot speak of urban vigilantism without the name of Bernhard Goetz becoming part of the
conversation. The question of law it presented was a fascinating one:
If a person is fearful, because of a prior experience or some subjective imagined terror, is he justified in preemptively assaulting the
person he fears? What if the person he fears has not made a verbal
or physical threat—has not even shown a weapon? What is the law
on justification? Should that law be modified in view of the lurking
terror in a contemporary urban environment?

On Saturday afternoon, December 22, 1984, four young black
men boarded an IRT express subway train in the Bronx and headed
south toward lower Manhattan. They rode together in the rear portion of the train. Two of the four, James Ramseur and Darryl Cabey,
had screwdrivers inside their coats, which they said they intended to
use to break into the coin boxes of video machines.

Bernhard Goetz boarded this subway train at Fourteenth Street and sat down on a bench toward the rear section of the same car occupied by the four youths. Goetz was carrying an unlicensed .38 caliber pistol loaded with five rounds of ammunition in a waistband holster. It appeared from the evidence before the grand jury that one of the youths approached Goetz, and stated, "Give me five dollars." None of the four youths displayed a weapon. Goetz responded by standing up, pulling out his handgun, and firing four shots in rapid succession.

The first shot hit one of the youths in the chest; the second struck another in the back; the third went through another's arm and into his left side; the fourth was fired at Cabey, who apparently was then standing in the corner of the car, but missed, deflecting instead off of a wall of the conductor's cab. After Goetz briefly surveyed the scene around him, he fired another shot at Cabey, who then was sitting on the end bench of the car. The bullet entered Cabey's back on the left side and severed his spinal cord.

Joe told me it was Cabey, still paralyzed and suffering brain damage, who was suing Goetz.

On December 31, 1984, Goetz surrendered to police in Concord, New Hampshire, identifying himself as the gunman being sought for the subway shooting in New York nine days earlier. Later that day, after receiving *Miranda* warnings, he made two lengthy statements, both of which were tape-recorded with his permission. In the statements, which are substantially similar, Goetz admitted that he had been illegally carrying a handgun in New York City for three years. He stated that he had first purchased a gun in 1981 after he had been injured in a mugging. Goetz also revealed that twice between 1981 and 1984 he had successfully warded off assailants simply by displaying the pistol.

According to Goetz's statement, the first contact he had with the four youths in the subway came when one of them, sitting or lying on the bench across from him, asked, "How are you?" to which he replied, "Fine." Shortly thereafter, two of them walked over to Goetz and stood to his left while the other two youths remained to his right, in the corner of the subway car. One of them then said, "Give me five dollars." Goetz stated that he knew from the smile on that one's face that they wanted to "play with me." Although he was certain that none of the youths had a gun, he had a fear, based on prior experiences, of being "maimed."

Goetz then established "a pattern of fire," deciding specifically to fire from left to right. His stated intention at that point was to "murder [the four youths], to hurt them, to make them suffer as much as possible." The next time they asked him for money, Goetz stood up, drew his weapon, and began firing, aiming for the center of the body of each of the four.

Goetz recalled that the first two he shot "tried to run through the crowd [but] they had nowhere to run." Goetz then turned to his right to "go after the other two." One of these two "tried to run through the wall of the train but . . . he had nowhere to go." The other youth, Cabey, "tried pretending that he wasn't with [the others]" by standing still, holding on to one of the subway hand straps, and not looking at Goetz. Goetz nonetheless fired his fourth shot at him.

He then ran back to the first two to make sure they had been "taken care of." Seeing that they had both been shot, he spun back to check on the latter two. Goetz noticed that the youth who had been standing still was now sitting on the bench and seemed unhurt. As Goetz told the police, "I said, '[Y]ou seem to be all right, here's another,'" and he then fired the shot that severed Cabey's spinal cord. Goetz added that "if I was a little more under self-control . . . I would have put the barrel against his forehead and fired." He also admitted that "if I had had more [bullets], I would have shot them again, and again, and again."

When the grand jury began its deliberations to decide whether Goetz should be indicted and tried for attempted murder, it was read the "justification statute." This statute provides that a person could use physical force against another person "when and to the extent he reasonably believes such to be necessary" to defend himself. When one of the grand jurors asked the district attorney to clarify the term "reasonably believes," he was told that the grand jury had to determine, under the circumstances of the incident, "whether Goetz's conduct was that of a reasonable man in his situation."

As I noted, the grand jury indicted Goetz for attempted murder and assault.

Mark Baker, an outstanding appellate advocate, along with his partner, the renowned criminal defense lawyer Barry Slotnick, sought to have the grand jury indictment dismissed, claiming that the instruction given to the grand jury was in error. They argued that the test should not be whether Goetz's conduct was that of a "reasonable man" but rather whether the conduct and reaction were "reasonable" given the mind-set and circumstances not of a reasonable man but of Bernhard Goetz.

The lower courts agreed, and the indictment was dismissed.

The dismissal was greeted with great public approbation. Goetz had become a folk hero. A citizenry beset with the fear of crime had a hero who had the courage to say to the marauders, "No more!"

But what did the decision of the lower courts do to the law? Did their decisions dismissing the attempted murder charges mean that, no matter how absurd Goetz's perception of reality, it was nevertheless a proper standard to measure the justification of his actions?

What if Goetz, or someone similarly situated, believed that all men with tattoos must have been in prison, and that all ex-prisoners were dangerous? Would that person be "justified," because of this subjective belief, in gunning down all persons with tattoos because he was in fear? Should the law of justification allow the perpetrator of a serious crime to go free simply because that person believed his actions were reasonable and necessary to prevent some perceived harm? To completely exonerate such an individual, no matter how understandable his thought patterns, would allow citizens to set their own standards for the permissible use of force.

Goetz's case may have been one that aroused sympathy, but when a court decides a case, the law that it articulates in its decision becomes a precedent. That precedent controls the determination in future cases that may not arouse so much sympathy.

It occurred to me, and ultimately to my colleagues, that the test of "justification" had to be a blend of subjective as well as objective criteria. First, the jury would have to consider the *objective* circumstances, those facing a defendant at the time he takes action. Would a "reasonable person" under those circumstances believe that deadly force was necessary?

Second, the jury would have to consider whether the defendant had the *subjective* requisite belief under the statute, that is, whether he believed deadly force was necessary to avert being the victim of one of the enumerated felonies.

The courtroom was packed during oral argument of the Goetz case. In an article that appeared in the April 1996 issue of *Lifestyles* magazine, Mark Baker, the appeals lawyer representing Goetz, described the scene and the outcome:

> Following the prosecution's presentation (during which I felt confident that the dismissal of the indictment would be upheld) and before I even completed my assent to the podium to defend my position, the Chief Judge was all over me. He challenged this premise, or raised that point or nuance which I had little opportunity even to contemplate . . . Ultimately, the full Court, by a 7–0 vote, in a thorough and cogently reasoned written opinion by Chief Judge Wachtler, reversed the lower court's decision, reinstated the indictment, and sent the case back for trial. (Mr. Goetz was later acquitted, in June, 1987, of all shooting-related charges.)
>
> For the first time in 150 years, the law of justification in New York had been explained with clarity of thought and syntax—by Judge Wachtler. This lucidity is the hallmark of the more than 450 opinions he wrote in his law-book filling, 20-year career on the court. His opinion in the Goetz case is now a widely cited national precedent in the many comparable cases that have followed.

When Joe left, I was handcuffed, strip-searched, led by guards past the stares of my fellow convicts, and put back into my solitary confinement.

December 7, 1993

This morning at five A.M., a shout came through the slot in my cell door. It was to awaken me for my daily medication.

I rose from my sleeping pad, put my feet on the floor, and started for the door. But before I reached the slot shelf that held my pills, I lost my balance and fell backward; I used my elbows to break my fall. One elbow tore open and started to bleed profusely. It was later to swell, Popeye-like, to twice its size and become a source of red-hot infection.

December 8, 1993

It has been eighteen days since my transfer to seclusion. Joan told me to keep a calendar—if I didn't, I would have no way of keeping in touch with reality and knowing how much time I've spent in this airless and solitary place. Actually, it is not completely solitary. The other night, I noticed a cockroach crawling across the shadows of the bars that appear on my cell wall at night.

Because there is no way of turning on my light from the inside of my cell, I did my best to follow the path of the roach with the help of the security compound lights shining through my window. It was not alone. Although I had not seen the nest during the day, there were dozens clustered near the base of my toilet.

December 14, 1993

This morning—very early this morning—I awoke with a start. Since the stabbing, and the infected elbow, my sleep is easily disturbed so that the shuffling noise over my cot, although barely audible, was enough to awaken me. There, not two feet from my head, was the largest, hairiest, and most sinister-looking spider I had ever seen. Although it had the size and characteristics of a tarantula, it had the ominous hourglass marking of the black widow.

As a rule, insects do not frighten me. But this one, larger than my fist, caused me to bolt out of my bed in frantic search of a light switch. Remembering that the lights must be turned on from outside my cell, I began shouting through the food slot for the duty officer.

There I was on my hands and knees shouting through the door slot, "Officer! Officer! Officer!" My voice became part of the nocturnal chorus. I was trying to yell louder than any of the others who were shouting, barking, singing, and screaming. I had become one of them. And although I thought the spider was enough of a reason for me to require special attention, I am certain that whatever devil, fiend, or specter had moved in with them was at least as disturbing.

When the officer put on the light, there was no spider. This news came as no surprise to him. He had witnessed the simple turning on of a light put flight to vampires, mummies, devils, and once, the four horsemen of the apocalypse. My spider was no challenge at all. But it frightened me. Not the spider. The fact that I saw the spider.

December 16, 1993

I have been in solitary confinement for almost a month. They apparently have no additional clues as to my assailant, so they don't know where to put me. They feel it would be dangerous for me to be put back where my stabber may be waiting to finish his job, and they know that keeping me in the hole very much longer could affect my sanity. They have to decide what to do with me.

At a conference held in a small room near the seclusion cells, Dr. Johnson, an assistant warden and herself a psychiatrist, and other members of the psychiatric staff held a meeting. After the conclusion of their meeting, I was escorted into the room and told of their solution.

First, they said that the tentative diagnosis that the doctors at But-ner had reached was far more serious than they, or even my own doctors, had initially thought. They said that during the commission of my crime, I was delusional—psychotic. That the imagined brain tumor that had plagued me for months as well as the characters that I had conjured up during my manic episodes took on such genuine proportions as to become, in my mind, more real than imagined. In fact, said one, "If you had been sent here on a study we would have found you mentally incompetent."

Second, they felt that I am in further need of treatment. I could not understand this. Except for the aberrational episode with the "spider"—which I was convinced was generated by my elbow infec-tion fever—I thought my behavior normal. In fact, I thought that my ability to endure this interlude in seclusion with equanimity was evidence of mental stability, not weakness. I also felt that the Prozac that had been prescribed and that I was taking with regularity was easing the pain of my depression.

But they were of a different mind, and I realized that trying to convince a group of psychologists and psychiatrists that you are mentally well is difficult, particularly when they are convinced that you are not.

And so they told me of their plan. They intended to have me flown to Minnesota to a prison affiliated with the Mayo Clinic. The name of the prison: Rochester.

December 17, 1993

I heard this morning that Frank Altimari and his wife, Angela, were coming to visit me today. This is not a visiting day, so it is almost im-possible for anyone to arrange for a visit. But Frank Altimari is not just anyone—he is a federal judge. And not just a federal judge—he is a judge who was appointed by President Reagan to sit on the Second Circuit Court of Appeals. This is an appellate court one notch below the United States Supreme Court in the federal judicial hierarchy.

I first met Frank in 1955. I had just been discharged from the army and had gone to New York for the sole purpose of finding a job in a law office. I came to believe, after my brief experience as a law clerk in Florida, that the most able lawyers were those who had practiced in the larger Northern cities.

In those days, Florida had what was known as the "diploma privilege." This meant that if you graduated from a Florida law school, you were automatically admitted to the Florida Bar; whereas if you had graduated from an out-of-state law school you were required to take the Florida Bar examination. This was an incredibly difficult three-day examination designed to make it almost impossible for an out-of-stater to compete with the local homebred and home-educated natives.

Those lawyers who left their New York practices to retire or make a more comfortable life for themselves in Florida and who were able to pass the Florida Bar examination made a great impression on my young legal mind. Many Florida lawyers were also excellent, but it struck me that I could be a better lawyer if I went to New York for a short training period before starting a Florida practice.

It was easy to convince Joan, whose mother and other family members lived in New York, that this New York sojourn for the learning experience would be worthwhile.

Because I had graduated from law school with honors, had been president of the student bar association and head of the moot court team, and, more recently, had military experience as the head of the Courts and Boards Section of the Provost Marshal General's Center, I thought that it would be relatively simple for me to get a job as a law clerk. After all, New York City had thousands of law firms; surely one of them would need or could use my talents.

After three weeks of interviews and rejections, I concluded that perhaps I had less talent than I thought.

When I was about ready to give up and go back to Florida, I was hired by a firm in Jamaica, Queens, not Manhattan—and not the major Wall Street firm I had envisioned. The firm, Austin & Dupont, handled everything from wills and estates to real estate closings and criminal trials.

My salary was thirty-five dollars per week. Once again I was forced to depend on the financial assistance of my father, and for the first time in my life I learned what it was like to be in debt.

My "office" at Austin & Dupont was a seat at the library–conference room table with a window that was on the same level as and adjacent to the Jamaica Avenue elevated railway. Of course there was no air conditioning, and when a subway train rumbled by the open window, which happened every fifteen minutes, all conversation, telephone and otherwise, stopped until the rattling, screeching, and sound of rushing air generated by the passing subway cars stopped.

It was at Austin & Dupont that I met Frank Altimari and his law partner, Ted Hoffmann. We became close friends, and I was able to persuade them that practicing law adjacent to an elevated subway line was not the best way to make a mark in the legal profession. I convinced them that the burgeoning suburban neighborhoods of Long Island, once thought of as only bedroom communities for the city dwellers of Manhattan, were developing an industrial and commercial identity of their own, that where there is growth and commerce, there is a need for lawyers.

Ted and Frank became convinced, and in 1957 joined me in leasing space in Mineola, New York, the governmental seat of New York's most populous suburban community, Nassau County.

For weeks we sat waiting for the phone to ring. I was pained to notice that as the barren and tedious days continued, Ted and Frank stopped looking at the silent phones and started staring at me. Even the noise of the subway was preferable to this stillness.

Fortunately, before our patience and financial resources were exhausted, we started to develop a client base. I would like to say that this was due to our legal skills and business acumen, but it was not. We were just incredibly fortunate.

It was I who first encouraged Frank to become involved in politics. His ambition in life was to be a judge, so in 1963 I introduced him to the Republican leadership, and sponsored him for his first nomination to run for the office of district court judge of Nassau County from the district that embraced the town of North Hempstead. At the time I was a councilman of that township and a vice chairman of the Republican county committee.

We were successful in getting Frank the nomination. Unfortunately, the year of that election was 1964, the year that Barry Goldwater's presence at the head of the Republican ticket spelled disaster for almost every Republican candidate that year.

Frank's district court campaign became a subject for the history books and a constantly cited example of the importance of a person's single vote. Of the over 112,000 votes cast (112,484, to be precise), Frank and his opponent ended up in a dead heat—a tie. After several recounts and the counting and recounting of the absentee ballots, the vote was still a tie.

Inasmuch as a tie vote elected neither Frank nor his opponent to the judgeship, a vacancy in the office was declared, and, pursuant to the county charter, the county executive, a Democrat, was to appoint someone to fill the vacancy. Predictably, Frank's opponent, the Democrat, was chosen. The following year, sympathy dictated that Frank receive bipartisan endorsement, which he got, and he became a county district court judge. A few years later he was elected to the county court, and then the state supreme court. He then gravitated to the federal district court and, as I have noted, now sits as a federal appellate judge on the Second Circuit Court of Appeals.

I was prepared for Frank's visit in the usual "seclusion" manner by being given khakis to wear in place of my orange jumpsuit and shoes to wear instead of the orange slipper sneakers. I was then handcuffed and taken across the compound to the private visiting room that had been arranged for me.

Because this was a weekday, the compound was filled with inmates. I felt more self-conscious than usual as my four-member guard escort surrounded me and led the way.

Two of the guards were discussing this extraordinary visit and speculating as to its nature and reason. One of the others apparently knew the answer: "I understand he's getting a visit from a big-time federal judge."

No more had to be said.

Frank and Ange's visit was just this morning. I remember how pleased I was to see them both, how distressed Ange was to see the size and redness of my injured elbow, and how we laughed at shared remembrances. But I recall very little of our conversation. I remember the silences, and my own thoughts of the strange situation presented by this longtime friend and law associate of forty years ago, now an important federal judge, visiting me in prison. But for the life of me I can't recall what we talked about.

Frank stopped by here on his way to Palm Beach for a three-week vacation. I, on the other hand, was told just yesterday that I am soon to be sent to spend the next seven months in a prison in Minnesota. At least one of us can hold himself fortunate to be traveling to an agreeable climate this winter.

December 20, 1993

I didn't sleep last night. It was a combination of things. The roach population in my cell seemed to grow by multiples. I was accustomed to seeing them crawl along the walls, but now—perhaps because of the sudden onset of winter or the phase of the moon or the new occupant of the cell next door—for whatever reason they have taken to the invasion of my bunk. I have had to remake it four times.

Or maybe my sleeplessness was caused by the pain from my stab wounds or the infection in my elbow or my anticipation of the trip to the federal medical center in Rochester, Minnesota. I've been told that I will probably be going the day after tomorrow.

While lying awake in my solitary confinement, I remembered a fall day when Joan and I took Alison to her first day at Skidmore, a small upstate New York college. Alison and I walked across the leaf-strewn campus, and in the most fatherly tone I could manage I put my arms around her and said, "Tootie, remember one thing: Nothing is more important than self-respect. Once you do something or allow something to be done to you that diminishes your own self-image, then you have lost the firmest foundation of good character."

I remember that thought as I lie in this filthy dungeon—that's what it is—and ask myself, "How can you still respect yourself when, by your own deeds, you placed yourself in a cage like the most feral of animals?"

The only peace that came to me that night was remembering the remarkable good news I had heard during the past few weeks. Alison and my daughter-in-law Robin had recently told me they were pregnant, and tonight my daughter Marjorie told me her good news as well. Thinking these thoughts, the expectation of three more grandchildren, brought me some serenity. This was abruptly interrupted by a banging on my cell door: "Weshler, get dressed!"

"What time is it?"

"Five o'clock. You're supposed to be ready to leave in fifteen minutes."

"Leave for where?"

"Damned if I know. I was just told to get you up."

Of course, I knew where I was leaving for. Prison transfers are almost always unannounced. Butner had learned that a prisoner was being flown from Jessup, Georgia, to Rochester, Minnesota, for a surgical procedure. All they had to do was arrange for a slight detour to have me picked up and rid themselves of me.

To prepare me for this excursion, I was trussed like an oven-bound turkey. First, a chain was fastened about my waist. I was then handcuffed to that chain. Both of my ankles were then shackled, and those shackles, linked together, were joined to the chain girdling my waist. I should have been used to chains by now—accustomed to their heavy weight and coldness, to the leadened sound when the links pulled apart and then came together, to the way in which they seemed to pinch and burn and bruise while constraining your freedom—but I wasn't.

Walking—I should say hobbling—was awkward, painful, and slow. When we arrived at the private airport at Durham, I noticed that the other prisoner, the one being transported from Jessup, wore only handcuffs. It was explained to me that although he was serving a six-year sentence, all of his time was served at camps. He was not considered dangerous. I, on the other hand, was classified as a security risk.

The guard from Jessup who explained this to me was twenty-five years old, chewed tobacco, lived in Waycross, Georgia, and had never been north of South Carolina. He looked at my chained form, crammed into one of the four passenger seats, spit tobacco in a Styrofoam cup that he carried for that purpose, and asked me, "Have you ever been up in a plane, Washtler?"

If someone asks you how long it takes to fly in a twin engine prop plane from Durham, North Carolina, to Rochester, Minnesota, tell them four and a half hours. If they ask you how long it seems when you're immobile because of being chained from your waist down during the entire trip—unable to even scratch your nose, no less cross your legs—triple it.

We arrived midday at the Rochester airport, and I was not surprised to see the ground covered with snow. The fact that this was winter in Minnesota was made apparent by the blast of frigid air that greeted me as I was extracted from the plane and assisted to a waiting van. Employees of the small Rochester airport self-consciously tried to look the other way. They didn't want to appear to stare at this sinister creature, wrapped in chains, whose crime must have matched that of Hannibal Lecter.

My fellow prisoner and traveling companion, who was spending his fifth year at a camp, was being sent to the Federal Medical Center for an operation on his back. Inasmuch as the Federal Medical

Center, the F.M.C., is much like an adjunct of the Mayo Clinic, he considered himself fortunate. After seeing the way I was compelled to travel, he considered himself even more fortunate.

If I hadn't been so cold, miserable, and humiliated I probably would have found some humor in the scene that was played out at the Rochester air terminal between the guards who had accompanied me and those from the correctional facility who had come to pick me up and bring me to my new place of confinement.

Guard from the plane: "You can't take him with those chains."

Guard from Rochester: "Why not?"

Guard from the plane: "Because those chains belong to Butner, and we're responsible for bringing them back."

Guard from Rochester: "But we can't take him if he's unchained."

Guard from the plane: "Hey, we were only supposed to deliver him, not the chains. You gotta get your own chains."

Guard from Rochester: "No, you were supposed to deliver him chained. In fact, he should have been wearing a black box. Where's his black box?" They were referring to a small black box that dangerous prisoners in transit have secured between their handcuffed wrists to further restrict movement.

Guard from the plane: "He didn't come with a black box."

Guard from Rochester: "He should have had a black box. But I'll tell you what. We'll take him in these chains and then we'll send the chains back to Butner."

Guard from the plane: "No deal—we don't leave here without the chains."

The debate lasted far too long, but it was finally resolved when one of the Rochester guards discovered a set of chains in the transport van. As one set of chains was taken off me, the others were simultaneously substituted, until the Butner chains were freed for return to North Carolina.

When we arrived at F.M.C. Rochester, we were taken to the receiving office, where my companion's handcuffs were removed and I was unchained. He was told that he would be assigned a cell pending his physical examination. I, on the other hand, would be assigned to seclusion on a temporary basis.

"Excuse me, sir," I inquired. "By seclusion do you mean solitary confinement?"

"By seclusion, I mean the hole," he answered.

If someone were to ask me to identify the worst moment of my confinement, this would be it.

I had just been released from one month in the hole at Butner. When you are so confined, you are not permitted to change your underwear or to shower and shave during the weekend, so I looked—and must have smelled—like one of Hannibal Lecter's victims. My nearly five hours of being chained in transit had caused every muscle and bone to ache. I had not slept for two days. My stab wounds still throbbed, my swollen and infected elbow was hot and aching. And now I was being told that I was to be interred, once again, in the airless vault of seclusion.

Except for the fact that the issued uniform was a dark green jumpsuit instead of bright orange, seclusion at Rochester was very much like seclusion at Butner. Fortunately, I was to stay in seclusion for only three days. I remember nothing about those days, except for the visit from Dr. Ruth Westrick, a psychiatrist who served as the assistant warden.

She was the first person I saw. She was visiting the inmates in seclusion and showed genuine concern for my condition. She arranged for the immediate examination of my elbow by a physician who provided antibiotics that stemmed the infection.

I was to learn later from personal experience that Dr. Westrick spends every morning, from six A.M. on, visiting each and all the psychiatric patients in the mental health unit. And her visits are not perfunctory. She exhibits inordinate patience and seems to know all their afflictions. In addition, she is available day and night to those who want to see her, no matter what the reason. She is living proof that prison personnel can be firm and efficient, maintain discipline, and at the same time allow an inmate to retain dignity.

Rochester

Rochester, Minnesota

THE ROCHESTER RAP

Why you laughin', ain' nothin' funny,
Don't nothin' move, 'ceptin' the money,
Locked up, han'cuffed, now I'm on the stand,
Fifty Kees, fifty Gees, just part of my plan,
Finally got to Rochester, three hots and a cot,
Fed up, bulked up, here till I rot.

Lawrence (Strick) Strickland, an inmate

Christmas 1993

December 22, 1993

My new place of confinement here in the Federal Medical Center at Rochester bears no resemblance to Butner. The red brick buildings, built in the fifties originally as a state mental hospital, house some eight hundred prisoners, about the same population as Butner. The grounds are surrounded by two very tall, parallel razor-wire fences with a perimeter traveled twenty-four hours a day by a truck manned by guards. The truck substitutes for a guard tower. As of this date, there has never been an escape from Rochester, but there have been attempts.

As I anticipated, I have been assigned to Rochester's mental health unit. The officials at Rochester have no way of knowing exactly what my mental condition is. Their sole reliance is on the report from Butner, which, as I have noted, still categorizes me as mentally ill. The Bureau of Prisons obviously feels that I'm too lacking in mental health to be sent to a camp—so lacking that I cannot even be allowed to become part of the general population of this prison.

I know that I am still depressed, but considering my condition of some months ago I feel relatively well, at least well enough to cope with my imprisonment. Strange, when I knew I was mentally afflicted, the government in the person of the prosecutor took the position that I was well, and now that I feel myself to be well, the government, in the guise of the Bureau of Prisons, takes the position that I am sick.

I am once again dressed in a jumpsuit and am trussed in the Martin unit, which is a steel-barred enclosed section of the mental health unit. It's namesake, Dr. Harold Martin, was a psychiatrist at the Mayo Clinic. He envisioned a unit that was secure but not harsh, somewhere between the total isolation and security of seclusion and the less rigorous confinement of the general population. His idea led to the establishment of the housing unit that bears his name and which will confine me during the next few weeks.

Meals and medication are delivered to the rather small Martin unit which comprises ten cells occupied by inmates who are all seriously mentally ill but not dangerous. The steel door of each cell is locked at ten-thirty P.M. and is opened at six-thirty A.M. The unit itself is always locked behind heavy steel bars; however, inmates have the freedom of leaving their cells to walk in the unit's corridor, which leads to a small conference or game room.

Meals are delivered in trays. The inmates eat either in their cells or seated in one of the chairs installed in the unit corridor.

Unlike in "seclusion," showers and shaves are permitted every morning, one inmate at a time, under the watchful eyes of a guard assigned to make certain that no inmate injures himself.

December 24–25, 1993

I've just been told that Joan and my son Philip will be visiting me today and tomorrow. I know it must have been difficult to arrange transportation on Christmas Eve. I'm very glad they did.

Seeing them brought a renewal of spirit. Although we have never celebrated Christmas as a holiday, it has always been a time of year for some kind of family gathering. When the children were very young, we would go to California, Florida, or Bermuda or charter a yacht in the Virgin Islands or the Grenadines. We would visit farms or ski resorts—always something to do or someplace different to go.

This would have been the first Christmas that Joan and I were apart. Thanks to her, that did not happen. Thanks to me, we spent it in an overcrowded room with prison inmates and vestiges of their families. The sadness became a forceful and real presence among the false paper decorations and plastic Christmas tree.

January 1994

January 1, 1994

The first of the year, when newly elected public officials take their oaths of office. Some wait until the second or third, but most want to create the appearance of continuous government and so opt for January 1. Still others are anxious to taste the fruits of their November victory at the first possible moment. For them there are two swearings in, one at midnight on December 31, usually private; and the other the next day, a public inauguration.

I was much sought after as the person to conduct the swearing-in ceremonies, not because of any particular skills, but because I was the state's Chief Judge. It was in that capacity that I swore in Governor Cuomo on two occasions and Mayor Koch after his last election, in 1986.

The first time I swore in Governor Cuomo was for his second term, in January 1986. It was a unique experience. The first family of New York State invited me and my family to join them at the governor's mansion on New Year's Eve. Our two families dined together, and after dinner, on the stroke of midnight, I administered the oath of office. The entire audience consisted of our wives, Joan and Matilda Cuomo, and the Cuomo and Wachtler children. That ceremony was much more memorable to me than the public inaugural that followed, although the latter was attended by thousands and was accompanied by bands, choirs, and the firing of cannons.

I recall going with Mario to his new offices on the second floor of the Capitol Building after the swearing in. I looked at the massive desk, which had been used by such distinguished New York governors as John Jay and Franklin D. Roosevelt, and mused at how great an honor and challenge the governorship of New York must be.

"All you have to do is give up your entire life and work and campaign twenty-four hours a day, seven days a week, and it could be yours," Mario told me.

"Sounds easy," I said, "and if I ran against you, I would have a perfect campaign slogan."

"What would that be?" he asked.

"I would simply say, 'How can you vote for Mario Cuomo? Anyone who appointed me Chief Judge isn't fit to be governor.' "

I was also given the opportunity to officiate at the swearing in of the majority leader of the state senate and the speaker of the state assembly. Indeed, at my last swearing-in exercise, I was given the unique privilege, for the first time in history, of swearing in the entire membership of the New York State Senate and Assembly en masse.

Remembering this my thoughts turned to a wedding that my friend Bernadette Castro gave for her daughter. It was only a year ago. Joan and I were seated with Rudolph Giuliani and his wife, Donna Hanover. Donna said to Joan, "Just think, in a couple of years Rudy and I will be in Gracie Mansion and you and Sol will be in the governor's mansion."

There are only seven residents in the Martin unit. Mr. Harrison, who lives across the hall from me, is a toothless, painfully thin, elderly black man who hasn't bathed in months, maybe years. He walks the length of the unit constantly, back and forth. As he walks, he claps his hands softly and whimpers. If you were to close your eyes, you would think you were hearing a baby's bare bottom being gently spanked and the baby responding with a muffled cry.

He stops walking only to eat in his room. Every now and again he stops to tell you that he is God, and that none of us are where we think we are. Yesterday, when one of the unit guards tried to convince him that he should bathe, he went into a rage. "You're not fit to tell God what to do!" When Simon, another resident of the unit, shouted his agreement that Mr. Harrison was indeed God and that we should open our minds and hearts to him, Simon was thrown into the hole. As soon as Simon was handcuffed and escorted from his room, God, né Harrison, went into Simon's locker and stole his instant coffee.

Now that Simon has made the ultimate sacrifice for his god, there are six residents in the unit. Garcia, who shouts epithets in Spanish, seems to be constantly angry. His crime is never mentioned. Duarte is a very young bank robber. And then there's Elliot, a twenty-three-year-old who is proud of the newspaper article that tells how he bilked major corporations out of $10 million by selling stolen computer parts and computer chips, which he pilfered while serving as a security guard for various companies. At twenty he owned a Porsche, a Jaguar, and a Corvette. At one time, he told me, he had in his possession a Vermeer, a Monet, three Rembrandts, and three Degas, all stolen from the Isabella Stuart Gardner Museum in Boston.

Elliot will be released on January 29, but he has a number of detainers filed against him (as soon as he's released he's turned over to another jurisdiction to be tried for another crime). One of his detainers relates to the museum heist.

Then there is Hughes. He's another one who threatened the life of the president. He is an absolutely incoherent twenty-five-year-old who claims to be a veteran of World War I. He spends most of his time striking poses—standing, sitting, bending—poses that his six-foot, six-inch frame maintains for long periods. He is also fond of spitting at people, particularly the nurses.

These were my companions during this holiday season. With them I marked the end of 1993 and the beginning of 1994, and I wasn't invited to a single swearing-in ceremony.

January 4, 1994

I feel as though I have been in an inescapable labyrinth. My universe has become so small and confined that I have lost touch with the outside world. Today one of the guards brought me a newspaper. It is from Des Moines, Iowa, and it is two days old, but it is a newspaper and I am glad to have it.

As part of the review of happenings in 1993, one of the feature stories is the story of the massacre of Long Island Railroad passengers by a man named Colin Ferguson. It happened on December 7, but word of this atrocity did not reach me when I was in solitary. His was an act of heartless depravity.

Predictably, it has revived the clamor for the death penalty in New York, an issue that bedeviled Governor Cuomo, who year after year, for twelve years, has vetoed legislation that would bring back New York's electric chair. The electric chair itself still exists; I saw it stored in an attic in Sing Sing Prison. It goes by the sobriquet "Old Sparky."

It was New York that was first to use the electric chair. The year was 1890, the victim, a murderer by the name of William Kemmler who argued before the New York State Court of Appeals that death by electrocution was cruel and inhumane. "Not so," said the court on which I was later privileged to sit. It held that the miracle of electricity would result in instantaneous and consequently painless death. *The New York Times* went so far as to call it euthanasia by electricity.

Thomas A. Edison, who was attempting to commercialize the use of direct-current electricity at the time, and George Westinghouse, who was marketing alternating current, were each hoping the other's current would be chosen for the electrocution. After all, how could they market their brand of electricity as a safe source of energy if it was used to kill Kemmler?

Direct current was chosen, but the instantaneous and painless death promised by the court was not to be. The newspaper *New World* described the execution:

> The current had been passing through his body for 15 seconds when the electrode at the head was removed. Suddenly the breast heaved. There was a straining at the straps which bound him. A purplish foam covered the lips and was spattered over the leather head band. The man was alive.
>
> Warden, physician, guards. . . . Everybody lost their wits. There was a startled cry for the current to be turned on again. . . . An odor of burning flesh and singed hair filled the room, for a moment, a blue flame played about the base of the victim's spine. This time the electricity flowed four minutes.

Old Sparky did not live up to its promise. But the real question is whether the death penalty can live up to any promise, aside from ratcheting our civilization back a few notches on the evolutionary charts, venting public frustration, and allowing us to offer up an occasional human sacrifice to appease the howling gods of rage.

If Mario Cuomo is defeated in the next gubernatorial election, or when he retires, we will have a death penalty in New York. It will cost a fortune: in California each capital case costs between $2 million and $5 million to prosecute. They have had the death penalty for sixteen years and it cost them $90 million a year. But in sixteen years they have executed only two people.

We have executed two hundred fifty people in this country during the eighteen years the death penalty has been legal. There are now three thousand waiting to die. Speak to some of the chief justices of other states, as I have—in Florida, Louisiana, Texas, states that have the largest per capita number of executions—and they will tell you that they also have the highest murder rates. The death penalty is not a deterrent. It is extremely costly; it clogs the courts; it doesn't reduce prison populations. But make no mistake, it's coming to New York.

The great irony in the current climate is that the last death penalty bill vetoed by the governor allows for execution only in limited circumstances, none of which fit Colin Ferguson. Those who murder police officers and prison guards can be executed as well as those who murder witnesses to be certain of their silence. Hired killers and people who kill in furtherance of other crimes, or those murderers who make their victims suffer—they are all on the list. But the crime that Colin Ferguson allegedly committed, the mass murder of innocent civilians, is not.

January 5, 1994

Today I was taken out of the Martin unit and assigned to the mental health unit. For the first time I have a roommate—or, to be more precise, a cellmate. A "celly," as they are called. He has a very full, red beard and bright blue eyes. He chews tobacco, snores, and speaks with an almost incomprehensible Kentucky drawl. He was once a coal miner and is proud to claim the appellation hillbilly.

Arvil Lake is from Knox County, Kentucky. His father was also a coal miner; his back was broken in the mine when Arvil was thirteen years old. Being the oldest of seven children, all of whom lived in one room, Arvil set himself the task of supporting his family as best he could.

In 1968, at age eighteen, he was drafted and was sent to Vietnam, in time to engage in the Tet Offensive of 1969. He was wounded in combat and returned to Kentucky in 1970 to do what his father and most other people in Knox County did: He went into the coal mines.

After thirteen years as a miner, he decided to become an entrepreneur—he was going to own his own mine. This did not require much of a capital investment. He leased mining equipment and made an arrangement with the owner of the land to be mined whereby the owner would receive a percentage of the proceeds from the sale of the coal.

There were some 350 such small independent mines in Knox County. The average mine hired some twenty miners. The one significant way in which these independent mines differed from such giants as Consolidated Coal Mining was that the independents were nonunion, whereas the large operators contracted with the United Mine Workers.

Arvil's mine was successful. After paying rental on the equipment, wages, and the percentage to the land owner, he averaged some $60,000 net from $500,000 gross per year over his ten years of operation.

But the United Mine Workers, who wanted to represent the miners, and the Bituminous Coal Association, which represented the owners of the larger mines, were unhappy with these independents. The independents like Arvil, without worrying about dealings with the union, could sell coal for less than the Bituminous Coal Association members.

One day—Arvil says it came without warning—a special investigation from the United States Department of Labor informed Arvil that his mine was to be closed. The reason given was "safety violations" (failure to properly ground powder magazine and bench grinder; failure to have a wind curtain; a rock obstruction; failure to have a safety cover on the fuse box). Although I have no way of knowing, Arvil tells me that all of these deficiencies could have been remedied by him, at very little cost, in about three hours. But he was not given the opportunity.

It was difficult for me to believe that a federal agency would be that arbitrary and severe. But Arvil insists that the Department of Labor was determined to get rid of the independents and lay in wait to "hit 'em like a snake" when given the opportunity.

Despite Arvil's protestations, I could not help but believe that he had probably been given a warning—perhaps more than one—that went unheeded.

Nevertheless, Arvil, and the owners of most of the independents, were hauled into court for these petty violations. The judge dismissed the charges, but the appellate court reinstated them. Under the sentencing guidelines, which mandate punishment on a sliding scale, Arvil Lake was sentenced to six months' incarceration and six months' supervision.

The process of trial and appeal began in 1989 with the closing of his mine. He will be going home in two weeks. The government spent four years and an enormous sum of money to prosecute Arvil Lake. But he was only one of many. Of the 350 independent mines in Knox County, he tells me only 10 remain in operation.

Of course, some will tell you that the strong political and lobbying arms of the United Mine Workers and the Bituminous Coal Association were the powerful influences that caused the federal government to be so draconian in its treatment of violations that amounted to no more than misdemeanors. I don't know enough about the situation to make that appraisal.

Arvil was originally sent to Butner by the Bureau of Prisons for a study relating to a posttraumatic stress syndrome that has been plaguing him since Vietnam. Butner, finding no evidence of mental illness, sent him to Rochester for further testing. After seven visits to the Mayo Clinic, four of which involved MRIs (magnetic resonance imaging), it was discovered that he had a brain tumor that affects the functioning of his left leg and necessitating that he walk with a cane. His symptoms are the same as those I had during the time of my depression. But his tumor is real, whereas mine was imagined.

Arvil will go home for an operation at the Kentucky Veterans Administration hospital. The protracted litigation and six months' incarceration caused him to lose his mine. He will live on disability if his tumor is successfully eliminated. He remains a deeply religious and patriotic man, but I wonder how much his country or his faith have really done for him.

January 9, 1994

Philip and Joan came to visit today. We shared the visiting room with a large group of very tough-looking men who had come to visit an elderly gentleman. Several of the visitors wore sweatsuits; all of them seemed menacing by virtue of their size.

I introduced both Philip and Joan to this kindly old man who greeted them with a benign, almost tender smile. What I didn't tell Philip and Joan was that this very amiable eighty-six-year-old inmate, Joe Aiuppa, also known as Joey (Doves) O'Brian, was the reported head of the Chicago crime family called the "Outfit." Those muscular visitors who came to see him were also from Chicago.

Aiuppa's nickname, Doves, was derived from his one and only prior arrest. It seems he was caught with some two hundred doves in the trunk of his car after a hunting trip, a number far in excess of the legal limit. His influence and presence go all the way back to Al Capone. I'm certain he deserved the deference his visitors bestowed on him, and after observing his visitors, you can be sure that I will also defer to him during my stay here. My deference will also come from the story of his career.

The F.B.I. long contended that Aiuppa, as one of the bosses of the Outfit, participated in the decision to murder the one-time "Top Boss" Sam Giancana. That was in 1975. In 1983, when the Outfit's Las Vegas operations became the subject of an indictment charging a vast conspiracy to skim millions from the Las Vegas casinos, Aiuppa, along with fifteen crime leaders from five cities, was named as the leader of a conglomerate of crime families known as La Cosa Nostra.

One of the witnesses by affidavit in Aiuppa's detention hearing was Ken Eto, one of the mob's capos who had been the subject of an aborted assassination attempt. He testified that his murder was ordered by Aiuppa or another leader of the Outfit, "because the Outfit did not think I could do my time and that therefore I would cooperate with the government." Eto was shot three times in the back of the head from the rear seat of a car he was driving, but miraculously managed to crawl to a phone and call the police. His two would-be assassins were both killed as payment for their ineptitude.

Another witness was Aladena (Jimmy the Weasel) Fratianno, who swore by affidavit in the same detention hearing that Aiuppa ordered the murders of at least six other persons. One was Johnny Roselli, Al Capone's emissary to Las Vegas, who was found in a barrel floating in Key Biscayne. Another was Ray Ryan, William Holden's Kenya partner whose car was blown up after he testified against a mob member.

But the most detailed picture of Aiuppa's rule as boss of the Outfit came from the affidavit of Angelo Lonardo who, prior to the defection of Sammy (the Bull) Gravano, the underboss to John Gotti in the Gambino family, was the highest-ranking member of the Cosa Nostra to become a witness for the government. He described Aiuppa as "being a very tough disciplinarian. . . . Those who testified or provided information against the family would be silenced, including by their death."

Aiuppa was sentenced in 1986 when he was seventy-eight years old. Now, in his eighty-sixth year, he uses a walker to travel across the prison compound. He is shown enormous respect by the other prisoners and even the guards. Perhaps it is because of his age or his very pleasant demeanor—maybe it is because he has been here so long, or perhaps because his exploits as a major figure in organized crime for so many years have given him some sort of status. Whatever the reason, he is shown great deference—far more than former Chief Judges.

When Joan's visit was over, the usual closing ritual took place. Tearful good-byes and then the dramatic return to the harsh reality of brusque orders, single-file lines, and the strip search. But for whatever reason, Joey "Doves" was not required to "bend and spread 'em."

January 27, 1994

Arvil has left and I miss him. I wish I could rid myself of this pain I feel whenever I have to say good-bye to someone. He's on his way back to Kentucky to undergo surgery for his tumor.

My new "celly" is Chet Choi, whose parents came to America from Korea. He's twenty-two years old and was arrested last year for trafficking in LSD. His story is typical of many of those arrested for dealing drugs. They are undone, not by law enforcement investigation, but by being turned in by a confederate seeking to lessen his own jeopardy. In addition to other charges, he faces imprisonment for the catch-all crime of conspiracy.

LSD, a hallucinogen that was a popular drug in the sixties, has been making a comeback. It first came to national attention in 1957, when *Life* magazine actually praised it as a new antiaggression drug. It was classified as illegal in 1966, as it had become popular as a recreational drug and had been linked to suicide and prolonged psychotic states.

LSD is an odorless, colorless, and tasteless derivative of ergot, a fungus that grows on rye; LSD can also be synthesized in the laboratory. A little bit goes a long way toward bringing the user visions and a great increase in conscious awareness. The big problem is that it decreases the user's ability to logically deal with this rush of perception.

Its potency is such that an extremely small amount, a "microdot" on blotter paper or sugar cubes, is sufficient to disable the user's perceptional filter system for twelve hours. A three-by-three-inch blotter cut into small pieces is good for a hundred hits. Put another way, a normal hit of LSD is 50 to 150 microprograms, which means that there are approximately 200,000 doses to the ounce. LSD is considered to be by far the most potent drug known.

Chet has been doing LSD since the eighth grade, when he was fourteen years old. He is also a loyal follower of the Grateful Dead. Whenever the Dead were on tour, Chet made every effort to attend their concerts, following them from city to city. He was and still considers himself to be a Dead Head.

It was to attend a concert of the Dead in Oakland, California, that he left his home in Springfield, Illinois, during the summer of 1992. While there, he bought a blotter of LSD to send home to his friend in Illinois. He knew that what he was doing was illegal, but he figured that there was no way he could get caught. He placed the blotter in a plain number 10 envelope, without a return address. There was nothing in the envelope except the blotter, therefore there was no way to trace the illegal substance to him. Or so he thought.

Unfortunately for Chet, while he was in California, his friend in Illinois was arrested for dealing drugs. In order to escape punishment, the friend "gave up" (turned in) everyone he knew who had anything to do with drugs, including his own sister. While he was in the process of saving himself, the envelope containing the LSD-saturated blotter arrived from Chet. When Chet returned to Illinois, the F.B.I. and a three-year sentence were waiting for him. He is here for observation concerning a depression that has been with him for almost a year.

January 28, 1994

Yesterday I came into our cell to find Chet talking to another inmate who looked to be fifteen years old. He told me he was eighteen.

"What are you here for?" I asked Chet's friend. His name was Pepe.

"Bank robbery," he said.

"How much did you rob?"

"Eighteen hundred dollars."

"Did you use a weapon?"

"Naw, jes' a note what said, 'Put all your money in this bag. I've got a powerful weapon here,' it was jus' an empty box. The lady gave me the money and I took off."

"Did they get your picture?"

"Naw."

"Did someone identify you?"

"Naw."

"Did they go after you when you left the bank?"

"Naw."

"How did they catch you?"

"They didn't."

"Then what are you doing here?"

"They arrested someone else for my crime—he was in jail for four months. An' then I saw Jesus—he come to me an' tol' me that 'someone else should not pay fo' y' crime,' an' so I give myself up."

"That must have been difficult to do."

"Naw—the only hard part was persuadin' the F.B.I. that I was the one what did it. I had to keep goin' back an' tell them other things I 'membered that only the robber would know, afore they'd believe me."

The innocent man was freed, and Pepe was sentenced to forty-eight months, less than the guidelines called for, but because of his diagnosed mental illness, his sentence was reduced on the basis of "diminished capacity." He feels comfortable with his decision to confess, and even elated by the circumstances that led him to be "born again."

The reason Pepe has been kept in the mental health unit is his profound religiosity. It manifested itself in many ways, from resentment toward those who would not verbalize their acceptance of Christ, to frequent audible conversations with his Savior. It was this latter propensity that caused the other inmates to ridicule him.

I was reminded of Thomas Carlyle's observation: "If Jesus Christ were to come today, people would not even crucify him. They would ask him to dinner, and hear what he had to say, and make fun of it."

Interesting, when you think of it: Someone talks to Jesus, it's called praying, but if Jesus talks to someone, the person is put in a mental health unit.

Interesting from another perspective.

Pepe was convicted after he had confessed. This is true in a great many cases — confessions have been the predicate for a great many convictions. After a person admits that he has committed a crime, the presumption of innocence becomes weakened in the mind of the fact finder. A confession, presented to a jury, is compelling evidence of guilt.

Of course, in Pepe's case his confession was voluntary. He was guilty and wanted that to be known. He wanted to be punished for his crime.

But in other cases and in other contexts the issue of "confessions" has been troublesome. Because getting a conviction is made relatively simple when a suspect confesses to his crime, there is always the suspicion that a confession is not altogether voluntary, that law enforcement lessened its burden of ferreting out evidence and building a case by taking the easier path of forcing the suspect to "confess." To deal with this concern, the United States Supreme Court handed down a decision in *Miranda v. Arizona*, according to which a police officer arresting someone for a crime is required to inform him that he has a right to counsel and a right to remain silent.

The genesis of *Miranda* is the Fifth Amendment to the United States Constitution, which proclaims that the government may not compel a person "in any criminal case to be a witness against himself." The framers of our Constitution knew, from the bitter lessons of history, that it was not difficult to obtain a confession by the use of the rack, the thumbscrew, or other coercive measures like threatening to send a colonist back to England for trial if he did not confess his crime. To prohibit this kind of abuse by government, the framers said, in effect, that a person could not be forced to confess. The question then became a determination of whether force or some other coercion was used to obtain a confession.

In certain earlier cases, this determination could be made quickly and easily. For example, in the thirties, when a black man in Mississippi was beaten with a metal-buckled leather strap as a prelude to confession, the Supreme Court had no trouble in setting aside the conviction that his confession spawned.

But what of the more subtle ways of coercing confession? Actual cases: A defendant is kept in isolation and questioned for three days without being allowed to see an attorney; a suspect is told that if he does not confess to a crime, his ailing wife will be arrested and brought to the station house for questioning; a mother is told that if she doesn't "cooperate" with the police her children will be taken away from her.

These were the kinds of fact patterns placed before the courts in the 1940s and 1950s, and the appellate courts were called upon to determine whether confessions elicited under these circumstances should have been admissible. Before the *Miranda* decision, the methods of police interrogation were so diverse and the effects of isolation, intimidation, and defendant ignorance so varied that the courts found it difficult to determine, after the fact, whether a confession was truly voluntary.

The 1966 decision in *Miranda* was an effort to put an end to this difficulty by establishing an objective standard—denounced by critics who classify themselves as conservatives—which requires that all persons in police custody be read their rights before being questioned. Failure to comply with this rule would under most circumstances lead to a suppression of the confession.

Talk show hosts, television "cop" shows, and some other critics have led people to believe that before the police may interrogate or arrest a suspect, the *Miranda* warnings must be given. That is not the fact or the law. Neither arrest *alone* nor interrogation *alone* (if there has been no arrest) requires the warnings to be given. A statement given to the police by a suspect not in custody is not subject to *Miranda*, which applies only to "in-custody questioning."

I was a young lawyer in 1966, when *Miranda* was decided. I had already served as a member of the military police and was at that time serving as chairman of the Nassau County Board of Supervisors' Committee on Public Safety. Law enforcement was very much a part of my life, and I, along with the members of the county police force, the prosecutor's office, and those charged with the general responsibility for maintaining law and order, were frightened by the decision. We envisioned the use of *Miranda* by wily defense counsel as a tool for the suppression of confessions, which, we all knew, were often the strongest foundation on which to build a conviction.

Over time, however, police compliance became second nature. Administering the warnings became a routine part of postarrest interrogation. Today the occasions for suppressing improperly obtained confessions, particularly in view of some of the modifications made to *Miranda* consistent with the common law process, are extremely rare. Acquittals on the basis of a *Miranda*-based suppression are even more rare. Indeed, I would be hard-pressed to name a single such case involving a serious crime in my court or any other.

When I was a judge, I concluded that *Miranda* was a sensible ruling that did not present any problems for law enforcement while at the same time allowing the courts to use a helpful device to vindicate the Fifth Amendment protection against self-incrimination.

Now, after having spent a year in prison with prisoners, many of whom confessed or made self-incriminating statements after having the *Miranda* warnings read to them, I am prepared to go one step further. I have concluded that when an arresting officer reads from that small card in his hat or pocket telling a suspect in custody that "you have a right to remain silent, anything you say may be used in evidence against you," etc., he may just as well be reading the batting order for the New York Mets.

They've all heard it before—on TV or when they were last arrested. The incantation is neither as meaningful as I once thought it was, nor as sinister as the critics of *Miranda* think it is. Ask an inmate who has incriminated himself why he did so, and the answers are predictable: the attempt to shift blame when an accomplice is involved; the protestations of innocence because he "didn't know what was in the bag"; the attempt to dupe the "dumb cop"; the promise or hope of leniency; or just plain remorse or conscience.

These thoughts cross my mind as Pepe tells me of his epiphany and confession. His was a confession of conscience, and I am certain that it would have been forthcoming even if Jesus had given Pepe his *Miranda* warnings.

January 29, 1994

This morning my hair froze. I had to go for blood tests on the other side of the compound—about three city blocks away from my unit. I had just finished my morning shower, my hair was not yet dry, and on my way to the lab it froze. This will give you some idea of what a −73° chill factor can do to a damp head.

One of the inducements for my plea of guilty had been the promise of a sentence of confinement in warm and sunny Florida. This thought crossed my mind as my hair froze.

January 30, 1994

F.M.C. Rochester is divided into three parts: psychiatric, medical, and work cadre. The work cadre consists of sentenced prisoners who attend to the orderly and kitchen duties as well as assist in attending to the patients in psychiatric and medical. They are the drones, and any day now I am expected to join their number in the general population. In the meanwhile, I work with the therapy department of the psychiatric unit.

Some of those in the psychiatric unit have committed violent crimes and will be here for decades. There is one who cut his wife's heart out and then calmly collected her insurance. Another, who looks like he is fifteen, shot and killed his grandmother. These crimes were committed on a military base and an Indian Reservation, respectively, which explains the federal jurisdiction.

But there are others in the general population serving ridiculously long sentences for crimes not serious enough to merit long-term incarceration. Whether you are for or against the legalization of controlled substances—and I, for one, am opposed to legalization—we must realize the costs to society when we use our prisons to warehouse low-level drug dealers and users for long periods. In most instances, one-, two-, or three-year maximum sentences would provide a sufficient deterrent.

Marijuana, also known as cannabis, grass, weed, pot, reefer, herb, tea, Mary Jane, ganja, and dagga, was known in colonial America as hemp. As early as 1630, all of the rope and half of the clothes made in America were made of hemp. Presidents Washington, Jefferson, and Adams grew it for its fiber use. In 1762 it was our second-largest export.

During the 1930s marijuana became popular as a recreational drug, and a campaign was begun to outlaw its use. The Marijuana Stamp Act of 1937 was enacted for this purpose. Of course, the act had the side effect of outlawing hemp production, and some historians suggest that the burgeoning synthetic-fiber industry worked hard to enact this legislation. The Stamp Act was ruled unconstitutional because as soon as a grower paid the tax, he was prosecuted. This was held to be a violation of the Fifth Amendment right against self-incrimination.

Until 1973, marijuana possession was punished with lengthy prison sentences. In Georgia and Missouri, selling marijuana to a minor was punished by death. But marijuana use continued. In 1974, 43 million Americans admitted using marijuana, and penalties for personal possession were reduced in most states. Still, there are marijuana dealers—I have met four already—who are all serving terms of ten years or more because of federal sentencing laws that make no sense. There must be hundreds if not thousands who have been similarly punished. Let me tell you about one.

For reasons that will become apparent, he was called "The Hermit." He is tall and has movie-star good looks. The year 1974 was when the Hermit decided the legalization of this substance was imminent.

To prepare himself for a career as a grower of marijuana, he went to Colombia to learn growing techniques from the experts. He spent two and a half years in Colombia raising, harvesting, and learning about marijuana, the flower, and hashish, the resin. He learned that the THC (tetrahydrocannabinol) chemical content determined the potency of the product; that the flowers and outer leaf of the female plant are where the THC is found. He learned how to raise a higher-potency marijuana (sinsemilla) that had no seeds.

He also learned about corruption. He tells stories of Drug Enforcement Administration and customs employees of the United States government who came to Colombia to buy large amounts of marijuana. They would arrange to seize certain shipments consisting of stems and male plants, both useless, while allowing the sinsemilla and choice marijuana to be shipped to prearranged destinations untouched. He knew of one such scam involving twenty-seven tons of pot.

President Nixon had developed a plan to close the borders of drug-exporting countries through subsidy payments to them. This caused the price of marijuana to increase from $10 to $80 an ounce. During the same year the price of domestic sinsemilla increased from $80 to $100 an ounce. One year later the price had doubled.

It was in 1976 that the Hermit came home from Colombia and enrolled in the University of Santa Cruz School of Horticulture, in California's Humboldt County.

He introduced sinsemilla to Humboldt County and Santa Cruz. With what he told me was a corrupt constabulary and a weak economy, marijuana growing supported whole communities. But in 1978, when marijuana was targeted by the war on drugs, federal agents moved in and the Hermit decided it was time for him to move out. In that year alone there were 400,000 marijuana-possession arrests in the United States.

The cost of real estate in the Santa Cruz area in 1978 was $85,000 to $90,000 a lot. After some research, the Hermit discovered that land in Minnesota was selling for $250 an acre. He bought 240 acres and moved to that state. It was here that he was going to start a family and establish himself.

He made the small rural community of Akeley, Minnesota, his home and discovered that there were farmers there who could not pay their taxes. Others were facing bank foreclosures. He made a proposal to several: He would use a small part of their land, grow marijuana on it, sell it, and give the farmer part of the proceeds. He would average approximately fifteen plants per farm, so that a farmer could receive approximately $1,000 per plant or $15,000 for the six-month growing season. This windfall was enough, in many instances, to allow the farmer to keep his land.

In 1980, the Hermit hit his peak. He planted marijuana crops sufficient to fill two suitcases with $175,000 in cash. To do this he had to live in the woods and tend the crop from May to September. This earned him the nickname Hermit.

Having made his first substantial "score," he decided to quit the marijuana business, and establish himself as a legitimate citizen, which he did in 1982. In the same year he married a divorcee who had two sons. Together they had three daughters, and the Hermit felt the obligation of supporting a growing family.

There came a time, in 1987, when he touched the edges of poverty. He was an accomplished carpenter, but outside of the occasional deck, fence, or house alteration, there was no work. He did everything he could to put food on the table, including shoveling snow for neighbors. In the spring he tried selling plants as part of a nursery operation, without success. He could not help but notice that he could sell a bushel basket of corn for $3.18, whereas the same basket filled with marijuana would bring him $13,000. Estimates placed marijuana, a $33 billion crop, as this country's most valuable cash crop, larger than corn ($14 billion) or soybeans ($11 billion), even though one fourth to one third of the illegal pot is kept from the market by law enforcement.

By 1989, he and his wife were divorced and his effort to survive in the plant nursery business was derailed by an order for 400,000 tomato plants that was placed by a customer who left town before paying.

He decided that he would go back into the marijuana business while at the same time giving his marijuana-growing enterprise a nobility of purpose by establishing a "food shelf," a place where people in need of assistance could go, in commune style, to be fed. With the profits from his operations he would be able to accomplish this with great ease. But he never saw the profits.

The Hermit was picked up in his motor home with 1,185 marijuana plants. He was swept into the federal system, where the law provides that if you have over 100 plants, each plant is presumed to weigh one gram. Under the Reagan-era approach of "zero tolerance," the punishment for possession of one hundred grams of marijuana is the same as for the possession of one hundred grams of heroin: a mandatory five- to forty-year sentence with no chance of parole. The average time spent by a murderer in American prisons is nine years.

There is a move afoot to eliminate this one-plant-equals-one-gram weight presumption, because after you discard the male plants, the stems, and other unusable parts of the plant, the average weight is far less. But any such change in the law will not help the Hermit, who has already spent four years in prison and is looking at another five years on a ten-year sentence. Under the Crime Bill recently signed into law, if he had been found with 60,000 plants his penalty could have been death.

He is bitter. He will show you the longitudinal study of 1,380 U.C.L.A. undergraduate marijuana users which found that there was no relationship between the use of marijuana and grades. Or the La Guardia Commission study of chronic pot smokers in New York City, and the India Hemp Commission, and studies in Costa Rica and Jamaica, where no psychological or physiological difference was found between users and nonusers. The Costa Rica study of eighty men who smoked an average of ten joints daily for twenty years found "no organic brain damage, medical or psychological differences after they had quit for two days."

When the Hermit points to his mandatory ten-year sentence, he notes the burden his incarceration brings to the American taxpayer—over $30,000 per year. But his profound sorrow lies in the effect his ten-year absence will have on his children. He feels that in a real sense they are being punished and deprived because of an unjust law and an unrealistic sentence. He also feels that society may ultimately pay for this imposed neglect.

The needs of his ten-year-old daughter, deprived of her father for a decade, are reflected in a letter she wrote him:

Dear Papa,

I love you very much more than you can ever think. What if you never get out of jail and never see us again. I worry about that sometimes. But I know in my heart you will see me when you get out of jail and I will see you a lot. I love you very, very much.

Papa, I love you.

In 1992, according to the F.B.I., 535,000 people were arrested for the possession, sale, or manufacture of marijuana. In six cases, life sentences were imposed, bringing the number serving life sentences to thirty, despite the fact that history does not record a single death as having been caused by that drug.

I hesitate to recommend that marijuana be made legal for the reason that no drug is completely safe. And I am persuaded that smoking marijuana does provide a gateway to the use of stronger drugs. But the current federal laws regulating marijuana, with their outrageously long sentences, are absurd.

One of the prisoners occupying a cell next to mine, a very young Minnesota farm boy named Arlen Floyd Angell, was caught up in this marijuana sentencing net. His sentencing judge, Paul A. Magnuson of the federal court for the District of Minnesota, is one of the judges who recognizes this absurdity in sentencing. The transcript of Arlen's sentencing is edifying.

This was Arlen's first arrest. A year passed after his arrest while the authorities debated whether the state or federal courts should try him. As Judge Magnuson, constrained by the sentencing guidelines to send Arlen to prison for ten years, put it: "A charge in the state court would constitute a petty misdemeanor, a charge in the federal court would mean ten years of incarceration." He continues:

> I cannot help but reflect on the day I sat beside the former director of the Federal Bureau of Prisons and listened to the Chairman of the United States Sentencing Commission speak with such great confidence about the ten year sentences which were going to be mandated in certain instances. And the Director of the Federal Bureau of Prisons leaned over to me and said: "Does the chairman not realize that any person that spends ten years in one of my institutions comes out of that institution dysfunctional, without exception?"

February 1994

February 6, 1994

"Respect." That word is a constant source of conversation. "Don't disrespect me, man." "If anyone showed me such disrespect, I'd show him my fist." "I don't care what I have to do—I'll do it—but the man has to show me some respect." "Don' dis me, man!"

If you asked a prisoner what means most to someone in this environment, he would tell you, "Respect." That is not to say deference, or special treatment—just the respect due to any person who is a decent human being. If you assume, as most people do, that a person in prison has no decency, then of course you will not show him or her any respect.

I can remember visiting prisons as a judge. I attempted to avoid eye contact with the prisoners. I did not fear them, or hold them in low regard, but I could not relate to them as people. They were society's rejects, paying a price for their antisocial behavior. I was there to see how they lived, worked, and were treated. I always felt they should be treated humanely and decently, but I am not certain that I was prepared to respect them.

But my definition of respect has changed. I would now define the word as meaning the demonstrated awareness that the prisoner is a person. That each person is unique and each person's life is singular. Indeed, it is the uniqueness that makes a person responsible for his actions. If we are to say he is responsible for doing wrong, we are recognizing this uniqueness in that context; to deny it in another context is to be inconsistent and unfair. You don't have to condone a person's misdeed to acknowledge and respect his humanity. You can respect the sinner without respecting the sin.

Frankie, my executive assistant, and Neil, my security officer, used to tell me that by virtue of my high office and the constant assistance of those surrounding me, I never knew the pain of others' indifference: the rudeness of the clerk behind the counter or motor vehicle bureau window. During my incarceration these past months I have known what it is to be ignored and subjected to incredible rudeness.

I am reminded of something that J. B. Priestley wrote: "I can't help feeling wary when I hear anything said about the masses. First, you take their faces away from 'em by calling them masses, and then you accuse 'em of not havin' any faces."

I think of this every time I say "Good morning" to a guard and get not so much as a glance or grunt to acknowledge my greeting or even my presence. Or when an officer approaches me with a snarl and an inquiry like "Washtler, what's your cell number?" or "Washtler, where are you going?" or "Washtler, come over here" or "Get over there" — never an acknowledgment that you are any more than a subhuman or an inanimate object.

February 12, 1994

"Hey, Washtler, the warden wants to see you."

The directive has the ability to get your attention. All I could think of was the Edward G. Robinson or James Cagney characters getting a similar summons. When they got to the warden's office they were usually thrown in the hole, there to spend endless hours of torment.

Under normal circumstances we have what is called "controlled movement." That is, you cannot be out of your unit except during decreed periods of ten minutes each, on the hour, and then only to go to or from an assigned location. But when the warden wants to see you, the prescribed limitation is waived. You go immediately, every step of the way monitored by sentinels with walkie-talkies.

Allowed to walk across the compound under the watchful gaze of the guards, I bundled up against the cold and walked to the warden's office. When I arrived I was met by Dr. Westrick, the assistant warden, and the warden.

"We have a surprise visitor here to see you," said Dr. Westrick.

When I walked through the door, I was greeted and embraced by Justice Harry Blackmun of the United States Supreme Court.

During my time as a judge, I was privileged to meet and spend time with several different Supreme Court justices. On two different occasions Justice William Brennan and I shared the limelight as guests of honor. I was similarly honored with Justices Thurgood Marshall and Potter Stewart. My closest relationship was with Justice Lewis Powell, who had attended and was a benefactor of my alma mater, Washington and Lee University. He sent me an inscribed copy of his biography while I was here at Rochester. When I was chair of the New York State Bicentennial Commission, I spent considerable time with former Chief Justice Warren Burger, who was the national Bicentennial chair. And now I was being honored by a visit from Justice Harry Blackmun.

I had met Justice Blackmun several years ago, when we both served on a televised panel show in Philadelphia, one of Fred Friendly's Socratic panels on "medicine and the law." More recently, we both had been given honorary doctoral degrees at the Claremont Colleges in California. On that occasion Joan and I had spent a weekend with the Blackmuns and the president of the college and my longtime friend and former classmate, John McGuire. I never could have imagined that the next time Harry Blackmun and I would be together, the justice would be visiting me in prison.

The warden and Dr. Westrick left the room, thoughtfully allowing us the privacy of the warden's office. The justice was dressed in a dark suit, white shirt, and tie. He looked as though he belonged in the spacious and comfortable office. I, on the other hand, was dressed in army fatigues: an olive-drab uniform originally made for and previously worn by a soldier. It bore nondescript stains and was faded—suitable for a prisoner but not tailored for the reception of a justice of the United States Supreme Court.

He told me that he was in town for a physical examination at the Mayo Clinic, that he had often thought about me and was wondering how I was doing.

"You're looking well," he told me.

I returned the compliment—but in fact, he looked tired.

"Are they treating you well?" he inquired. And then, with the verbal precision of a judge, he corrected his question: "I should say, are they treating you all right."

I told him that, yes, they were treating me as well as a prisoner should expect to be treated.

He then proceeded to tell me of his admiration of me—*his admiration of me.* Of his belief that I had made a considerable contribution to the law and that, when this is all behind me, my experience and understanding will enable me to add a new dimension and perspective to our system of justice.

I know that much of what the justice said was to bolster the spirits of someone who must have looked very pathetic. But his visit and words had a dramatic impact on me. We continued to speak for a while and, when he was preparing to leave, we both stood and again embraced.

The visit of the senior justice of the United States Supreme Court, the author of *Roe v. Wade,* his embrace and words of praise and encouragement meant more to me than I can possibly say. The memory of what I once was brought me renewed hope for what I could be in the future. I also wept, thinking of what I once was but will never be again.

February 18, 1994

Dr. Campbell, one of the prison doctors, has told me that calcium has been found in my blood. Because this could suggest the presence of a cancerous lesion or tumor, he has arranged for me to have a bone scan at the neighboring Mayo Clinic. This morning I went to the prison infirmary to be escorted to Mayo.

A guard carrying a black case approached me. He asked me to step into a small room and there opened the case. It was filled with chains.

"What are they for?" I asked.

"We're going into town," he answered.

"I know," I said, "but what are the chains for?"

"You," said the guard, as he spread the leg irons, waist iron, and handcuffs out on the table.

It was the first time since coming to prison that I refused to do what was expected of me: "You're not putting those chains on me," I said.

"You're not leaving here without them," he answered. He then proceeded to tell me that by arrangement with the City of Rochester, no inmate subject to confinement is allowed out of the prison unless chained and shackled. I had been told, although this was never verified to me, that even corpses of prisoners are transported to the city handcuffed before a death certificate is issued by the Mayo Clinic. Corpses in body bags with handcuffs on! I could think of no greater indignity.

"If being chained like an animal is a condition of receiving medical treatment, then I refuse medical treatment."

The guard made a hurried call and then gave me a form to sign which noted the fact that I refused treatment.

I told Dr. Campbell that I would rather allow a cancer to go undetected and kill me than to again subject myself to leg shackles and chains. The idea of going into town and a public hospital, trussed in the same manner as I was when I came here from Butner, was to me unthinkable.

February 21, 1994

Mark Putnam, thirty-five years old, was a young, bright, and ambitious F.B.I. agent. He was, and is, an outstanding athlete married to a beautiful woman. On visiting days, together with their two children, a boy and girl, they present an ideal family portrait.

A few weeks ago Mark was the subject of a made-for-TV movie and today he was on a television talk show with his wife, Kathy. Tomorrow, as on other occasions, we will be walking around the compound track together, trying to keep warm. Neither of us will discuss why we're in here—we both know.

Mark is here for the crime of murder. He strangled his pregnant girlfriend.

It all began just seven years ago. Right out of the F.B.I. academy, Mark was assigned to the Appalachian region of Pike County, Kentucky, one of the poorest parts of the country. His duty station, Pikeville, Kentucky, was right on the West Virginia border, the border that marked the boundary between the infamous Hatfields and McCoys.

The region was marked by the same kind of distrust that was exhibited by those two feuding families. The area's resources had been plundered by railroad, lumber, and coal robber barons who left an embittered citizenry in their wake, a citizenry distrustful of Northerners like the Putnams. Even more so when the Northerner was a federal law enforcer.

The first significant case to come over Mark's desk in this, his first duty assignment, involved a notorious regional bank robber named Lockhart, who because of his remarkable green eyes was called Cat Eyes. Although Cat Eyes, by virtue of his sudden wealth and certain suspicious activities, was a prime suspect in a series of bank robberies, Mark was unable to build a case sufficient enough to make an arrest.

Through a member of the local sheriff's office, Mark managed to meet a young woman whose husband was friendly with Cat Eyes. In fact, Cat Eyes was staying at her home. The woman, Susan Smith, agreed to become Mark's paid informer and was soon able to report that Cat Eyes had come home with two sawed-off shotguns and some ski masks. He boasted of his next robbery, which, through Susan's assistance, the F.B.I. was able to make his last.

Susan became more than just a source of information for Mark. Being seen with her, a local, gave Mark an acceptability in the community that increased his effectiveness. In time, Susan began to feel that Mark needed her comfort and support more than he needed a mere companion or informer.

Mark soon became involved in a major investigation involving stolen vehicles and a multistate chop-shop operation. That investigation was to take a year—a year marked by veiled threats against the Putnam family made by those being investigated. It was also a year marked by marital friction between Mark and Kathy, and the development of an adulterous relationship between Mark and Susan.

There was a time when I thought of adultery as the kind of transgression that was unforgivable. It was a violation of one of the Ten Commandments, a violation of a sacred vow and obligation. I was filled with rectitude and a sense of virtue that categorized adultery as a sin, one not easily forgiven. I was one of the first to criticize a person, male or female, who strayed into those forbidden pastures. I am no longer of that mind. My own transgression, which was the beginning of my undoing, convinced me that adultery should be avoided and resisted, but now I understand it as a peril that is a man-ifestation of human weakness.

I now find myself wondering how many humans, even the most moral, given a certain juxtaposition of circumstances and timing, would be strong enough to resist. Many, I hope. I was not one of them, but I wish I had been.

Because of the threats against his family, Mark applied for and was given a change of assignment. After two years in Pikeville, he was transferred to Miami. He had done extremely well during his difficult baptismal F.B.I. assignment, and was about to begin the second phase of what promised to be an extraordinary career.

His world began to fall apart when he was summoned back to Pikeville to testify in the chop-shop trial that was about to begin. Susan was waiting for him with news that she was pregnant.

There was the ugly confrontation, threats, and an angry visit by her to his motel room. In order to contain the vicious quarrel, he convinced her to take a drive with him. The quarrel and exchange of insults was accompanied by blows. Mark parked on a lonely mountain road and Susan continued to scream at and threaten him. After she put her fingernail in his eye, he tried to strike her, but missed. His fist struck the windshield and began to bleed. She bit his bleeding hand and he put both his hands around her neck. He said that he didn't think his hold would do more than silence her.

She did fall silent. He couldn't believe he had killed her, but he had.

I have never been, and do not believe that I could ever be, capa-ble of committing an act of physical violence. By the same measure, I do not believe that Mark had the calculated intent of killing Susan anymore than he intended to compromise the F.B.I. by having an affair with an informant, or jeopardizing his marriage by commit-ting adultery. Does that mean his deed should be excused? Of course not. His career and idealism were destroyed by his weakness and a momentary impulse of violence. Neither the law nor society can let such an act go unpunished. But as I look at Mark—even knowing this story and his evil and sinful deed—I cannot think of him as a person beyond redemption.

He carried Susan's body in the trunk of his car during the next day, imagining any number of scenarios: fake a car accident, confess and accept the consequences, commit suicide? He rejected them all and buried the body off the road near a ravine.

Mark returned to Florida a few days later. Because Susan's life had been marked by drug abuse, a bad marriage, and association with many of the lawless and ragged citizens of Pike County, her absence was not a matter of great concern. Some even felt that she was in hiding because she feared reprisal for having been an F.B.I. informer.

Although they did not find Susan's body and, because of a construction project at the ravine where Mark had left it, probably never would have, Mark's conscience got the better of him and he eventually confessed to his crime. Without his confession, he could never have been convicted.

Absent his confession I would not have conceded the possibility of his redemption.

Although Mark Putnam was guilty of the state crime of first-degree manslaughter in Kentucky, he agreed to plead guilty only on condition that he be permitted to serve his sentence in a federal prison. He obviously feared for his safety if incarcerated in a Kentucky penitentiary. He was first sent to Otisville, New York, and was later transferred to the general population here at Rochester.

His plea agreement and ultimate sentence in June of 1990 called for sixteen years. Because the sentence was under state law, he will not be required to do more than twelve years and will be eligible for parole in 1998.

Kathy left Florida and moved for a short while to Minnesota to be near Mark. She has remained committed to him and eagerly awaits his return. He talks of little else but Kathy and his two children.

March 1994

March 10, 1994

When you are a prisoner, few people on the street care what you have to say—particularly when you are talking about the length of your sentence. "After all, you are a criminal." "You have violated society's rules and you are being punished." "Yes, we know you think you have been treated unfairly—all prisoners say that—but you probably haven't been. And who cares, anyhow?" "Whatever unfair treatment you have been given, you deserve." "Sure you are critical of the police and the prosecutors. They put you where you are—where you belong." "If you hadn't committed a crime, you wouldn't be in prison, so keep quiet." "You shouldn't have done the crime if you couldn't do the time."

In prison, every inmate has a complaint about law enforcement. Most feel they were unfairly singled out for arrest and then were victims of malicious and ambitious prosecutors. They also feel that no one on the outside, except perhaps for family members, gives a damn. And they're usually right. That is why, when it comes to our punishment systems, you see so many books, articles, and treatises by criminologists, penologists, wardens, prison guards, and—most of all—members of the law enforcement community.

There was a time when authors like Bunyan, Gramsci, Genet, Oscar Wilde, and Henry David Thoreau wrote of the prison experience. But you won't find many writings by prisoners these days. They all have much to say, and many are able to express themselves very well, but no one really cares about what they have to say, so they don't say it. Let me tell you about their chief complaints.

Some find fault with the laws they are accused of violating. They come to me griping that certain laws are arbitrary. They're right, but I tell them the legislative bodies, federal or state, are permitted and entitled to be arbitrary, so long as they act rationally, constitutionally, and without discrimination. When the government decides that you can drive on the right-hand side of the road and not on the left, it is being arbitrary, but it is certainly permissible. If the government says that taxes are to be paid on a certain date, the selection of that date is arbitrary, but it is also legal and appropriate.

The legislative and executive branches must also discharge the state's obligation to prevent crime and punish wrongdoers. To do this, laws are passed whose purpose is to protect society's interests, and police and prosecutorial agencies are vested with power to enforce those laws.

It is the abuse of that power—the arbitrary enforcement of these laws by the police and prosecutors that poses a problem, one that I in my former life, and many others have grappled with for years. For example in 1970, when Congress passed the Racketeer Influenced and Corrupt Organization law (RICO) it was seeking to stop the influence of organized crime in legitimate businesses. But in arbitrarily enforcing that law, prosecutors were handcuffing, arresting, and prosecuting Wall Street executives for everything from insider trading to stock fraud. These men were certainly not "racketeers" and were not engaged in "racketeering." If they violated the laws of the Securities and Exchange Commission, they could be punished for those violations. But not under RICO. I believe the RICO law was being misused by some prosecutors usually for their own personal reasons and not necessarily for society's benefit.

This is but one example of the arbitrary enforcement of laws. Another is the police officer's looking the other way when the speed limit is exceeded by five or ten miles per hour. No one would find that bothersome, but if a white policeman looked the other way when a black motorist was being beaten without cause by his fellow officers, the arbitrariness might be more than troublesome; it could be illegal.

As a nation we vest enormous power in our legislative and executive leaders. Our constitutional forebears allowed for this by means of the checks and balances of our tripartite form of government. In addition, officials must meet their responsibility to the electorate in order to stay in office.

But law enforcement and law enforcers, unelected officials who have such an enormous ability to abuse power and destroy lives, are generally free of these strictures. Federal prosecutors are not elected and the populist trend is to vest them with more and more discretion. With more discretion comes more power. There is a danger in this, one the Founding Fathers anticipated when they enacted the first ten amendments of the Constitution, the Bill of Rights.

The Bill of Rights came into being because the Founders had experienced the unbridled power of the Crown in trammeling liberty. A full two thirds of the provisions of the Bill of Rights were designed to protect the prisoner in the dock, to be certain that the freedom granted the citizens of this new nation was not eclipsed by prosecutorial abuse, that every citizen was afforded due process of law, as guaranteed by the Fifth Amendment.

During the calm and prosperous 1950s, prosecutorial abuse was held in check by the courts and public opinion. It was not until the cultural insurrection of the sixties that the popularity of "law-and-order" issues introduced a whole new political agenda. I know because I capitalized on it, along with Richard Nixon, in the election of 1972. It was then that the courts, which had contained and checked the prosecutors, were called soft-hearted and soft-headed and such due process safeguards as the *Miranda* ruling were denounced. The United States Supreme Court, responsible for many decisions protective of defendants' rights, was vilified. I can remember seeing placards calling for the impeachment of Earl Warren, the Supreme Court Chief Justice, at the 1968 Republican National Convention.

In the seventies and eighties the economy smiled on the rich but did not smile so broadly on the poor and middle class. Unemployment increased, as did drug use and street violence. This, coupled with the anguish generated by the Vietnam War among both those who fought in it and those who opposed it generated a genuine hostility against what appeared to them to be an "indifferent" government.

Politicians, quick to seize on the increased public fear of this lawlessness, began a campaign to fight crime. The first salvo was, predictably, against the judges: "If these soft-hearted, soft-headed judges would put more of these animals in jail, we would have less crime" was the cry. During this period the prison population had tripled and was exceeding prison capacity. Not one of these prisoners had gone there voluntarily; they were all sent there by judges. But when you're campaigning for office, these facts become unimportant. Another was "It's about time these judges thought more about the victims and less about the criminals." This is a not-so-subtle suggestion that certain constitutional guarantees should somehow be diminished instead of being protected by the courts. Which ones? The guarantee against unlawful searches? The right not to be forced into confession? How about the protection against double jeopardy or the rights to counsel and a speedy trial? Maybe even the presumption of innocence?

The politicizing of the issue of constitutional rights versus crime fighting reached its high, or low, watermark during the 1988 presidential campaign, in which George Bush wrongfully blamed

Michael Dukakis for the parole of Willie Horton, a black male who, after being freed on parole, raped and tortured a white woman. The incident inflamed racial passions and provided yet another opportunity to denounce and undermine so-called "failed liberal reforms" in criminal justice.

The most tangible result of this political energy, aside from the conservative nature of judicial appointments during the Nixon-Reagan-Bush years, was to take sentencing discretion away from the judges. The rationale for this was simple: If the judges would not punish wrongdoers severely enough, then the legislature would mandate what punishment was to be meted out.

Commissions were established in several states and the federal government created the United States Sentencing Commission to determine categories of offenses and establish the punishment range for each offense. The crime committed was to determine the punishment, without consideration of all of those factors that were weighed by judges when they still had discretion: What was the nature of the crime and its effect on the victim and victims? How many and what sort of prior convictions did the defendant have? Did he use a weapon? What was his mental condition at the time of the offense? Did his family background and status, his position in the community, his education, employment, and job training, as well as his life's history, indicate that he could be rehabilitated, or would he continue to be a danger to society?

The federal guidelines include many of these factors but specifically exclude some of these elements from consideration—age, education, and vocational skills. Instead, the judge simply applies a graded scale, mechanically adds up points (which has already been done by the prosecutor) and, voilà! there's the sentence.

Mike Kelly is handsome, blue-eyed, and extremely likable. He is in his late twenties and will be in prison until he is fifty. He's here because he pled guilty to the armed robbery of a bank and possession of cocaine. The federal sentencing guidelines made certain that the taxpayers will pay more than one million dollars to keep Mike off the streets for another twenty years. His only prior offense was for the possession of a small amount of cocaine.

Mike was an addict. He committed his first and only robbery while high on cocaine. He went into a bank in a South Boston neighborhood not two blocks from his home, brandished a starter pistol, and ordered a teller to fill a paper bag with cash. He was wearing a Stetson hat to conceal his face from the overhead camera. The teller was in the process of emptying her cash drawer when a twenty-dollar bill fell to the floor. As Mike bent over to pick up the bill, his hat fell off. Instinctively, he looked up at the camera and then fled. His total take from the robbery was $1,850, which he spent that afternoon for cocaine.

Mike was arrested at his home that evening. The F.B.I. identified him by a perfect eight-by-ten photograph of his startled countenance. The cocaine he had purchased after the robbery, or what was left of it, was still in his pocket.

I could tell you a dozen stories like Mike's, of people who commit crimes that, viewed in the abstract, are serious, but when punishment is to be meted out, should be the subject of contextual and individual analysis, tempered by the wisdom and discretion of judges. Absent the sentencing guidelines in his case, there are few judges who would even consider a twenty-year sentence. This would have been an ideal case for medium-term incarceration—say five years—coupled with a drug program. After-care would be a condition of long-term supervised release. Under the sentencing guidelines no such option is available.

Another example of the treachery of the sentencing guidelines and their misuse is the case of an inmate I met at Butner who was serving time for bank fraud. He was an elderly pig farmer from a southern state who mortgaged his livestock in order to secure a bank loan. When he couldn't keep up with his mortgage payments, he sold off some of the pigs. This diminution of collateral used to secure the bank loan was categorized by the U.S. attorney for his district as bank fraud, and the farmer, in his seventies, was sentenced to over twelve months in prison under the sentencing guidelines. Another inmate who worked an intricate scheme to larcenously defraud another bank received the same sentence. Technically, the two committed the same crime: They both defrauded banks. If we were to say that motivation and circumstance make no difference, that justice demands that they should both be similarly punished, what kind of justice are we asking for?

Making the name of the crime determine the sentence almost invites injustice. For example, in a barroom brawl, the victor—the one left standing—may be guilty of the crime of assault. Under sentencing guidelines his punishment would be the same as it would be for the marauder who beats up a frail elderly person. A young chain snatcher could be found guilty of the same robbery charge as a sophisticated bank robber.

As was predicted, the impact of sentencing guidelines and mandatory sentencing on the prison population has been staggering. This country leads the world with a rate of 500 incarcerated persons for every 100,000 population. Compare Japan (45 per 100,000) or England (97 per 100,000). Our prison population has increased from 330,000 in 1980 to over 1,000,000 in 1994 with predictions of 6,000,000 by the year 2015. The cost to operate this nation's prisons is $30 billion a year.

What is happening in New York illustrates the fiscal problem created by mandatory sentences for drug crimes. When I became Chief Judge in 1985, there were some 35,000 people in our state prisons. There are now over 60,000. Between 1983 and 1990, we built twenty-seven new prisons, which will cost the citizens of New York $5.5 billion over the bonding period of the next thirty years for construction alone.

As Burton Roberts, the administrative judge of the Bronx, New York, and a former district attorney of that county, recently observed: "We are unable to build prisons fast enough—and, instead of exploring alternatives, we continue to criminalize things which should not be criminalized, and we continue to lengthen sentences." Worst of all is our continued reliance on mandatory sentences and sentencing guidelines, which has the effect of distorting the entire criminal justice system. Because judges have been deprived of their sentencing discretion, the only person who decides what the penalty will be is the prosecutor. The prosecutor, and not a judge, decides what to charge, and what charges should be ultimately retained or dropped.

In a recent poll conducted by the American Bar Association, federal judges from Chief Justice William Renquist on down, charged with the burden and obligation of applying these guidelines, concluded "that only one in four of the sentences now imposed are fair and just." These are judges appointed by both Republican and Democratic presidents. As Judge Magnuson put it when sentencing Arlen Angell to ten years for his first marijuana offense: "Society has chosen to take the responsibility for the amount of sentence that people receive out of the hands of judges and into the hands of prosecutors and police officers."

The constitutional oracles on the far right, who in other contexts advocate a return to the original intent of the framers of the Constitution, must or should know that such prosecutorial abuse would be anathema to our Founding Fathers.

March 15, 1994

I was just told of a television interview given this week by Michael Chertoff, the U.S. attorney who prosecuted me. He is about to leave office, and saw fit to review his prosecutorial triumphs. He considers my scalp to be his most impressive trophy.

In one of his essays Montaigne observed: "A man never speaks of himself without losing something. What he says in his disfavor is always believed, but when he commends himself, he arouses mistrust."

That is one reason why I am reluctant to use my own case as an illustration of any observation I make on mandatory sentencing. I do so not to commend myself—I have done nothing commendable—but to demonstrate the shift of power from the judicial branch to the prosecutorial arm of the executive branch. It also illustrates what the commentators mean when they speak of the power the sentencing guidelines have given to prosecutors. As David Margolick of *The New York Times* put it: "Rather than eliminate discretion for the sentencing process the guidelines have merely moved it from judges, who exercise it in open court, to prosecutors privately deciding who to charge with how serious a crime and at what stage of the criminal act."

Which is precisely what happened in my case. The U.S. attorney from New Jersey, Mr. Chertoff, decided that I should not be given any warning before my arrest, which would have terminated my bizarre letter-writing campaign and compelled psychiatric treatment. Mr. Chertoff decided when to arrest me; rather than having that done immediately after he discovered that I was engaged in harassing Ms. Silverman, he put me under surveillance for over a month. My criminal activity was watched and nurtured during this period. He also decided what the charges against me should be, which was decisive of whether I should go to prison and for how long.

I certainly do not blame Mr. Chertoff for my criminal activity. I destroyed my life and hurt any number of innocent people by my own conduct. My crime, stated by the prosecutor at the time of my plea, was to send "threatening communications with the intent to harass." Mind you, I never stalked Ms. Silverman by following her or even observing her from afar, nor did I ever touch her. Had I not sent letters from New Jersey across a state line to New York my crime would not have been a federal one and, under New York State law, would have been a misdemeanor.

But the letters were grotesque, written by me, as I have already noted, while in a clinically manic state. Once Chertoff had me in his sights, and to heighten the drama of the case (as if this aberrational conduct of the Chief Judge of the State of New York weren't drama enough), he marshaled a veritable army of F.B.I. agents to follow my every move. According to published accounts, between eighty and one hundred agents from the New Jersey F.B.I. offices were deployed.

When Chertoff decided that I had gone about as far as I would go he gave the command decision to—as he was quoted in *The New Yorker*—"take him down."

From my training as a member of the military police, and as part of the law enforcement community for forty years, I know that the approach used in my apprehension is reserved for desperate and armed felons either escaping from or going toward a criminal enterprise. Even John Gotti, charged with multiple murders, was allowed the dignity of self surrender.

In Chertoff's television interview this week he said, "Wachtler's prosecution and long-term imprisonment prove that no one is above the law, and all violators of the law must be treated equally."

I was hoping his interviewer would have asked the question, "If all the violators of the law must be treated equally, can you name a single prosecution similar to Wachtler's in the history of your office?" The answer to this question was given in an Op-Ed piece written by the noted attorneys William M. Kunstler and Ronald L. Kuby. They wrote of a case involving an assistant U.S. attorney from New Jersey by the name of Judy G. Russell who was working in the office now headed by Chertoff.

During an extradition trial that she was conducting, a series of six anonymous threatening communications, created by words cut out of magazines, were received, five addressed to her and one to the judge. It was assumed that the notes were sent by terrorists, so extraordinary security was imposed, including bodyguards for Ms. Russell and the judge, rooftop sharpshooters, and the shackling of the defendants.

It was soon discovered that Ms. Russell herself was sending the threatening communications. She claimed that she had no memory of sending the letters in question to either herself or the judge. As was noted in the Kunstler and Kuby article:

From the moment in early 1988 that her crime was detected, she was never arrested or subjected to any conditions of release. Instead, she was permitted to commit herself voluntarily to a psychiatric facility for a period of fifty days, after which she was freed to return home.

Before sending her home the judge observed that he would be reluctant to put a former U.S. attorney in prison because of the dangers she would face from inmates she had prosecuted. He also ordered the record sealed in order to spare the defendant any unnecessary publicity and directed that, while the public could be informed of further court appearances in the matter, any releases by the Justice Department would be "limited strictly to the fact that there will be a proceeding" but would not indicate the nature.

Every day I read of some case of harassment, most far more egregious than mine—many involving actual stalking and physical assaults—where the sole punishment is an "order of protection" or mandated psychological treatment. Or other cases like that of the Surrogate of Bronx County, one of the highest judicial offices in the State of New York who, after months of following and stalking his victim, with whom he had an extramarital affair, that resulted in her losing her employment and having to change her address, was finally brought before the Commission on Judicial Conduct. He was removed from the bench, but was never arrested or prosecuted. He is still practicing law.

After six months in prison, and after meeting and talking to hundreds of prisoners, I have yet to find or hear of one other inmate serving time in a federal prison for a crime similar to mine. So much for equal treatment under the law.

March 17, 1994

When they speak of their sentence, the inmates use months instead of years. It sounds shorter. "How long have you got to serve?" I asked the pale and frail-looking fellow sitting next to me at Friday-night service. "Seventy-one months all together," he answered.

I quickly computed six years. Now what could this gentle-looking soul have done to warrant a six-year sentence? It's considered bad form to ask an inmate the nature of his crime, but they usually volunteer it.

"I stole books," he said, as if reading my thoughts. "*Harper's* magazine featured my story in its January issue. Would you like to read it?" "Sure," I said. He brought it to me a few minutes ago. Fascinating.

Stephen Blumberg stole books from 327 libraries and museums in this country and Canada over a twenty-year period. He came to rest in Ottumwa, Iowa, where, with an income from a trust, he lived alone with his hoard of priceless books, many of them first editions, all of them rare. Books such as the 1480 Coburger Bible, a world history that was the last not to mention Christopher Columbus, or the actual diaries of pioneers conquering the Old West; or the first editions of Walt Whitman's *Leaves of Grass* and Mark Twain's *The Celebrated Jumping Frog of Calaveras County*. His was a bibliomania fulfilled by theft.

The French writer Gustave Flaubert once described a bibliomaniac as one who "loved a book because it was a book; he loved its odor, its form, its title." And so it was with Stephen Blumberg. He never sold a book; his was not a crime of greed or violence. He earnestly believed that he was benefiting mankind by saving fine works from extinction. He also felt that what he was doing was not morally wrong. "No one has a right to monopolize learning," he said to me. "I preserved a collection of American history from the destruction and misuse often inflicted by libraries."

An example of his criminal ingenuity was his robbery of Widener Library, one of the Harvard University libraries. He used a false faculty identification to obtain a ninety-day library pass. He then removed the stacks lock cylinder and replaced it with one that any key could open. While the blank cylinder was in place, he took the real cylinder to a locksmith in Canada to have a key made for it. He then replaced the blank cylinder with the real one. He now had a key to a veritable treasure trove of rare and valuable books.

From Harvard in Massachusetts to the Claremont Colleges in California, Stephen plied his skills as a book thief. At Claremont, from which he stole the most valuable book of his collection, the Nuremberg Chronicle of 1493, he gained entrance to the library with a popsicle stick. He later stole a ring of keys with which he effectuated more normal entry.

How did they catch him? The same way the vast majority of inmates here were caught: someone "snitched him out."

His collection of some nineteen thousand books, valued in the millions, was hoarded in his Ottumwa, Iowa, house. Into this house he took Kenneth Rhodes, a friend with whom he had dealt antiques for fifteen years. Two years after the F.B.I. had abandoned its own investigation, Rhodes went to the F.B.I. in Detroit with pictures of the interior of the house showing books from floor to ceiling. The government paid Rhodes $56,000 for this information, and, after executing a search warrant, arrested Blumberg.

Blumberg's thievery was branded by the F.B.I. as "the crime of the century." The agency valued the thefts at $40,000,000. This was an inflated estimate, as was the significance of the case. In court, the U.S. attorney, with the usual hyperbole accompanying prosecutions, said Blumberg "stole the cultural history of the United States."

Blumberg was unsuccessful in convincing the jury of his insanity and he was sentenced to seventy-one months' imprisonment and fined $200,000.

I asked him the real value of his thievery. He told me that all of the books were worth less than $3,000,000, and that only three thousand could be identified as belonging to particular libraries. This means that some sixteen thousand books will be waiting for Stephen Blumberg when he is freed, valuable books that libraries all over the country are missing. Blumberg tells me that the way many libraries are managed, they are not even aware of their loss.

March 18, 1994

Now that I'm in the general population I have three cellmates. The four of us sleep on two double-decker bunk beds in a twelve-by-fourteen-foot cell. Each of us is given a small metal locker to store our uniforms and possessions. The combination locks used on these lockers are purchased by us at the commissary. Each lock can be opened by a key in the possession of the guards. This enables the guards to open our lockers at will, which they often do.

One of my cellmates is a large and very muscular Nigerian who very seldom speaks. Another is an Orthodox Jew, who is very seldom silent; his name is Michael Goland. Infantile paralysis left him with a withered left arm, which either hangs limply by his side or is tucked, as far as possible, into his pocket. Michael seems to become more devout each day. He wears a yarmulke under the prison-issue blue knit cap and never shaves.

His beard is black, tufted at the bottom with gray. If you were to see him on the street, your first impression would be of an impoverished but obviously devout Jew. Your next impulse would be to give him all of the change in your pocket—maybe even a dollar bill.

But there was a time when, Michael tells me, he was very wealthy. He told me of living a luxurious life as a real estate investor with a lavish home in Beverly Hills. His avocation was politics—assisting candidates to be elected who supported Israel and working and contributing to defeat office holders who did not. It was in pursuit of this avocation that he ran afoul of the law. It seems that he contributed too much toward the defeat of a member of Congress who was an avowed enemy of Israel. He was also indicted and convicted of an attenuated conspiracy in connection with a savings and loan association.

Michael is probably more disliked—perhaps I should say detested—by the staff of this prison than any other inmate. He has what they call an "attitude"—an attitude that drives him to file written complaints concerning what he considers wrong with the facility or its employees. He has filed over one hundred such complaints, mostly relating to the food service. You see, Michael is kosher—very kosher.

The prison chaplain, a Catholic priest, asked me to try to keep Michael from irritating everyone from the unit guards to the warden. Considering that Michael had been sent to the hole on eleven separate occasions for disciplinary reasons and still persisted in committing acts of defiance, I doubted that I could help the father in lessening Michael's passion for disruption.

Michael's current crusade is to see to it that the Jewish inmates have a kosher Passover. He is not content with a kosher seder, the traditional Passover meal. He wants a kosher week of meals (three a day) to be given to each of the Jewish inmates. Now, mind you, the Jewish inmates would be more than satisfied with just a kosher seder, and none of them has chosen Michael as his spokesperson. But the facts don't deter Michael from his self-appointed mission. "I want to be certain," says Michael, "that in the future, Jewish inmates do not have to go through what I have gone through to remain true to their traditional beliefs."

To make his point, he has stopped eating in the dining hall, despite the fact that the prison does provide what is called "common fare," which purports to be kosher meals for those who are observant. In fact, "common fare" has been designed to satisfy all religious dietary codes.

"Not kosher enough," says Michael. "In fact, not kosher at all. The ingredients and preparation of the food, the food service personnel who are handling nonkosher food at the same time, and the mixing of dairy and meat dishes are just a few of the problems."

And so he continues his self-imposed fast. He will eat only fresh fruit or kosher bread from a sealed package. He has lost thirty-two pounds and looks haggard beyond his forty-six years.

March 25, 1994

Today the Jewish inmates were summoned to the chapel by Father Jerry. There the chaplain tells us that he, with the warden's assistance, has arranged for the Jewish inmates to have three kosher meals a day for the entire week of Passover. I look at Michael to see some recognition of his victory—a smile, or even a nod of his head, some expression of gratitude to the father for his efforts. Nothing. When we left the chapel I asked him why he was so taciturn, unusual for him if not entirely unique.

"Because I don't believe them," he said.

March 30, 1994

As it turned out, Father Jerry was true to his word. Kosher meals were flown in, frozen and double-wrapped, from a kosher kitchen in Florida. At Michael's insistence, when they arrived they were handled by a Jewish inmate who saw to it that they were in no way contaminated by any violation of Jewish law.

It was arranged for the Jewish inmates to eat their kosher meals a few minutes earlier than the meals scheduled for the other inmates. They decided—I should say Michael decided—that they should all sit together in one section of the dining room. Unfortunately, this evening they sat in the section usually occupied by the Native Americans—far more in number than the Jews. When the Indians came in, there were Goland and his minions eating their kosher pot roast.

Because they were one kosher meal short, I volunteered not to join the others on this particular evening. Although I was not there, from what I was told, the scene could very well be described as "Goland's Last Stand." He stood his ground, his yarmulke giving scant protection to his scalp, defiantly warning his Sioux, Winnebago, and Chippewa antagonists to back off.

"Sit elsewhere, you're *trayf*" said Michael, using the Yiddish word for "unkosher."

"We may be safe, but you're not," said Chief Bear Claw, the tall and muscular pride of the Sioux, whose mastery of the Lakota dialect was far better than of Yiddish.

As they stood nose to nose (and in the nose match-up I think Goland was a winner, but not by much) one of Michael's companions pulled him away to another section of the dining room. He convinced Michael that his tribe was badly outnumbered, and that these Indians were not about to give up their native territory to this crowd of newcomers and their bearded, one-armed leader. Michael told me later that he did not consider this a defeat.

"I reserve my energies for my real enemies," he said, referring to those responsible for running the Federal Medical Center at Rochester.

But the Passover seder itself was excellent. Rabbi Friedman from Rochester conducted the service and several members of his congregation were in attendance. Rabbi Esor Ben Sorek from New York, someone who has been writing me regularly, sent a package filled with Passover delicacies, which were distributed to the Jewish inmates. It was a pleasant afternoon. Even Michael smiled.

April 1994

April 1, 1994

Stan Bolle never had much to say. We all knew he was in for dealing drugs, and he made no apologies for having been involved in
what he considered a "good business." It's just that "it has its risks,"
he once told me. Taking those risks had gotten him indicted on
thirty-five counts of possession, trafficking, and selling cocaine, for
which he was convicted and is now serving a mandatory sentence of
twenty years.

This morning he asked if he could talk to me. Because I had
never heard him say more than one or two sentences, I quickly
agreed to hear him out.

As should be expected, a prisoner has an enormous grasp of the
facts and law applicable to his case. He has spent days, weeks, and
months in courtrooms, conference rooms, and law libraries. He has
consulted with his lawyers and dozens of "jailhouse lawyers," he has
read books, briefs, trial records, articles, and treatises on the subjects
relating to his case. And he has had a great deal of time to do and
contemplate all of these things.

Stan wanted to discuss the exclusionary rule with me. This is a rule of law that has been at the heart of most of the criticism leveled at judges and judge-made law. It is a court-fashioned rule dictating that evidence secured by the police, evidence that can prove guilt, must be suppressed if the police violated an accused's Fourth Amendment right against "unreasonable searches and seizures" when acquiring that evidence.

Many critics of the rule blame the modern-age liberality of the Supreme Court for its formulation, but as far back as 1914, in *Weeks v. United States,* the Supreme Court held that the product of an unlawful search and seizure could not be used as evidence against an accused in the federal courts. The evidence was suppressed as much to provide a remedy for the party wronged as it was to vindicate the integrity of the judicial process.

The Supreme Court of that day felt there was something wrong with a court's countenancing a wrongful act committed by law enforcement to obtain evidence. To discourage warrantless searches, evidence obtained in that fashion could not be used in a court of law to convict a defendant. I personally find no fault in the rule. Courts should be no more anxious to receive evidence gathered by the police by breaking down a door than to receive a confession taken at the end of a rubber hose.

In 1961, this rule was extended to the states. Of late it has been watered down (e.g., if the police are acting in an emergency and the "exigency" does not allow time or opportunity to get a warrant, or if the court feels the seizure of evidence was in "good faith," or if the "totality of the circumstances" justified the police intrusion, etc.) but the exclusionary rule is still the law.

After reviewing the history of the Fourth Amendment to the United States Constitution, and he knew it well, Bolle told me of how his rights had been violated when the F.B.I. broke into a lake cottage that he used for vacationing in Wisconsin in the summer — he apparently used it to store cocaine in the winter.

"No warrant," he told me, "didn't even try to get one. Just busted down the door."

If what he told me was true, it seemed he had a good chance for a reversal. And sure enough, one afternoon he ran through the unit. Stan Bolle — "Silent Stan" — was leaping and shouting the news: The circuit court of appeals had reversed his conviction. The search had been held illegal, the contraband seized in the cottage suppressed, and thirty counts of the thirty-five-count indictment dismissed.

When Stan regained his composure, I warned him against an excess of optimism. The history of the exclusionary rule suggests, except in those rare cases where *all* of the evidence is suppressed and *all* of the counts dismissed, that a retrial usually results in a reconviction. A reversal of a conviction, contrary to popular belief, does not mean that the defendant "goes free."

In the spring of 1996 Stan was retried and convicted on the five remaining counts. His sentence: the same twenty years. Stan's probable disappointment aside, this was a good result. The Fourth Amendment was vindicated and the warrant requirement elevated by the use of the exclusionary rule. The F.B.I. will be more careful next time — and Stan is probably on his way back to Rochester.

April 3, 1994

When you are housed in a mental health unit, you don't have to leave the building to receive medication. There is a pill line in the unit. But once you are in the general population, you must walk to one of the medical units to receive your prescribed dosage of medicine. In my case, the initial high dosages of Lithium and Prozac taken to stabilize my diagnosed bipolar disorder required me to take two trips to the pharmacy pill line every day, one at twelve noon and the other at eight P.M.

The medication has helped me considerably. Although the depression is still with me, it has diminished in intensity. I have had no more manic episodes. I don't know whether that is because of the medication I am now taking or the drugs I have stopped using.

April 6, 1994

Today I met Ted. He's a marijuana smuggler. He has been here for five years, and spends much of his time telling stories of how marijuana is brought into this country from Mexico. He has five more years to spend telling these stories.

I can remember reading stories of balloons filled with radar equipment that were to be placed every hundred yards or so to detect border crossings from Mexico.

"Don't hear about those anymore," said Ted. "Know why? Because they were the best friends a smuggler could have. We used to pay boys one dollar a day to watch them. When one came down for repairs, or was blown down by the weather, why there was the opening we would go through. But we didn't need that help—we brought tons right through customs."

He went on to explain how, for example, when roadwork was being done in Tijuana, large asphalt trucks would travel with heated asphalt from San Diego, unload in Mexico, pick up bales of marijuana, and go back across the border with a smile, a wave, and tons of weed. Here we were spending millions for radar balloons, aircraft equipped with infrared sensors, and ground-implanted motion sensors, and the illegal pot was coming in by the truckload, undetected, through customs. The fact is that customs officials did not suspect the truckers and were not eager to inspect, nor were the dogs anxious to sniff, truckloads of hot and redolent tar.

One of the most inventive avenues used by the traffickers was a tunnel discovered in the spring of 1990 by customs agents. It was 250 feet long and five feet wide and provided a concrete and steel reinforced conduit between a construction supply warehouse in Arizona and a private home in Mexico.

Then there were the planes that would fly at night. As soon as the border was crossed, the bales of marijuana would be kicked out to waiting accomplices on the ground.

He told me of planes that would fly from Mexico, through the Dakotas, across the Canadian border, and then back down into Minnesota, where the drop was made. There were stories of motor homes, custom built with false walls, ceilings, and floors where the marijuana was stored—and furniture, machinery, and even portable privies. In later years when dogs were used to sniff out the contraband, pepper was sprinkled and glued in places to dull their sense of smell.

But the stories of our government's complicity in some of these smuggling operations were the most interesting. Ted believes that a large percentage of the bulk wholesale marijuana from Mexico was sold to dealers by C.I.A. operatives, not to expose the smuggling apparatus but to exploit it. "I'm doing ten years for doing the same thing the C.I.A. was doing" was his usual plaint.

"No one knows that for sure," I said.

"I do," came a voice from over my shoulder. "My celly in Lewisburg was with the C.I.A. and he told me that funding covert operations was their biggest problem, and drug money was their best solution." He went on to talk about the millions of dollars of drug money funneled by the C.I.A. to the guerrillas in Nicaragua, the *contras*.

Convicted felons are not an unimpeachable source of information. On the contrary, truth telling is not considered a virtue among the inmates, so that many of the things you are told must be either disregarded or reshaped to conform to known realities.

I do remember seeing a CBS documentary by Bill Moyers, "The C.I.A.'s Secret Army," where this same type of secret government operation was explored. And now I was hearing the same story from someone who claimed he competed with the government in the drug business.

"C'mon," said one of the inmates, "the only reason they keep pot illegal is to maintain its value. For Chrissakes, it's a weed which can be grown anywhere, but if the government allowed it to be legal, and grown legally, it would be worthless to them."

Of course, there is an inmate bias against the government and all things governmental. It must be remembered, it was the government that sent them here. I don't believe for a minute that marijuana is kept as a controlled substance in order to inflate its value.

But I am starting to believe that our government has been and may still be involved in dealing with the drug trade.

April 8, 1994

"Hi!"

He's twenty feet away, and I know he can hear me.

He didn't even glance my way, but I know he heard me. I'm only five feet away from him. I'll try again.

"Nice morning, isn't it?"

Nothing, but now I'm right next to him. My face is no more than inches from his.

"Beautiful day isn't it?"

He does not respond. He does not look at me. To him I am invisible and mute.

When I was a small boy my fondest wish was to be invisible. To walk about unseen. The guards (hacks, screws, cops, turnkeys, "Call me officer!") have made my wish come true. To many of them—not to all, but to many—inmates are nonpersons to be seen only when they can be disciplined.

I have neither the time nor the pages to detail the many affronts that have been visited on me, and I have a strong sense that the guards are even more outrageous in their treatment of others.

I was given an example of this kind of "hack attack" last month.

The patients in the mental health unit have their vital signs checked once a month. When my turn came, the nurse felt my blood pressure was far too high, and suggested that I come back that evening to have it checked again. When I returned from religious services that night, I noticed the same nurse leaving the building.

"Are you leaving for the evening?" I asked.

"Yes," she answered.

"Who's going to take my blood pressure?"

"There's another nurse on duty—she's expecting you."

"Thank you. Have a good night," I said, and walked into the unit.

No sooner had I returned to my cell, than I heard the boom of the intercom loudspeaker:

"Washtler, Washtler, report to the one-two officer's station NOW!"

I walked as quickly as I could to the small room occupied by the guard responsible for maintaining order in that part of Unit 1, second floor. A female guard was seated and a male guard—I would have guessed him to be twenty-five years old—was standing awaiting my arrival. Neither was as old as my youngest child.

"Sit down, Washtler," he said brusquely, trying his best to impress the woman with his machismo. "What did you say to that nurse downstairs?" His tone suggested both his authority and his anger.

"I was surprised to see her leaving," I explained, "so I asked her who was going to take my blood pressure."

"I asked you what you said to her," he said, raising his voice to a menacing pitch, as much to intimidate me as to impress the female guard who was watching my belittlement.

"I told you. I asked her who was going to take my blood pressure in her absence."

"Didn't you say 'high blood pressure'?" he asked. "I was there, buddy—I heard you say 'high blood pressure.' "

"I may have said something about 'high blood pressure'—like, 'Who's going to take my high blood pressure?' "

With the look of an inquisitor who had gleaned a confession, he stopped his pacing, and stood square in front of me. He bent over and put his face not two inches from mine:

"If I ever hear you make another wise-ass remark like that, I'm going to throw you in the hole. You better watch your mouth—and don't ever forget who and what you are!"

The guard's name was Smith. He is slim, six feet, four inches tall, and in desperate need of a haircut as well as training and discipline.

He orders me to remember who and what I am. I know "what" I am—I'm a prisoner, a nonperson.

April 9, 1994

Attica. The name conjures up memories of the prison riot that claimed forty lives in September of 1971. It was a four-day racially motivated uprising that saw fifteen hundred state police and other law-enforcement agencies stage an air and ground attack on the prison, which was under the control of the inmates. Nine guards and twenty-eight prisoners were killed. I was a trial judge at the time, and visited the prison when it was still in a post-riot state of disrepair.

Last night the Attica riot was revisited in a made-for-television movie. Once again I was struck by the overwhelming irony of my life: As a prisoner I was seeing a drama involving a prison that I had visited as a judge.

The TV room was crowded, the inmates anxious to escape their own imprisonment for a couple of hours by watching the story of other inmates who suffered even more.

The movie depicted the indifference of the guards to the loneliness and deprivations of the prisoners. It illustrated the prison regulations, which seemed to have been designed more to create inmate discomfort and suffering than to provide prison efficiency. And it showed the mindless violence that follows oaths like the one spoken by an Attica inmate: "If we can't live like men, at least we can die like men." A reprise of the oath of Emiliano Zapata: "It is better to die on your feet than to live on your knees."

When the movie ended and the epilogue scrolled silently across the screen, the room was equally silent. Then one in the room spoke. He addressed a question to me: "How many Atticas will it take before the people who run the prisons learn that we're people too?"

I said nothing out loud. To myself I said, "Forget it. As prisoners, you will never be thought of as people."

* * *

In 1975, after the Attica riots, New York prison officials learned that the Ku Klux Klan was actively courting prison guards for membership. Benjamin Ward, himself an African-American and then the commissioner of the New York State Department of Correctional Services, promulgated a directive forbidding employees from joining the K.K.K.

Some prison guards promptly sought to have the commissioner's directive declared illegal, claiming that under the First Amendment to the United States Constitution they were free to join, assemble with, and express themselves through any group they wished, and that included the Ku Klux Klan.

They were correct to a degree. Abridging the freedom of association is prohibited for a mere advocacy of doctrine without the advocacy of unlawful action. In most cases, as with the danger posed by subversive activity to national security, merely belonging to an organization without the specific intent of furthering its illegal aims is not enough to declare membership illegal. In such cases, like those involved in Communist Party membership, the United States Supreme Court held that the likelihood is slight that grave and immediate harm will flow from membership alone.

But in this case involving prison-guard membership in the Ku Klux Klan, the commissioner was not seeking to punish prison guards for harboring unpopular beliefs. Rather he was seeking to rid the prison system of racism by relieving the institutional strain that would erupt into another Attica.

It was the commissioner's contention that the mere presence of a guard who believes in Klan doctrine may subtly, if not blatantly, infest the prison environment with the taint of racism, an affliction that can paralyze the rehabilitative process. He considered this a grave and immediate harm that would be caused by the communication of racist attitudes even in the absence of specific illegal intent.

The question we anticipated when the case was brought to our court was this: "Was the New York State prison system or persons confined in New York State prisons placed in grave and immediate harm if the guards were members of the Ku Klux Klan?" The lower courts held that membership in the Klan by prison guards constituted no such danger, and so the commissioner's regulation was declared unconstitutional and was nullified.

The commissioner appealed to the Court of Appeals. The answer seemed self-evident to me. The idea that members of the Klan would be allowed to hold the whip handle over the head of prisoners, most of whom were black, struck me as intolerable. I was strongly in favor of reversing the lower court and upholding the commissioner's regulation.

As usual, each of the seven judges of the court had read the briefs in advance of the oral argument. Also as usual, we did not discuss the case before allowing both sides to be heard. There was always the chance that one of the lawyers would advance an argument or make a point during his or her oral presentation that you might have missed when reading the briefs. For that reason, a judge would resist the urge to come to a conclusion too early in the process.

And it was for that same reason that we did not discuss a case among ourselves before each side had the opportunity, by way of written brief and oral argument, to persuade us as convincingly as possible. It would have been inappropriate to indicate a personal predisposition to a colleague, when that premature impression might preempt a more informed determination.

Of course, there were cases where the result seemed so apparent, the ultimate determination so self-evident, that no preliminary conversation among the colleagues was necessary to learn how the other judges felt. You knew how your fellow judges would react to certain fact patterns—at least you thought you knew.

The attorney for the prison guards understood that arguing a case that supported membership in the K.K.K. would not be easy. Rather than trying to convince the court of the virtues of Ku Kluxers, he took an entirely different tack: a procedural technicality.

On the day of argument, the entry of the judges of the Court of Appeals is announced by the court crier: "The judges of the court."

Everyone in the magnificent oak-paneled courtroom rises and remains standing as the black-robed judges walk to their places on the bench in order of seniority. The crier then tells all assembled: "Hear ye, hear ye, hear ye. All persons having any business before this Court of Appeals, held in and for the State of New York, may now draw near, give their attendance, and they will be heard."

The Chief Judge then takes his seat, and the other judges and spectators do the same. The Chief Judge then calls the first case and the arguments by the attorneys are heard.

When we took the bench for the oral argument in the case of *Matter of Curly v. Benjamin Ward, Commissioner,* I felt certain that the commissioner would prevail. What I did not foresee was the argument made by the attorney for the prison guards. He did not argue the First Amendment right of his clients, as I believe we all expected he would. Instead he went off in another direction entirely. He informed the judges that there was no "record" made in the lower courts with respect to any propensity or bias that the Klan might have against members of the negro race. Without proof of that antagonism being in the record, he argued, the Court of Appeals could not consider that to be a fact.

He knew that an appellate judge cannot decide a case on emotion alone or on presumed facts. A judge must be conscious of the law, and the law tells us that an appellate court is bound by the record of the lower-court proceedings. Even though an appellate judge might disagree with the determination of the court below, that determination can only be affirmed or reversed on the basis of what is in the record. In other words, judges on the Court of Appeals do not take testimony or receive new evidence. Their review is limited only to matters that were in evidence in the prior proceedings before the lower court.

Seven cases are usually argued during each session of the court. After oral argument, the judges of the court retire to a small room adjacent to the courtroom. The Chief Judge then spreads seven index cards facedown on a table, each bearing the name of a case argued that day. Each of the seven judges of the court then draws one of the cards, and the case identified by that card is assigned, for reporting purposes at conference, to the judge drawing it.

The case conferences are held in private, in a large and imposing room with only the judges of the court, the chief clerk, and the "opinion" clerk allowed in attendance. The pattern of these conferences, like much of the work of the court, is dictated by precedence.

First, the Chief Judge calls the name of the case. The "reporting" judge, the one who drew that case the day before, then tells his or her view of the case and recommends either affirmance, reversal, or modification of the determination made by the lower court. Then each judge, in reverse order of seniority, expresses a view either agreeing or disagreeing with the reporting judge.

The reason the judges speak in reverse order of seniority—the more recent or newer members of the court first, and the Chief Judge last—is so that the less experienced judges will not be influenced by the others. When the junior judges speak, they will have no way of knowing what the more senior judges have to say and therefore will not be inclined to defer or be intimidated by the latter's experience and seniority. (Although this reasoning might be theoretically sound, my actual experience has always been that the more recent additions to the court are usually the most outspoken, and not at all in awe of their senior colleagues.)

At the time the prison guard–K.K.K. case was argued, I was not yet the Chief Judge, but I was considered a senior judge. As the conference progressed, and I awaited my turn to speak, I was astonished to note that the majority of my colleagues were accepting the argument advanced by the attorney for the prison guards. They were agreeing that the "record on appeal" did not fully explicate the extent of the Klan's activity—at least not sufficiently enough to permit a conclusion that being a member of the Klan would predispose someone to treat a member of the black race with undue harshness.

When it came to my turn, I was genuinely upset. There is something in the law known as "judicial notice": when a fact is well known and beyond doubt, a judge can take "judicial notice" of the fact without requiring exacting proof. This has been called a short-cut for doing away with evidence. We all know, for example, that Washington, D.C., is the nation's capital. If that became a relevant fact in a case, no evidence would be needed for proof.

"Why, then," I argued with my colleagues, "can't we take judicial notice that the Klan, since the Civil War, has preached hatred, violence, and genocide?"

"Because," came the response from one of my more senior colleagues, "judicial notice can only be taken of facts which are of"—and here he opened the casebook in front of him—" 'common and general knowledge, well established and authoritatively settled.' "

"So?" I said. "Isn't that what we're talking about?"

"No," said my senior colleague. "What the Klan stands for might be general knowledge, but how a Klansman might behave as a prison guard is not, and that should be subject to proof."

"But it doesn't matter how a guard who is a member of the K.K.K. will actually behave," I argued. "The mere fact that a black prisoner knows that a Klansman will have a club over his head is enough to breed frustration, hatred, and disruption."

Maybe that would not have been enough to override the First Amendment right of a prison guard to join the Klan, but the very least our court should have done, or so I thought, was to reach that constitutional issue. However, the majority would not go even that far.

My argument went nowhere, and the New York Court of Appeals, in a brief memorandum, agreed with and affirmed the lower court and struck down the commissioner's directive outlawing the membership of prison guards in the Klan, not on constitutional grounds but because it felt, as it wrote in its brief memorandum of affirmance, that it was "nothing more than speculation as to the effect which such membership might have upon the correctional facilities."

On more than one occasion I disagreed with my colleagues, and I am certain there were occasions when they exhibited more wisdom than I, but never did I disagree more strongly. To this day I cannot understand how the judges in the majority could have considered the Klan's blatant racism and their vows of enforced racial dominance as "nothing more than speculation."

I dissented, noting:

> The Klan's reputation for violence and illegality indicates that the employment of Klan members as prison guards will surely trigger a recurrence of violent disruption. The terrorism of the Ku Klux Klan is a matter of common knowledge. . . . The prison population in this State is more than 70% Black and Hispanic. The Klan openly professes hatred towards these groups. Inmates forced into daily interaction with Klan members who are prison guards will inevitably face the indignity, degradation and threat of violence spawned by racial discrimination.

In that same dissent, I addressed another concern. I wrote of what I then perceived to be the helplessness of those who are in prison, noting that though society has a "right and obligation to punish those convicted of criminal offenses," in so doing it should be certain that prisoners not be stripped of all protections. I believed then, and now have confirmation for my belief, that "during a criminal's imprisonment the State must" afford that protection, "for the prisoner himself is incapable of doing so."

When our decision came down, I thought the public would be outraged to know that the Klan would be permitted to operate in our New York prisons; I thought the editorial writers and good-government groups would be up in arms. But nothing happened. Judicial opinions that seem to favor inmates usually go unnoticed. No lessons were learned from Attica.

And here I am writing again of this public indifference to the lot of prisoners. I accomplished nothing as a judge; how much could I ever hope to accomplish as a prisoner?

From what I was told by correction commissioners and prison officials—when they still communicated with me civilly—there are still Atticas all over America, penitentiaries that breed hate and malevolence. When stories of prison brutality surface, the public attitude is either applause or indifference. And now, given the new populist trend that would deprive prisoners of legal assistance to redress these wrongs, they will go without remedy and without notice.

Although I have never been subjected to this kind of depraved treatment, I do know from firsthand experience about the callous and dehumanizing ways of some prison guards, people who refuse to recognize that we were sent to prison *as* a punishment, not *to be* punished.

The way in which our prisons are run does not lead to rehabilitation. If a person's life turns around in prison, it is usually a tribute to that person's inner strength or overwhelming desire to regain and retain his freedom. On the other hand, prisons can be responsible for lowering an inmate's self-esteem to the point where not only does rehabilitation become impossible, but antisocial behavior becomes inevitable.

When I first went on the bench, in 1968, there was still talk of rehabilitation as the goal of imprisonment. I remember questioning the ability of the prisons to accomplish this result. In a speech delivered before the League of Women Voters I noted: "Our prisons do not rehabilitate. They act instead as breeding grounds for hatred and act as schools for advanced studies in criminality. The only thing our prisons seem to cure is heterosexuality."

I was falling into the same pattern as the vast majority of our citizens in assuming that "nothing works." That these are bad people, who have done bad things, and that it would be more productive to devote our efforts toward a more attainable goal than prisoner rehabilitation.

Neither I nor the public at large was entirely wrong—at that time. But that was before the days of sentencing guidelines and the drug epidemic. That was a time when the reform of prisoners was elusive because almost all of the prisoners were perpetrators of vio-

lent crimes and most were malefactors who were beyond being restored as productive members of society. That is no longer the case.

Today over half the prisoners in our system are here because of
nonviolent drug crimes. Another large percentage are here because
their "category" of criminal conduct indicates a serious criminal act,
even though the underlying facts of the case belie such a definition.
They are here for longer than they should be because the sentencing judge was deprived of discretion by the mandatory sentencing
laws and was powerless to consider those underlying facts.

Some prisoners are capable of rehabilitation. I am not saying
that with this new prison population "rehabilitation" will suddenly
become the method by which the prison can make good citizens of
lawbreakers. But we make a mistake in depriving prisoners who will
utilize them of programs and self-development opportunities.

Given the fact that we have over one million Americans behind
bars, we have to consider ways to deal appropriately with them—not
just for their sakes but also for ours. When a guard abuses or brutal-
izes a prisoner you can be certain that when the prisoner is released
he will be more antisocial and dangerous than when he was sent
away. It is a simple but accurate equation: Violence begets violence.

One of the first lectures a prisoner receives is called A and O, Admission and Orientation. When I attended A and O at Rochester, a
young female guard addressed our small group of newcomers. After
telling us of the awesome power vested in a guard she cautioned,
"Just because some of us may be friendly, don't think we are your
friends." It would have been more appropriate if she had said, "Just
because some of us will treat you like dogs, don't bite."

April 10, 1994

"We've got our own judge and he's more important than any of
them."

It was an inmate talking to one of the guards.

"Difference is, these are *real* judges," said the guard. "Washtler will be standing with the rest of you at the four o'clock count."

The guard's reference was to the daily attendance check, when every inmate is to stand silently next to his bed to be counted. The inmates were talking about an anticipated visit from a group of judges to F.M.C. Rochester.

Prison visitations are often made not out of concern for the imprisoned but out of curiosity. Before I ever thought I would be a prisoner, the fearsome aspect of "the prison" only heightened my interest in visiting one. It was probably the same kind of curiosity that brings people to horror films, or entices them to see sharks in the aquarium or large reptiles in the zoo. Monsters and other fearsome things compel our attention. The same can be said of prisons.

Jails should not be confused with prisons. Jails, which are run by local communities, cities, and counties, house people who have committed lesser crimes and misdemeanors. Prisons are where felons who have committed serious crimes are incarcerated. State prisons, which came into being in this country shortly after the ratification of our Constitution, should not be confused with federal prisons, which were not built until the end of the nineteenth century.

The federal prisons were built to incarcerate those who violated federal law (laws enacted to deal with large conspiracy crimes or other enterprises that cross state lines), whereas the murderers, rapists, and other violators of more traditional state laws were incarcerated in the more numerous state prisons. As a state judge, my concern was with state prisons, and my visits were to these prisons.

There was a time in our history when prisons in this country were visited by sociologists and students from all over the world because they represented a new era and a novel approach to crime and punishment. It was our prisons that lured Alexis de Tocqueville from France to visit this country in 1831. He stayed on to write his classic *Democracy in America*, but it was our prison system that first attracted his attention.

The creative approach in fashioning a new punishment system in this country was understandable, given our displeasure with British justice, a system that dealt harshly with the colonists. In addition, our independence from England brought with it a desire to do better than the mother country in addressing the problem of crime and criminals. Our forebears recognized that the English system of sending most criminals, from pickpockets to horse thieves, to the gallows seemed not only inhumane but ineffective in reducing crime.

The alternative to execution devised by the citizens of our new nation was incarceration. It was the belief of the Founders that this punishment, certain and humane, would cause crime to disappear. They were wrong. Crime increased, prison riots ensued, and Jacksonian America looked desperately for an alternative. Rehabilitation seemed to be the answer.

New York State was the first to experiment with imprisonment designed to rehabilitate the offender. The year was 1820, and the prison was Auburn. The system was called "congregate" and was premised on the belief that solitude and regulated labor would eliminate the propensity to do evil acts. It was called congregate because for the first time prisoners were allowed to eat and work together.

When I visited Auburn I was shown reminders of this penitentiary system, where the inmates lived in single cells and were prohibited from either talking to or even looking at their fellow prisoners. This enforced silence and solitude was intended to encourage inner reflection and the rehabilitative forces of self-examination. The only time the prisoners were together was when they ate or worked, and that too was done in silence. The Auburn experiment took hold and became the model for most other states. Prisons were built all over the country that adopted not only the Auburn method of inmate regimentation but also its prison architecture, which resembled and reflected the impregnability of a medieval fortress.

Increased prison populations, budget constraints, and a sense that the Auburn method was not curing criminal propensity brought an end to the concept of rehabilitation. In the 1860s the sole concern of the prisons, and those who ran them, was to keep the facilities secure and the prisoners under control. New York, which once had prided itself on the humane treatment of its convicts, introduced the harshest of corporal punishments.

On one of my tours, a warden told me of some of these punishments, which were not unique to New York, he believed. There was the yoke, which the prisoner was made to wear, consisting of a heavy six-foot bar with a center ring for his neck. The hands were shackled to each end of the bar. Another, the punishment of "bucking," forced the prisoner to squat with his wrists tied under his knees. A stick was then threaded under his knees and over his arms. He was compelled to remain in this painful position for hours at a time. There were also more conventional punishments of the lash or being hanged by the thumbs.

It wasn't until the latter part of the nineteenth century that reform brought an end to such treatment.

Standing in my prison uniform I watch the visiting judges parade two abreast across the Rochester compound. I remember the prison tours that I took when I was a judge: the tour of Attica while the embers of revolt still smoldered, and Greenhaven, Elmira, Auburn, and Sing Sing—New York State prisons located in the most beautiful parts of my state. Prisons in the hearts of communities that welcomed their presence because of the jobs and revenues that they produced. And if the residents of these communities welcomed the prisons, you can imagine the welcome they extended to the Chief Judge of the state. I was made to feel like royalty.

The wardens would detail the reforms made in the state penal system since the turn of the century, how they coped with shifting prison populations, how the Department of Corrections showed its concern for the inmate population and how well the training programs were succeeding. I had the sense that all that could or should be done was being done, and I greatly admired the men and women who undertook the difficult task of guarding and assuming the responsibility for monitoring the behavior of large numbers of convicted felons.

I always knew that I was seeing only what I was supposed to see, and I didn't expect to stumble upon some defect in the system that would merit my attention. My visits, in addition to satisfying my instinctive curiosity, were in large measure to demonstrate to the inmates that I cared about their conditions of confinement.

Now that I am a prisoner, and judges are being shown the facility that imprisons me, I realize how deluded I was in those years by my own vanity and by the escorts who so carefully planned my itinerary.

In 1975 the Committee on Codes of the New York State Assembly, headed by Assemblymen Stanley Fink and Milton Jonas, proposed legislation that would have compelled any sentencing judge elevated or appointed to judicial office to spend two days in a prison for the purpose of familiarizing themselves with various aspects of incarceration. The judicial branch fought this legislative imposition but agreed by court rule to require periodic prison "tour visits" by criminal court judges.

Preplanned tours of such short duration as an afternoon cannot lead to a meaningful appraisal of a prison or the prison system. On the contrary, they can lead to false impressions that eventually become an accepted mythology of what prison life is all about. If I were empowered to reappraise the efficacy of having judges visit prisons, I would be opposed to continuing the practice.

This thought occurs to me as I watch these judges being shown a part of the mental health unit that is air-conditioned and spacious enough to accommodate two single beds. The prison system has very few units of this type. The visitors will not be escorted through the vast majority of the units, which have unventilated, cramped, double-bunk cells built for two but each holding four inmates. My home is in one of these. Or the even more crowded dormitories that are filled with work cadre inmates who freeze during the Minnesota winter and swelter in the mosquito-infested summer.

For the judges' benefit, the guards are on their very best behavior, troublesome inmates are either put in the hole or tucked away in some remote locale, and the cabinets that house television sets, always padlocked, are miraculously opened. And if we have the good fortune of having the visitors present during lunch, the meals are actually edible and the soda fountains, which are used very seldom, give forth soda. Apparently the visitors like seeing what they are shown, because they always seem to be smiling.

The only thing accomplished by these tours is to create yet another group of propagandists who spread the word that life in prison is pretty good or, far worse for the future treatment of the prisoners, life in prison is *too* good.

April 18, 1994

Lorenzo and I frequently sit together during meals. I met him when I was assigned to the mental health unit. He remains there for observation because of his bouts with depression and his two suicide attempts, once by cutting his wrists, and once by attempting to hang himself. He has served two years on a four-year sentence for conspiracy to sell drugs, the same kind of conspiracy charge that accounts for so many inmates: the crime of low-level operatives who facilitate a drug transaction in order to feed their own addiction.

The first day we met he told me he was from Cuba but was not a Marielito. "That's good to know," I said, "but what is a Marielito?"

"Those who came here from Mariel in Cuba," he said, reminding me of the time in 1980 when the Peruvian embassy in Havana was stormed by thousands of Cubans seeking to escape the repression of the Castro regime. Fidel Castro told those who wanted to leave that they could and at the invitation of then President Jimmy Carter, 125,000 Cubans left from Mariel, on the island's northwest coast, in a boat lift to what Carter described as the "open arms and open heart" of America.

What we didn't know was that 25,000 of these "Marielitos" came from Cuban prisons and mental hospitals; when many were arrested for crimes they committed here, Castro refused to take them back. That left our Immigration and Naturalization Service with the burden of detaining over 3,000 Cubans. At first they were kept in old army bases, and later at the federal penitentiary in Atlanta, Georgia. In a 1983 ruling the United States Supreme Court said these Cubans were not protected by the U.S. Constitution, so they could be held for any or no reason for as long as the Justice Department saw fit.

In 1986, when Atlanta became overcrowded, an "alien detention facility" was built in Oakdale, Louisiana, at a cost of approximately $20 million. Oakdale and Atlanta were having a great deal of difficulty holding this explosive population and so some Cubans were sent to the penitentiary in Leavenworth, Kansas. The real problem with the Marielito population began in 1987, when Castro agreed to take the Cubans back. They didn't want to go, and to demonstrate this fact they literally burned and tore down the Atlanta and Oakdale facilities at a cost to U.S. taxpayers of over $100 million.

Because Rochester has facilities for prisoners in the custody of the Bureau of Prisons who are in need of psychiatric and medical attention, some Marielitos have been sent here. But, as my friend Lorenzo reminds me, not all Cubans claim Mariel as the starting point of their ninety-mile voyage from Cuba to the United States.

There are a couple of Marielitos here whose presence is about as difficult to tolerate as a cockroach on a wedding cake. I first met Fernandez when he came into the television room where I and a dozen other inmates were watching a movie. Without a word he changed the station to a Spanish-language telecast.

"Hey man, what the hell are you doing?" shouted one of the inmates.

"Dees ees an ol' movie," answered Fernandez. "Everyone seen it."

"All these people were watching it," the inmate shouted in furious response.

They all looked at me. For some reason, either because of my age or my former station in life, I am looked to as the person most able to resolve disputes. I have done fairly well—but this is the first time that I was called upon to deal with a confrontation this explosive.

"Look, Fernandez—" I started. But before I could continue, Fernandez was standing in front of the television set brandishing a chair.

"You don' tell me what to do," said Fernandez. "I don' care what you was on the street, man. You here because you a criminal—I'm a political prisoner."

The rest was blur. One of the inmates charged Fernandez, who swung the chair in a well-aimed arc, striking his assailant on the side of the head. He continued to pound his downed opponent, breaking the chair over his huddled form.

Two other inmates grabbed Fernandez, one on each side, pinning down his arms. They looked at me: "Hit him, judge," they said in unison. "Hit him!"

I stood there, staring at Fernandez, who looked like a trapped animal. "Where are the guards?" I thought. They seemed to be everywhere all the time—where were they now? This looked to me like the kind of confrontation that could erupt into a full-blown riot.

"He dissed you, judge, hit him." One thing a real prisoner will not tolerate is to be "disrespected." But being dissed never bothered me very much, and on this particular occasion, it bothered me not at all.

"Let him go," I said. "He's not going to bother us anymore."

Fernandez showed his gratitude for my reprieve by spitting at me. "Now hit him, judge!"

When I continued to refuse, the two dragged Fernandez, kicking and screaming, to the shower room.

Five minutes later, Fernandez came out of the shower room, walked over to me, and said, "I deen't mean to diss you, judge. You accep' my sayin' I'm sorry?"

"Sure, Fernandez, but in the—"

He wasn't interested in hearing any more from me. He apparently had had the only lecture he could understand given him in the shower room.

April 22, 1994

My brother, Morty, came to visit me today. I waited in my cell for him to arrive, be searched, and clear the magnetometer. When he has been seated in the visitors' room and my name is called over the loudspeaker, I will go to Building 10 to see him.

According to "dress code" regulations, I will be in my army tans and black shoes. My clothing "will be neat, clean and presentable," and my shirt "will be tucked into belted trousers." My button shirt "will be secured up to the first button below the collar" and I will wear socks. I will look "well groomed." Visitors must "see you at your best."

You wait in your room for the visitor to arrive. When he has been searched and has cleared the magnetometer, he is seated in the visiting room, and your name is called over the loudspeaker: "Washtler, Washtler, you have a visit."

When you are cleared, you enter the visiting room and look over the faces, searching for those which are familiar. I quickly spotted Morty. Whenever I see him—even in this terrible place—I feel a surge of affection and nostalgia.

Morty and I see each other at the same time and embrace.

"What do you want to eat?" he asks me.

One thing visitors quickly learn is the necessity to bring change— quarters. The only way you can get a snack is to put quarters into one of the many vending machines that line the walls of the visiting room.

And my mind reels back almost sixty years to another time and place. It was the late 1930s. Dad was driving an old car, called, I believe, an Auburn (was there really such a car, or am I imagining it?). We're driving south, from New York to Florida along Route 1, the only highway that ran the distance between those two states. Morty and I were seated in the backseat, Mom and Dad in the front.

There were no such things as tape decks, or even radio stations strong enough to be picked up on the long lonesome stretches of road. My father complained that there were too few bypasses; Route 1 ran right through most towns and villages.

"The businesses and local Chambers of Commerce are responsible for this," he would say. "They want all the traffic they can get to go right through their business districts."

Morty and I didn't care what the reason was. We looked forward to driving through every city and every hamlet—all different, but each bearing some regional identity. Like the Confederate monuments in the South, and the smokestack factories in the North. And then, of course, there was the one link that knew no region: the ever-present Burma-Shave signs.

The Burma-Vita company was smart enough to realize that travel by highway was increasing, but was boring for drivers and passengers. They leased small sections of roadside land and placed rhyming signs, in sets of six each, spaced approximately twenty-five yards apart. Because they manufactured a brushless shave cream, ideal for traveling salesmen who didn't want to pack a mug and brush every time they went on the road, this roadside advertising was ideal. I was not yet old enough to read, but I could spot the signs at a great distance. The first sign had the name of the product. "Here comes Burma-Shave!" I would shout. And then Morty would read the signs. I still remember a few:

"Cheer up face / the war is over / from now on / you'll be in clover / Use Burma-Shave."

"Romeo / Romeo / Romeo / if you have a beard / go homeo / Use Burma-Shave."

Some of the signs encouraged safe driving:

"Heaven's latest neophyte / signaled left / then turned right / Use Burma-Shave."

Another source of amusement was picking restaurants and motor cabins, the primitive forerunners of motels. We would rent two cabins, one for Mom and Dad and one for me and Morty.

These long automobile trips were always an adventure. We could not complete a trip without some mishap: a flat tire, a speeding ticket, or a more serious event—when I was five years old I was hit on the head with an automobile chain hoist. It was that injury which I felt was responsible for my constant headaches and later blamed for what I thought was a brain tumor.

Standing in the prison visiting room watching Morty go to the vending machines to buy me something to eat reminded me of another one of those trips. We were in a motor cabin outside of Valdosta, Georgia. Morty, who couldn't have been more than ten years old at the time, got out of bed. It was still dark.

"What time is it?" I asked him.

"Five in the morning," he answered.

"Where are you going?"

"I'm going to the filling station next door to see if I can get a job pumping gas—it says 'Open all night—pumper needed.' "

I watched him leave, and a few minutes later there he was, pumping gas. In those days "pumping gas" men literally used a pump handle to pump, much as well water was pumped for domestic use.

He kept pumping for three hours, until it was time for us to get back on the road. He earned twenty-five cents for his labor. But the thing that moved me then, and moves me still, is that he spent the entire sum to buy me a doughnut and a bottle of chocolate milk. He spent not one cent of his hard-earned money on himself.

"Don't tell Mom and Dad," he said. "They'd kill me if they knew what I did."

As soon as we were back on the road, Morty fell into a deep sleep. I remember looking at him and thinking that I loved him more than anything in the world.

April 29, 1994

Today is my sixty-fourth birthday. My in-law and friend Fred Wilpon came to visit with Joan. My son and daughter-in-law, Philip and Robin, came along with their daughter—our granddaughter—Kimberly.

Kimberly is three years old. As I feel her hug and see her warm smile, I wonder how she will deal with the knowledge that her grandfather was a convicted criminal whom she visited while he was in prison. She too is an innocent victim of my crime.

But now she is too young to know or think about such things. She has found a friend her own age named Gail who is here visiting her father. The two of them are sitting at a table having an imaginary tea party.

I know the little girl's father. He was an army helicopter pilot in Vietnam who bought a plane of his own after his army discharge. He was going to be a crop duster, something he had done for the farmers in his Iowa home before he was drafted. All went well until one of his customers convinced him that flying some bales of marijuana was far more lucrative and healthier than spreading poisons on plants.

When his customer was arrested he "gave up" the pilot for a more lenient sentence. That career detour cost Gail's father his plane, all the money he had saved for his family's future, and ten years of his life. Gail will be a teenager when her father comes home, and she and her mother, who has been unable to find employment near Rochester, will be living on welfare until then.

After her tea party, Kimberly went over to one of the guards and spoke to her. She was treated rudely and with impatience.

At Butner the guards assigned to the visitors' waiting room showed some kindness to the family members who came to visit. They appreciated the fact that these people were innocents—victims, in a way, of the men they had come to see. The guards and reception personnel assigned to this same duty at Rochester were just the opposite.

Kimberly put it best. She came over to me, had me lean over to hear her, and whispered in my ear: "That lady doesn't like me."

Then there was the time that my daughter Alison came to visit me.

According to rule, I had donned my best khaki uniform and waited in my cell to be called. I knew Alison, seven months pregnant, was making the cross-country trek from Boston with her husband, Barry, to see me. Visitors usually arrive at ten A.M. but now it was noon and there was still no direction for me to go to Building 10.

Not until noon was I summoned.

It seems that when Alison was first seen by the reception guard for the routine search of visitors, she was refused admittance. The reason: The guard felt that the blouse she wore over her maternity leggings was too short. She was required to leave. She and Barry went to a local K mart and purchased a sweat suit, but when they returned another guard on duty said that she didn't need it: that her maternity outfit was perfectly proper—as indeed it was.

We had lost two precious hours of visiting time, and they had taken a long trip, all the way to Minnesota, to shop at K mart.

The other inmates ride me about the volume of mail I receive on a daily basis, but even I was astounded by the amount of birthday cards and other mail I received today. Perhaps the one that moved me the most was a card inscribed by all the judges who sit on the Supreme Court in Nassau County. My friendship with many of these judges goes back more than thirty years. To claim friendship with them would be honor enough, but this verification of their affections at this time and place hit me like an emotional tidal wave.

I cannot help wondering how they will view me when I return to New York. How will they think of their former leader and "chief" when he is back in their company as an ex-con?

May 1994

May 6, 1994

Today is Lauren's fortieth birthday, another milestone that the family will reach in my absence. When she was here with Paul last week, I told her how much I loved her and how sorry I was not to be able to be with her.

It's hard to believe that it is now forty years ago that Lauren was born. I was in the army at the time, stationed at Camp Gordon, Georgia. We lived in a small development called Thomas Woods, located between Augusta, Georgia, and the army base, in a district called Sand Hills.

When I think about that time in our lives, I remember Joan sterilizing Lauren's bottles while standing over a stove in 107° heat. Of course there was no air conditioning. Lauren's carriage was left in the coolest place we could find, our front porch. We thought better of that when we found a nest of black widow spiders building a web right in front of her unsuspecting blue eyes.

I was a sergeant in the military police, instructing company commanders on the finer points of the *Manual for Courts Martial.* To assist in my instruction, I prepared a monograph entitled "The Preparation and Trial of Summary and Special Courts Martial," which was later published and sent to army installations nation-wide. I was teaching others how to prosecute wrongdoers.

Life for Joan was not as interesting. She was living in the Deep South, among strangers, with her first newborn. Because we could afford only one car, she was forced to remain at home with the baby in the incredible humid heat of a Georgia summer. But I came home at five every afternoon, and our lives seemed carefree. We had nothing to do but plan and dream of our future.

Where should we live? How many children should we have? We both had great confidence in the future. We had our good health, the benefit of a good education, and had been blessed with a healthy baby. I had the promise of a professional career and, with the optimism of youth, we felt there was a certainty to our lives. We both look upon that time as two wonderful years.

May 7, 1994

Mike Trainor, my senior law clerk and friend for over twenty years, once told me that with my bodyguards and chauffeurs and position of exalted importance, I probably didn't remember what it is like being an average citizen, being an unknown face in an amorphous crowd. He put it this way: "Judge, you don't know what it is like to stand on line at the Motor Vehicle Bureau."

He was right. Although I never took improper advantage of the perquisites of my office, I never fully appreciated them—never, that is, until now.

On Friday, November 6, 1992, I was a speaker at a small Albany dinner party given for members of the New York State Bar Association. I was toasted and praised.

The next night, I was chained to a bed in a psychiatric hospital under the guard of two armed United States marshals.

That was one and a half years ago today. Today is another Saturday in my life. It is my turn to clean the art and activity rooms in the mental health unit, a job that falls to me on a rotation basis once a month. Today I sweep, mop, wax, and buff the rooms where I work during the week with Ms. Bighley, Ms. Burns, and Ms. Berg, three gifted mental health therapists. The cleaning routine is one part of my duties, for which I am paid 7 cents an hour, or $12.50 a month.

I would gladly spend the next one and a half years standing on line at a Motor Vehicle Bureau, if I could only stand there as a free man.

May 8, 1994

The inmates called him R.W. I called him Richard. The hacks called him Inmate Miller. He was a veteran F.B.I. agent stationed in California who was seduced by a female Russian emigré into giving government secrets to the Soviet Union. Her name was Svetlana Ogorodnikov and it was not known at the time whether she was a Russian K.G.B. agent or merely an opportunist.

At the time of Richard's arrest, F.B.I. officials said that "it was money problems more than his relationship with the Russian woman" that led Richard astray. Although he never discussed it with me, I doubt that was the case. In fact, Ms. Ogorodnikov herself admitted that in her Mata Hari role for the Soviet Union she had had an earlier love affair with another F.B.I. agent.

After his initial trial, Richard was found guilty of treason and sentenced to two life terms plus fifty years. That conviction was overturned and he was tried again. The second conviction resulted in a forty-year sentence, later reduced to twenty-four years.

He is a delight to be with. Although far too obese, he has a lightness to his step and an upbeat personality. He never talks about his crime, which received enormous publicity at the time; whenever a story appears involving traitors, espionage, or the activity of spies, the press invariably resurrects the facts of his case. On those occasions he is visibly saddened, and for good cause. He was the first F.B.I. agent ever to be convicted of espionage.

Yesterday he called me aside: "Your Honor," he said—he always calls me that, reminding me and him that our mutual disgrace did not change old habits—"I'm going home."

"How long have you been down?" I asked, using the prison term for time served.

"Thirteen years," he said.

"Why are they cutting you loose?"

"The judge thought I had been punished enough—he granted my motion and resentenced me to time served. I'm out of here, maybe even by tomorrow."

It often seems that everyone in prison has a motion of one sort or another pending before the courts. For a new trial or for resentencing; evidence has been newly discovered, or someone else has confessed to the crime; a juror has submitted an affidavit that something improper happened during deliberations; an inmate, after being advised by some jailhouse lawyers, has concluded that his attorney's representation at trial was ineffective—the list is endless.

And given the time a prisoner has to study his trial record, it is no surprise that errors are discovered. The questions are: Was the error serious enough to warrant remedial action by a court? And has the application been made to the court in timely and proper fashion?

When I was a judge, I can remember the endless number of applications made by prisoners. I knew that these petitions for court action were important to those in prison, but I didn't know how important they were.

Hope becomes an antidote for heartbreak. Much as a survivor in a lifeboat looks for a ship on the horizon, a prisoner looks for judicial salvation. In both instances, the hope and anticipation of rescue become the focal points of their existence. The odds are very much against a lone lifeboat being picked up in a vast ocean, and the chance of an appeals court finding error sufficient to warrant a reversal of another court's order is just as remote. Even more of a long shot is the reconsideration of a sentence by a trial judge who, having passed sentence after due deliberation, is reluctant to say later that he or she was too severe.

And there is another factor. Courts pride themselves on their ability to do justice free from the passions of the crowd or the moment. Unfortunately, prisoners recognize that judges are human. If there is a public clamor for eliminating the scourge that illicit drugs have brought to our communities, it is unlikely that a judge will reduce the sentence of a drug dealer.

The tide of public opinion as an influence on judicial sentiment became relevant in the case of the former F.B.I. agent Richard W. Miller. While his latest motion for the reduction of sentence was pending, a C.I.A. agent by the name of Aldrich Ames and his wife were arrested for selling military secrets to the Russians. The press immediately drew the parallel between the Miller and Ames cases and, in so doing, reignited the resentment that the public felt toward American spies.

When his name was again in the news, Miller feared that no judge would have the courage to mitigate his sentence. He resigned himself to serving the balance of his twenty-four-year sentence. He felt, and I agreed, that the likelihood of a judge's reducing his sentence under these circumstances was negligible. There was no possibility of a sail appearing on his horizon.

We were wrong. A judge in California had the courage to do what he considered just and proper, without concern for the negative publicity that his actions would engender. And so Richard W. Miller was rescued. He is leaving tomorrow morning.

While we were exchanging addresses, promising to keep in touch when I, too, was freed, I received word that my request for release to a halfway house for a six-month period, as recommended by my unit counselor, had been rejected by Washington. I was told that I would not receive more than two months in a halfway house. In other words, instead of leaving now, I will be here for another four

months and sixteen days. One hundred thirty-six more days of looking at a bare horizon.

May 10, 1994

About ten-thirty every morning the unit loudspeaker announces:
"Two, one work cadre, mainline!" Translation: "Those who live on
the first floor of Unit 2 and who are assigned to various jobs in the
facility can join the other inmates for lunch in the dining hall."

A policy in all the federal prisons provides that some of the
prison's more important officials "stand mainline" while the prisoners eat. That is, they line up in an area readily accessible to the inmates so that if any inmate should want to speak to them, they can
easily do so.

This accomplishes three purposes: (1) The everyday availability
of these officials precludes any prisoner from complaining about
not being able to see them. (2) If an inmate were seen speaking privately to one of these officials, he could be branded a snitch, a label
that would incur the enmity of all his fellow inmates. But speaking
to "the man" in plain view, and within earshot of everyone else, is
considered acceptable. (3) It serves as a subtle reminder that "they,"
although vastly outnumbered by "us" prisoners, are still in control.
"They" can arrive when they want to, stand where they want to, and
leave when they want to. "We" do as we're told.

Prisoners live in a unique world, by their own rules. Not even
guards and administrators who have spent years with the Bureau of
Prisons can fully understand the sense of brotherhood that exists
among the inmates. Even groups hostile to one another become
united when confronted by the common enemy known generally as
"the man."

"Beating the man," or putting one over on the system, becomes a
constant objective of those doing time. Sneaking food out of the
mess hall, a prohibited act, is beating the man. It's done by lining

your pocket with a plastic bag, once containing something bought at the commissary. Take out cookies and cake or, if you do a lot of cooking in your unit, take raw vegetables from the salad bar. Or spirit away a baked potato. Food tastes better when taken from the man.

Want some wine (prohibited by the man)? Get some oranges, raisins, or apples, a good measure of sugar and breads, rolls, cake, or any bakery product with yeast. Mix with hot water and put in a gallon jug, covered by a rubber surgical glove. In four or five days the fingers of the glove will inflate, indicating that the fermentation is done and you have beaten the man.

Or how about getting a tattoo, an adornment that the man says must not be acquired in prison? This mark of a professional convict—the dagger dripping blood, or the swastika; the skull, serpent, or spider; the roses and crosses; the teardrop under the eye—all can be supplied by a fellow inmate using tattoo guns made from motors stolen from tape players, paper clips, wire snipped off guitar strings. Need ink? You can always get the blue ink used for printing prison forms by boiling the forms and distilling the ink. If you want black ink, burn some Styrofoam; the ash is perfect. Need a stove? Take an electric wire with a plug. Split the wire on the opposite end, and attach each end to the ends of a metal spoon. Put the metal spoon in the substance to be heated, put in the plug, and you will find out how well a "stinger" works.

The list goes on—there are a hundred ways to beat the man. And every time an inmate beats the man and gets away with it, all the other inmates enjoy it. And if the man becomes repressive or enacts rules that don't make sense, all the inmates feel the pain and frustration. Just as the inmates all share the discomforts of prison—crowded into cells and dormitories built for fewer occupants; freezing when there is no heat; sweating and stinking when there's too much heat—so to do inmates become a part of the closeness that shared adversity brings.

When they hear a guard belittle or dehumanize a fellow prisoner—no matter his color, religion, or national origin—they sympathize with him and detest the hack for being a bully. No truer words were spoken than by Chekhov in his *Notebooks:* "Love, friendship, respect, do not unite people as much as a common hatred for something."

And if you want a philosophy to live by: "Gotta treat the man like you grow mushrooms—keep them in the dark and feed them shit!"

Mealtime is too brief an occasion to be considered a ritual, but it does have many ritualistic qualities. The order in which units are called to eat is determined by the ratings the units have received during the prior month's cleanliness inspection. If the floors were waxed to a high gloss, the cells immaculate, and the toilets and shower stalls sparkling, your unit stood a chance of being among the first—maybe even the first—to be called to the meal "mainline."

When your unit is called, the guard opens the heavy steel door of the unit and the inmates walk, as quickly as possible, to the chow line in front of the building that houses the mess hall, where they are under the watchful eyes of several guards ("Take off your hat, Washtler!" "What's that in your hand, McBaine? You know no books or papers are allowed in the mess hall." "Turn around, Cafer!").

Today was like any other. We were called to mainline, waited our turn, picked up our plastic trays with plastic utensils, and stood on the food line. As we walked along the cafeterialike counter, we took our food plates filled with the meal of the day. Today we had spaghetti with clam sauce (without clams), Parmesan cheese, garlic bread, salad bar, and chocolate brownies. There is a soda machine, but it never seems to be working. The more usual beverage, as was the case today, is water or Kool-aid. The meals are filling and fattening. You would not make this a restaurant of choice—oftentimes the food is inedible—but on the whole I can imagine it being worse.

The complaining mumbles of the diners were interrupted when an inmate at one of the tables began to cough and jumped to his feet. He was obviously choking. He put his hands to his throat, made a gurgling sound, and his face turned blue as he gasped for air.

Not many of the inmates are familiar with the Heimlich maneuver, a method of causing sharp pressure under the ribcage to expel a food particle obstructing the air passage. Unfortunately, none of us who knew this maneuver were near the victim.

"He's having a stroke," someone shouted. "No, it's epilepsy" came another diagnosis. "He's choking," shouted a bystander who proceeded to bang the choker on the back with both fists.

"No, you do it this way," said a fellow named Strickland, grabbing the now almost unconscious victim around the neck with a powerful arm.

There was instant panic. Strickland was in the mental health unit. He used to say (we always thought in jest), "I've killed before, don't make me kill again." It looked as though that's exactly what he was going to do.

Fortunately, at that moment the gagging inmate doubled over and spit out the offending piece of garlic bread. The incident was over and Strickland didn't have "to kill again" — but not every dining-room encounter has a happy ending.

It is not unusual to be "shaken down" when you leave the dining hall. An inmate is told to face the wall, and one of the guards pats him down to be sure he is not taking any food back to his unit. Last month one of the inmates was the subject of a shakedown and the guard felt a piece of bread in the inmate's back pocket.

"What's that?" asked the guard.

"Nothing," answered the inmate.

"Empty your pocket!" ordered the guard.

The inmate refused. Two other guards, hearing the disturbance, each grabbed one of the inmate's arms, while the third removed the slice of bread. For his refusal to obey the guard's order the bread thief was put in the hole. He was there for two weeks.

I saw him when he got out. "How ya' doin', Jamal?" I asked him.

He gave me a big smile. "I managed to save ten slices of bread from my trays in the hole. I smuggled them out in my clothing bag. I beat the man."

It was almost biblical. Proverbs 9:17 teaches us, "Stolen waters are sweet, and bread eaten in secret is pleasant."

I tried once to beat the man. It's a story I'm ashamed to tell—not because I made the effort, but because I made it so pathetically and, in the process, made such a fool of myself.

It was at Butner and the meal was hamburgers. Very hard, very dry hamburgers, on very hard, very dry buns. The one pleasant feature of the meal was a bag of potato chips that each prisoner was given at the end of the food line. It occurred to me that those potato chips would taste great in my cell, at night. All I had to do was get them out of the dining room.

I was wearing a bulky sweatshirt. It would be so easy: just tuck it under the shirt, out of sight, walk nonchalantly out of the chow hall, and that would be it. It wasn't that I wanted to get away with anything; it's just that the thought of those potato chips as a midnight snack was overwhelming.

My surreptitious concealment of the silvery bag was apparently witnessed by everyone in the dining room, especially the guards. As soon as I walked out of the door, three of the guards approached me.

"Whatcha got under the sweater?" one asked.

"Who, me?" I said, doing a bad job of feigning innocence.

"Yeah, you" came the predictable answer.

Rather than just confess and hand over the contraband, I clumsily pulled up my sweatshirt as if there were nothing there, and the bag fell to the ground. By now a large crowd had gathered, and everyone, the guards included, laughed.

Everyone except me. I saw nothing funny about a sixty-four-year-old former Chief Judge, in prison, caught in the shameful act of filching a bag of potato chips.

May 11, 1994

Because I cannot wear my contact lenses in prison (they will not provide the cleaning solutions) I must wear eyeglasses. After an enormous amount of red tape, Joan was able to send me a pair of reading glasses, the nonprescription magnifying kind available at Wal-Mart. Now, because of my advanced years, or poor diet, or attempts to read in the dim light of my solitary confinement cell—or for whatever reason—I can no longer rely on my Wal-Mart specials. It seems that while my mental condition has much improved this past year, my eyesight has deteriorated. And so I was fitted for prescription lenses by the Bureau of Prisons. Today I picked up my new pair of glasses. They are bifocals.

When they were fitted, the prison optometrist told me to select frames. He opened a large sample case and told me to pick whichever design I wanted. The case had about twenty frames—all the same.

"Not much of a selection," he said with a grin.

And so it has come to pass that, starting today, I will be wearing nondescript gray plastic framed bifocals, manufactured by UNICOR, in Butner, of all places, and issued by the Bureau of Prisons.

Some years ago Congress permitted the Bureau to establish UNICOR (Federal Prison Industries, Inc.) in most of the secure federal prisons. It is a light industrial facility that manufactures everything from T-shirts to mailbags, eyeglasses to electric cables—everything that can be used by the federal government, its prisoners, and its employees.

"Governmental use" was a critical prerequisite, because members of Congress did not want prison UNICORs competing with local community or other private industries. That would not be helpful to their constituents, particularly since the private sector could never compete with prison labor, which in UNICOR operations did not go much higher than two hundred dollars per month—an excellent wage for prisoners, but far less than a living wage on the outside.

In Europe they are experimenting with a "full-wages" prison where the prisoner is paid the same wages as he would earn for the same work on the outside. The inmate is then required to pay the prison for his room and board, send some money home to help keep his family off welfare, and contribute toward compensating his victim. It has yet to be determined whether such a system would be workable in this country or whether it would become bogged down in bureaucracy, bookkeeping, and a legislative agenda that prides itself on "taking from" rather than "giving to" prisoners.

At Rochester there is no UNICOR. When they did have one here, the high wages drew the very best of the workforce, leaving the hospital and mental health units vying for those workers without the seniority or skill of the UNICOR workers. The prison administration had two choices: increase the wages of the workers to compete with UNICOR, or eliminate UNICOR.

Needless to say, they eliminated UNICOR. But there is a UNISAT—a division of UNICOR where electronic components are assembled rather than fabricated. The wages at UNISAT, like those of the other work cadre positions at Rochester, range up to a maximum of one hundred dollars per month. As I have already noted, because of my short tenure I only earn twelve dollars per month. Michael Goland, because he has only one usable arm, works at sorting laundry. His highest monthly wage averages two dollars. He has been here for eight months and has earned a total of sixteen dollars.

May 13, 1994

Friday the thirteenth. This is as good a day as any to write about one of Rochester's prison officials and the mentality that grips some penal institutions.

I first saw and heard Roger Gabel at Admissions and Orientation (A and O), a time when the newly arrived inmates are told what to expect and what is expected of them. Butner's A and O took three days to complete; the one at Rochester was appropriately handled in one day.

To date I have never met Gabel nor dealt with him directly, but I know him to be the most detested individual here at Rochester. He is a man who enjoys the role of villain, and he plays it to the hilt. He prides himself on the enormous influence he has over the warden. The inmates remember him for his A and O opening remark: "You ain't got nothing coming."

Now that is really not bad counsel for a prisoner, but with Gabel it is given not as advice but as a promise. When he says, "You ain't got nothing coming," what he seems to mean is "I, Roger Gabel, will see to it that you'll never get anything. In fact I'm going to hurt you for even asking."

He will do everything he can to adversely affect an inmate's life in prison, for one apparent reason: He hates prisoners. And after he inflicts his psychic damage or physical discomfort, he takes pride in saying that his victim has been "Gabelized."

For example, there is in the federal, and most state systems, what is known as "compassionate release." When a prisoner is in imminent threat of death, he can apply for early release so that he can die in dignity, with his family. Not much to ask for.

A friend of mine who works in the hospital unit with terminally ill patients has given me a record of compassionate release requests that have been turned down during the past year. It is shameful. Although I have no way of being certain, he told me that Gabel had a great deal to do with the decision-making process.

It must be that for some reason granting such a release is considered not as an act of compassion but rather as giving "them" something, when, in Gabel's words, "they got nothing coming." And in a sense he's right; no one is "entitled" to compassion. It should, like mercy, come as a "gentle rain from heaven."

I have spread out on my bunk the very recent case records of six terminally ill patients, all of whom applied for and were refused compassionate release. Four of the six have died during the past few months, all of terminal cancer. Inmate Miguel Castillo was so ill with cancer that he lapsed into a coma while his petition was pending. He was still in a coma when his petition was denied. In fairness, I do have one that was granted; unfortunately the inmate died two days before his release was approved.

Some recent denials will, I am certain, result in the applicants dying in prison, like the seventy-six-year-old bank robber who has completed nineteen years on a twenty-five year sentence. After his sixth heart attack and an emphysema that causes him to receive oxygen sixteen hours a day, his doctor recommended compassionate release—it was denied.

The decision as to whether compassionate release should be granted is a difficult one, especially at a medical center where so many ill prisoners are billeted; and I'm not saying that all that are applied for should be granted, but I and the other inmates have a strong feeling that an unfortunate and cynical harshness has crept into the process.

This will soon become more of a morale problem for the Bureau in general and Rochester in particular, with its medical facility. The American College of Physicians and Surgeons is now completing a study, conducted with correctional health-care commissions, which will report that the incidence of AIDS is fourteen times higher in state and federal prisons than in the population at large. That's 200 cases for every 100,000 prisoners.

And then there is tuberculosis, sometimes linked with AIDS. During the time I was on the Court of Appeals in New York State, we watched with alarm as the prison tuberculosis rate soared. Between 1976 and 1986 tuberculosis—a particularly virulent strain— increased from 15 to 105 cases per 100,000 prisoners. During my last year as Chief Judge, 1991, thirteen prisoners died of this disease. Cumulatively, these two deadly diseases, AIDS and tuberculosis, constitute a plague.

Add to this the consequence of lengthening prison sentences to the point that inmates are kept in prison into their geriatric years, and we will find that more and more prisoners will be dying behind bars. Many ill inmates should not be released because of the danger of contagion; others, because they have nowhere to go if released. But many, out of compassion and so that other inmates have a sense that there is some humanity in the system, should be allowed to spend their last days in dignity—even if "they got nothing coming."

May 14, 1994

I wonder whether anyone other than Jesus' disciples fully understood his admonition on the importance of visiting someone in prison. I am reminded of this every Saturday when I see the inmate excitement generated by the anticipation of a visit.

I understand and share the excitement.

Today I will be visited by an old friend, Richard Heffner—author, historian, college professor, host of his own educational TV show, *The Open Mind*, for over forty years, and immediate past chairman of the Motion Picture Rating Board. I have already been visited by Matt Crosson, the former chief administrator of the New York courts and his new bride, Elaine. And Mike Tigar, the distinguished constitutional scholar and professor of law from the University of Texas. So many other good friends have traveled halfway across the country and suffered the inherent indignity of visiting a prison to bind me to the outside world.

One such visit was paid me on January 30, Super Bowl Sunday, by David Gould, who was my first Court of Appeals law clerk over twenty years ago. He is now a defense lawyer, having served as an assistant U.S. attorney.

He arrived at the prison the day after my hair froze, which occurred on the morning of the coldest day experienced by Minnesota during the last twenty years. David completed the usual visitor's form and then waited for me to be summoned. Half an hour later he was called to the reception desk by a guard, who looked over his shoulder and asked, "Where is your two-year-old son, Bryan?"

"He's home," David answered.

The answer seemed to agitate the guard, who asked, "He isn't here?"

"No," David said. "I didn't think I was supposed to bring him."

"He isn't here?" the guard repeated.

The guard shoved the paper David had filled out across the desk. "Why did you put down that you had your son with you?"

David quickly scanned the form he had filled out. He saw that in answer to the question "Do you have any children?" he had written down his son's name and age. It never occurred to him that prison security would not really care how many children a visitor had at home. He started to tell the guard that he hadn't realized that the question only applied to children accompanying the visitor, but was interrupted as the guard pointed to another of David's form responses.

"And when you put down that your car is a Mercury Sable, I assume that is your car at home and not the one you drove here?"

David didn't even try to make excuses. An honors graduate of Princeton and Harvard Law School, he was unable to fill out a visitor's form properly. As he left the guard he made an attempt to end the confrontation on a humorous note. "Ah, sir," he said. "We are thinking of having another kid. If we do, I promise to let you know immediately."

After David left, the guard told me that he "didn't think my friend was funny." I had the sense that he would have liked to put David in the hole. Fortunately for David, the guard's jurisdiction was limited. Fortunately for me, David left early.

Having David visit me in prison was difficult for me. I knew he always admired me. I had been his mentor, both professionally and in his personal life. I had performed the marriage ceremony when he wed another of my law clerks, Laurie Murdoch. I was the godfather to Bryan. Now he was buying me a dried-up hamburger from a food-vending machine.

•   •   •

The visit from Matt Crosson was also an occasion for reflection. Matt was the third of my chief administrators, people chosen by me to head the Office of Court Administration. The first, Joe Bellacosa, went on, as I have said, to become a judge on the Court of Appeals. The second, Albert Rosenblatt, went on to become a justice of the Appellate Division. Unfortunately for Matt, my untimely judicial demise brought his career in the courts to an abrupt end. As the president of the Long Island Association he is now a successful leader of the business and industrial community of Long Island.

All three of my chief administrators were vital components in meeting the challenges of managing the New York court system, once referred to as a "writhing monster." Together we were able to accomplish some very positive things.

Changing the system of case management and that of judge assignments was a difficult task, one made necessary by the overwhelming volume of cases. Dealing with gender bias and discrimination against minorities was another equally vexing problem, which had to be addressed if we were to have a truly just system of justice. These were challenges we knew we could meet—and we did.

But the one persistent problem that bedeviled me as well as my predecessors was the crumbling infrastructure of the courthouses in New York State. To improve and maintain our halls of justice seemed a daunting, almost impossible, task.

A survey of the court facilities showed that 60 percent of the some 270 courthouses in the state were in need of replacement or major renovation. The reason was apparent: When New York State absorbed all of the municipal city, town, and county court apparatus to establish the largest unified court system in the country, perhaps in the world—the municipalities agreed that if the state would pay all salaries and expenses incidental to the running of the courts, the municipalities would build and maintain the necessary facilities. The state kept its part of the bargain, but the municipalities did not.

City and county courthouses built a century ago and urban courthouses that had never been painted had plaster falling from the ceilings. The crowded housing courts in New York City resembled Calcutta on a bazaar day, and the family court in an upstate county had to remove seats from the waiting room so that there would be more standing room for litigants, lawyers, and family members.

In the Queens County courthouse, the attic was being used as a judge's chambers and a large safe was being used as an office. Examinations before trial, for which there was no room in the courthouse, were being held at a Burger King restaurant across the street. In Suffolk County, jury trials were being held in an unheated basement. Whenever a toilet was flushed on the floor above, the trial was interrupted until the sound of the water rushing through the ceiling stopped.

It was a scenario not only of "justice denied" but of "justice degraded."

It took five years of working with mayors, county executives, the state legislature, and the governor finally to enact the Court Facilities Law, on August 7, 1987. Within fifteen months of the law's enactment, every municipality in the state had to submit a plan for the renovation of existing court facilities and the construction of new courthouses. The law gave the Office of Court Administration the power to cut off state aid to any municipality that failed to submit a construction schedule or to meet an established and approved one, until the municipality complied.

The hundreds of hours spent arguing, cajoling, lobbying, and pleading paid off. After some months had passed, we saw the positive results in plan approvals and construction starts. Two courthouse projects were completed after my arrest. The Suffolk County Courthouse was completed and dedicated shortly before I went to prison, and the Queens County Courthouse shortly after I was released.

I was invited to neither dedication ceremony, and chances are I won't be invited to any in the future. But that is not important. What is important is that soon the courthouses, a necessary component to an efficient court system, will be built.

Another project that Matt Crosson adopted and we worked on together was the concept of the "community court," which we started developing in 1990.

Too often in a city the size of New York City, minor crimes such as graffiti, littering, solicitation—the misdemeanors that diminish the quality of life in a city—are dealt with ineffectively. The prosecution of these offenses falls through the cracks of the criminal justice system, and those who commit them are back on the streets repeating them within the hour.

What if we could deal with these minor offenses in "community courts" which we would establish in every police precinct in the city? The judges assigned to these courts would be unsalaried lawyers who would be trained for this purpose by the Office of Court Administration. Most lawyers would welcome the opportunity of rendering this community service, for which they would be rewarded by being called "judge," compensation enough for most lawyers.

For courtrooms we would use facilities in the community schoolhouses. People charged with misdemeanors who were in need of testing for diseases such as AIDS or tuberculosis would be tested, and those in need of treatment for addiction would be compelled to attend treatment facilities. The punishment to be meted out would be community service. The graffiti artist would think twice before marring a wall he had just been compelled to scrub down.

We met with the then mayor of New York City, David Dinkins, and his police commissioner, Lee Brown. Both embraced the concept with enthusiasm. The mayor, his deputy, and my former Court of Appeals colleague, Fritz Alexander, with the help of community leaders, located a city-owned building in the Midtown theater district, on West Fifty-fourth Street that was being used to store theater props. This was to become the Midtown Community Court.

We could not move the state legislature to consider the deputizing of lay judges at the moment, so under the aegis of the administrator of the criminal courts, Bob Keating, we had one of our criminal court judges sit as a judge in our first "community court."

If it hadn't been for the aggressive and tireless leadership of community activists like John Feinblatt, a lawyer who worked with the Fund for the City of New York, who was responsible for the court's layout and became its first administrator, and supporters like Amanda Burden, who worked with the community to develop the court's service programs, this idea never would have come into being.

The Midtown Community Court became fully operative during my imprisonment. It has become the model I hoped it would be. It is an arraignment court only: If the arrestee pleads "not guilty," he or she is sent downtown to the criminal court for trial. When the guilty plea is entered—and of the ten thousand defendants handled in 1994, seven thousand pled guilty—the sentencing is done on the spot. As envisioned, sentences involve cleaning, scrubbing, and sweeping in the Midtown area as well as working for nonprofit organizations. The court also offers a broad spectrum of social services such as drug and prostitute counseling, job placement, AIDS and TB testing, providing shelter for the homeless, and classes in English.

May 21, 1994

I remember reading somewhere that men are not hanged for stealing horses, they are hanged so that horses will not be stolen. And I remember reading somewhere else that the law is like a cobweb that catches small flies but lets the big bugs fly through.

I thought of these two aphorisms while talking to one of my fellow inmates, Elisha Jones.

"How long you been down?" he asked me.

"Eight months," I answered. "How about you?"

"Well," he said, "I got a break. The judge sentenced me to fifty, but the appeals court cut it down to forty."

I quickly calculated: forty months, with good time, would come to about three years.

"So how long have you been down?" I asked again.

"Since 1978" was his answer.

"On a forty-month sentence?"

"Who said months? My original sentence was fifty years, and it was reduced to forty years."

Elisha is one of my "homies": he comes from New York. He was one of fifty-two conspirators transporting and selling drugs between New Jersey, New York, and Pennsylvania. He and all of his co-conspirators have been down for sixteen years, and all look forward to many more in federal prisons. All except one, Leroy (Nicky) Barnes, who was the first major black organized-crime leader. He was sentenced to life imprisonment in 1978 for heroin trafficking. But like the big bug he was, he flew through the cobweb and is soon to be released on probation.

Elisha and his fifty-two co-conspirators were part of Nicky Barnes's drug enterprise. When Barnes was arrested in 1977, he "gave up" (i.e., "ratted out," "rolled over on," "snitched on") fifty-three people who worked for him and his empire.

"You see, judge," Elisha said to me, "the conspiracies laws are used to catch all the little guys, but Nicky is now in a witness-protection program."

He told me that Barnes cooperated with the government for the same reason that many arrested felons cooperate. "To get a break on their own sentence."

"A bunch of garbage," said Elisha. "He rolled over on all of us to save his black ass." There was no mistaking his deep hatred of Barnes, a hatred that justified Barnes's being put in a program for his protection.

There is only one class of persons detested more than the hacks and that is the snitches, more commonly called rats. The prosecutors use these informers to gather the names and information of others who were involved with them in criminal activity. In exchange for the information, the snitch is given a lighter sentence, or sometimes no sentence at all.

From the prosecutor's point of view, this has been most effective in dealing with drug conspiracies. An illustration of this is found in which the conspiracy laws are being handled by many prosecutors. The conspiracy laws were designed primarily to get the "kingpins," the heads of the drug operations. The theory is that the kingpins rarely deal directly with the drugs themselves; those are handled by lower-ranking participants. So the idea was to arrest the small-time participant and then make a deal with him. The small-time operator was to be promised leniency if he "gave up" (turned in) his kingpin boss. The prosecutor could make a case of conspiracy in order to get to the kingpins. Proof of any contact that the kingpin maintained, even at a distance from the everyday operations of the conspiracy, would be enough for a conviction.

But there is a deficiency in the system. Most United States attorneys have a very short shelf life. Their service is usually coextensive with the term of the president of the United States and is often measured by their ambition to reach another position that affords more job security. For that reason, some—not all—feel they must make a reputation as quickly as possible. They often allow their agendas to be shaped by the publicity that an arrest will bring—and the publicity is enhanced by the number of arrests the charges will bring. The largest number of arrests can be obtained by arresting many small operators, so there is an incentive for both the prosecutor and the kingpin to catch the small fish.

When a kingpin gets caught, he is often likely to save himself by "giving up" the other members of the conspiracy. Result: The kingpin, who was the original target of the conspiracy laws, escapes severe punishment, while all those who work for him, now or in the past, are sacrificed.

People often wonder why the prisons are so crowded with low-level dealers, pushers (salespersons), and "mules" (delivery persons) while the kingpins go free. The answer is in the abuse of the conspiracy laws.

May 22, 1994

Surprisingly few kingpins go to prison — but that is not to say that none do. One of my best friends here was a kingpin. He was a young kingpin, and an unlikely kingpin, but he was a kingpin, the boss of a retail drug operation — the kind of drug dealer some U.S. senators feel should be executed.

His name is Anthony J. Peters. In 1984, almost ten years ago, he was the subject of major headlines in the Milwaukee press. Then twenty-six years old, he had a Porsche and Jaguar, a mound of precious gems, condominiums in Chicago and Florida, and land in Colorado. For vacations he went to places such as Rio de Janeiro. His parties, complete with ballerinas, models, show girls, and half the Milwaukee Brewers, were legendary.

When he was sentenced with his younger brother, who was his partner, the judge said that Tony "lived like a maharajah." To be certain that Tony was cured of his extravagant habits and lifestyle, the judge sentenced him to serve thirteen years in prison. That was in 1984. If he were sentenced today, under the sentencing guidelines, he might have been looking at life.

Tony's brother, Larry, who had left Rochester before I arrived, was sentenced to less time. Tony showed me a statement his brother made to the press that seemed to say it all: "You gotta remember at that time, there were movie stars and there were professional athletes, doctors, lawyers doing cocaine. It was a socially acceptable thing. We never sat down and had a board meeting and said, 'Well, let's start selling this stuff.' It just happened."

Tony is six feet, three inches tall and extraordinarily handsome. When you see him competing on the athletic field you feel he could have been a professional baseball player. Instead, this man whose mother is a high school teacher and father is the communications coordinator for the Milwaukee Public Library will be here until his fortieth birthday. If ever you wanted a picture of an all-American boy it would be Tony Peters. He never committed or threatened an act of violence. But he is—or at least was—a kingpin.

May 23, 1994

Milton Mollen, a dear friend and the former presiding justice of the Appellate Division, is making national headlines. He is conducting hearings in New York City relating to police corruption. It seems that some New York police officers were running scams with drug dealers. The Mollen Commission is uncovering some of this conduct and subjecting it to public scrutiny.

"What else is new?" said Reggie Johnson, another of my "cribs" (fellow New Yorkers).

Reggie is doing fifty years on drug charges and was a substantial dealer before his arrest in 1979. His operation overlapped Nicky Barnes's, but only to a small degree. Barnes gave the F.B.I. Reggie's name, but Reggie had already been arrested, so the "rollover" did no good for Barnes or the F.B.I., and no harm to Reggie, either. But he resented Barnes for doing it.

Reggie spoke to me for hours about corrupt New York City policemen. There was one who shook him down whenever the two passed on the street. "He say, 'Reg, I'm a little short this week'—that meant he only wanted a coupla hundred. Or he'd see me standin' in a doorway and say, 'Lookee here—I jus' took this from your pocket, Reg,' an' he show me some blow [cocaine] an' he say, 'It'll cost you fifteen hundred to buy it back.' Now, I never carried shit, so you'd know he was lyin', but if he run me in, who they gonna believe, me or the man? So I give him fifteen hundred."

"Where'd you get the cash?" I naively asked Reggie.

"Judge," he told me, "fifteen hundred is chump change! I had that on me anytime. An' if I didn't have it, I couldn't be walkin' on the streets of Harlem. Shit, I supported one of those motherfucker cops. The nigger was like my partner, an' now he's retired, runnin' a candy store an' I'm still down and will be down 'til I die."

May 28, 1994

This is the start of the Memorial Day weekend. The inmates have scheduled competitive games—volleyball, softball, handball, etc.—to pass the time. A prison three-piece band plays Ricky Nelson and Everly Brothers hits from the sixties, and everyone tries very hard to forget that the perimeter of their playing field is the physical boundary of their lives.

There are a great many veterans here who have served in the military, almost all in Vietnam. Although doomed to spend many years as prisoners of their country, they are proud to have fought for it. Tragically, most became acquainted with weapons, drugs, and drug trafficking while in the service, and now they are paying a precious price for misapplying their knowledge.

Like Carl Terpac—affable, helpful, and very good company, except on those rare occasions when the temper born of the posttraumatic stress syndrome he brought back from Dong Ha would take over his personality. I first met Terp when I began working in the mental health unit where he was housed. I had occasion to read his military transcript, which detailed the incredible combat record and the heroism that won him numerous awards and three Purple Hearts (he was actually wounded four times, but because he was wounded twice in one action he only received one Purple Heart for that encounter).

He was raised in a good home in upstate New York. A devout Catholic, he neither smoked nor drank before he entered the Marine Corps at age eighteen. During training he proved himself a superb soldier who was anxious to fight for his country. He was soon given this opportunity. It came during the now infamous Tet Offensive.

Shortly after his arrival in Vietnam, his company was ordered to relieve a company of the 9th Marines then heavily engaged with a large enemy force along the Demilitarized Zone. Terp's unit had hoped to link up with the beleaguered unit by nightfall. Unfortunately, they encountered the enemy en route and, after suffering heavy losses, were forced to withdraw. Many in Terp's unit were killed, and he was detailed the next morning to retrieve the corpses of his comrades. Most had been horribly mutilated, some with their sex organs amputated and crudely stuffed in their mouths. After that, Terp became a killing machine.

On one occasion, after being severely wounded, he was loaded into a medevac helicopter, which was shot down immediately after takeoff. He was believed to be the only survivor. The battles detailed in the records that Terp shared with me were the stuff heroic legends and war novels are made of. In one battle after another he proved both his heroism and his ability to kill. He fought against the North Vietnamese army, not the Vietcong. These soldiers did not have sophisticated weaponry, but they made up for it with their perseverance, cunning, knowledge of the terrain, and a never-ending source of replacements whose ages ranged from nine to seventy. Because Terp carried the most lethal of the weapons in his company, including an M-79 grenade launcher, he killed over one hundred enemy soldiers.

Terp was introduced to marijuana and alcohol after his first battle. It helped him to forget the blood and the horror. His first use of heavier drugs came on March 3, 1968, when his arm was almost taken off by an enemy grenade. He injected himself with the morphine he had been issued and was transferred to a hospital ship. Within a month he was back in combat.

When Terp was discharged from the Marines he found himself in constant pain from his wounds and was embarrassed at having fought in Vietnam.

"Embarrassed?" I asked. "I've read your record. You were a hero."

"You don't understand, judge. No one who came back from 'Nam was a hero. It was a no-win war. So many good kids were killed. You'd take a hill one day—lose it the next—go back the next day. All the time having your friends killed. For what? There came a point when I enjoyed the killing. The guy with the most kills got R and R. I used to work like hell to get that reward and I never thought about the people I killed. I was like an animal. How can you be proud of being an animal?"

Terp's psychiatric reports detail the profound trauma he suffered and still suffers as a result of his Vietnam experiences. When he hit the streets he tried to obliterate his bad dreams and embarrassment with alcohol, marijuana, heroin, and methamphetamines. His drug abuse led him into a life of crime, from burglary and possession of a deadly weapon in New York to a kidnapping connected to a drug operation in California, for which he served five years in Vacaville. His most recent offense, which will keep him in prison until the year 2001, is for the manufacture of methamphetamine. He says that he was a low-level operative in this enterprise.

On this Memorial Day weekend I feel sorry for incarcerated combat veterans like Carl Terpac. There are thousands of them in prison. I also feel sorry for those members of society who will suffer from his conduct after he is released. In our haste to lock Terp up, we seem to neglect that he will be getting out one day, harboring the same hostility that leads to the commission of crimes. As one of his treating psychiatrists wrote while recommending comprehensive treatment, which Terp will never receive in prison:

> He has lost respect for all traditional institutions associated with the government as a result of his experiences in Vietnam and this is not atypical. I see no hope for Mr. Terpac without treatment. Incarceration will simply protect society and himself for a period of time and he will remain unchanged when he leaves the system.

But Terp was not the only thing on my mind this afternoon as I walked the prison compound track. I was lost in nostalgic remembrances of the Memorial Day picnics I had attended when I was in local politics. As North Hempstead town councilman and later town supervisor in the sixties, I was expected to attend the Sons of Italy picnic, and the Nassau Detectives picnic, and to "dance Greek" at the Greek picnic, and judge the Miss Polonia contest at the Polish-America club.

As a veteran, I was honored to walk at the head of Memorial Day parades given by many of the villages in North Hempstead:

"We have a place for you in the back seat of the convertible, Your Honor."

"No, thank you, I'd rather walk." At one time or another I headed every one of those parades, proud to wear a sash that read GRAND MARSHAL. Many of my fellow politicians dreaded the "Memorial Day drill." I loved it.

May 30, 1994

Today is Memorial Day itself and we were awakened by the smell of meat being cooked on an open barbecue grill. To its credit, the Bureau of Prisons is determined to make this as much like a normal Memorial Day as possible, going so far as to put tables out of doors at which we can eat our hot dogs, coleslaw, and baked beans.

The inmates even decided to have a parade. Some of the veterans (neither I nor Terp joined them) marched around the track. Seeing these men, most of whom had been in combat, marching around the compound under the watchful gaze of mostly younger, derisive guards—no band, no flag, no cheering crowd—seemed a sort of travesty. All I could think of were Rudyard Kipling's words in his poem "Tommy":

> But it's Tommy this, an' Tommy that, an' "Chuck him out, the brute!"
> But it's "Savior of 'is country" when the guns begin to shoot.

As I left the unit I was determined to forget where I was, if just for this one meal. I was going to fill my plate, close my eyes, and pretend that I was in my backyard in Albany, feeling the warmth of the sun, my friends, and family.

"Where are you going, Washtler?" It was one of the cops.

"To eat," I answered.

"Get on the L-to-Z line," he ordered.

It was then that I noticed there were two lines. At the foot of each was a uniformed guard with a clipboard. Just before you went past the food tables, your name was checked off on a printed manifest. So much for pretending to be in my own backyard.

June 1994

June 7, 1994

A. M. Rosenthal is a man of extraordinary intelligence. I first met him at a luncheon hosted by the then publisher of *The New York Times*, "Punch" Sulzburger. These "Punch's lunches" were an opportunity for public officials like me to meet the masthead and the brains behind the *Times*. They were not necessarily one and the same. But I had been an Abe Rosenthal fan long before meeting him, and still am. I had read his *Times* column for years and found that my thoughts paralleled his in many respects.

When I was attempting to explore approaches to resolve certain problems confronting the courts, I asked a small group of people from various disciplines to assist me. Abe accepted without hesitation and attended all of our informal gatherings and made an enormous contribution. I looked forward to being with him.

I wish I could be with him today to discuss a column he wrote for *The New York Times* News Service, which was carried today in one of the few papers I have access to, *The Reader Telegram* of Eau

Claire, Wisconsin. The column is headed: "How Prisons Save Lives." The first thing I thought when I read the piece was that Abe could not have written it: It was far too superficial. But my next thought was that I had written and said much the same thing during the twenty-five years I served on the bench. How could *I* have been so superficial?

The thrust of Abe's piece is that prisons save lives by taking criminals off the street. He concedes that "prisons cannot end crime," but says it is "intellectually slovenly to believe that they do no good and are filled mostly with gentle, first-time pot-smokers trapped by cruel law."

There is a fable about the mayor of the mythical hamlet of Chelm, the village of fools. It seems the mayor went to visit a prison and returned with the following observation: "Half the prisoners say they're guilty and half say they are innocent. So we should build two prisons. One for the guilty, and another for the innocent."

After eight months in federal prisons, I am convinced that there are very few people here who are innocent. I am just as convinced that half the people here do not belong here. Not that they are "gentle, first-time pot-smokers," but they are also not the violent felons and dangerous criminals who Abe feels, rightly, must be taken off the streets.

With the sentencing guidelines now in place in the federal courts, judges no longer have the ability to fashion a punishment to fit a particular crime or criminal. The woman who steals powdered milk to feed her baby must receive the same sentence as the man who steals powdered milk to cut heroin. Mandatory minimum sentences bring the same result of calling for the same sentence.

The New York Court of Appeals, Joe Bellacosa dissenting, recently affirmed a sentence that sent a teenage first-time offender to prison for fifteen years to life. She was a "mule," carrying a small amount of cocaine from one place to another at the behest of her drug-dealing uncle—with whom she was forced to live after being abandoned by both of her parents. No prior convictions. No violence.

Does anyone really believe that a fifteen-year-to-life sentence imposed on this teenager will reduce violent crime? Is it worth over a half million dollars of taxpayers' money to incarcerate Angela Thompson? As Judge Asche in the lower court noted:

> A system of justice which mandates a 15 year sentence, as a minimum, for a 17-year-old girl who was not cared for by parents and under the domination of her uncle also mandates a lifetime of crime and imposes on the community upon her release, a woman who may be incapable of anything but criminal activity. If we do not attempt to rehabilitate such young people, we condemn ourselves as well.

I would like to take Abe for a walk with me through my unit. In every four-man cell, there are two or three twenty- to thirty-year-olds doing a minimum of ten years. They are first-time offenders, usually in for dealing drugs or growing marijuana. Some are college-educated. Some have sentences of up to forty years. None are violent.

I can assure you that every one of them has been replaced on the street by someone else doing the same thing, but probably for more profit. Locking these people up doesn't come close to resolving the drug problem. Until we tackle that problem, we will never achieve a lasting solution to the crime problem.

When heroin (which puts the user to sleep) replaces crack (which produces mindless violence) and becomes the street drug of choice, then crime will be reduced. Locking up violent felons and keeping them behind bars as long as possible will reduce violent crime. Establishing foot patrols to maintain a police presence on the street will reduce crime. All of these reactive measures must be taken together with preventive ones: providing inner-city employment, strengthening family values, improving schools and housing—the list is endless.

But the new wisdom, which places our focus almost entirely on the lengthy imprisonment of law violators without distinguishing between violent and nonviolent conduct, creates more problems than can be imagined.

We must recognize the fact that between Abe's "gentle first-time pot-smoker" and the violent criminal whom he and I both agree should be behind bars are thousands in prison who do not belong there. And then there are thousands of others who do belong there for violating the drug laws—but not for ten, twenty, thirty years and more.

We should recognize that some 75 percent of crime is related to drugs. Using drugs, dealing drugs, committing crimes while high on drugs, and robbing to get money to buy drugs. Anyone who commits a violent act, whether on drugs or not, should be imprisoned for their act. But locking up low-level drug dealers who are nonviolent—addicts who use more than they sell—will not stop the supply of drugs anymore than carrying shopping bags with the legend SAY "NO" TO DRUGS will stop the demand for drugs.

Last year, 250,000 persons were incarcerated for drug offenses in this country and 80 percent of new federal prisoners since 1987 have been drug offenders. The effect on our communities, particularly our urban and black communities, has been devastating. Nationally, one out of every four black men eighteen to thirty years old is now under some form of correctional control. In Baltimore, 56 percent, in Washington, 40 percent, and in New York City, 35 percent of black males in this age group are either in prison, on probation, or on arrest warrants. And although the burden has fallen mainly on the black community, the suffering by innocent family members and by our taxpayers has been staggering.

During the Bush administration $100 billion was spent on the war on drugs by federal, state, and local governments, almost all for law enforcement. The courts were overwhelmed, attempting to process one million drug cases a year. But it didn't work. The use of drugs actually increased during Bush's four-year administration.

This year we will spend $20 billion for enforcement, and drugs will be more available than ever.

Shortly after I was elected to the New York State Court of Appeals, Nelson Rockefeller told me and the New York State legislature of his plan to deter the use of illicit drugs by enacting the nation's toughest drug laws. I thought he was right. We were both wrong. I know now that long prison sentences are not the answer, either in New York State or nationally. When these draconian drug laws were enacted there were 12,444 prisoners in our state penitentiaries. There are now 65,000, and drug use has increased tenfold.

And we already know that interdiction, although we must continue the effort, does not seem to work. If we built a fifteen-foot wall around this country, the drug cartels would build a sixteen-foot ladder.

There will always be the flow of raw coca from Bolivia and Peru and we already know the leaders of the Andean governments have rejected our State Department plans for wholesale eradication. Their position is that such an approach would both starve and radicalize the thousands of peasants who depend on the coca leaf as a cash crop. Heroin is also making a comeback thanks to bumper crops of opium in Myanmar. Incarcerated drug dealers tell me that Southeast Asian heroin traffickers are flooding New York and New Jersey with moderately priced, high-quality heroin, which they call China White.

From what my fellow inmates also tell me, the 800,000 poppy growers from Afghanistan who fled to Pakistan during the Afghanistan war are now back in Afghanistan doing what they do best. That means the importation of heroin from this quarter will be greatly increased. It will also mean that violent crime in the cities will probably decrease because heroin users, unlike crack users, are not violent while under the drug's influence.

So what do we do?

- Adopt a new philosophy based on public safety rather than punishment of sinners. One that is committed to locking up violent offenders to protect our communities, but uses more effective and affordable alternative programs and rehabilitative services for non-violent offenders who find themselves in the criminal justice system simply because they are drug users.

- Eliminate mandatory drug sentences and return sentencing discretion to the judicial branch, where it belongs. As Judge Bella-cosa wrote in his Angela Thompson dissent: "Prosecutors, as executive branch officers, should not enjoy the power to shackle judicial responsibility while they zealously seek to incarcerate masses of criminal drug offenders."

- Continue to explore punishment alternatives to imprisonment. For example, the government is in the process of closing military bases all over the country. Nonviolent first-time offenders charged with drug crimes should have their sentences vacated and be sent to one of these bases for between six months and two years, where they can do something useful and be trained. Any slipups and they go to prison. When they are discharged, the drug charges should be dismissed. They will reenter the community having been productive and having learned discipline and a trade—and without a felony conviction on their record.

Instead, these persons are now being subjected to a dehumanizing process that someone on the street cannot hope to understand. Many prison guards refuse to recognize that the punishment prisoners receive is to be taken away from family, husband, wives, children, family members, and communities—and to lose their freedom. Being sent to prison is their punishment, they are not, as some guards think, sent to prison to be punished. After ten to twenty years of humiliation and loss of self-esteem, these nonviolent offenders—almost all of whom have lost their families—come home to a hostile community with no job, no skills, and a prison mentality. And then we wonder why we have repeat offenders.

- No prison system—federal, state, or private—should be funded unless it provides treatment facilities for drug and alcohol abusers. Furthermore, all defendants who have a history of drug or

alcohol addiction or abuse should not be allowed probation or supervised release unless provision has been made for their continued treatment or after care.

• The federal government or some private foundation should
undertake a comprehensive study to find out what kind of drug rehabilitation should be used—which treatment or combination of
treatments will work best. The same applies to education about
drug abuse.

If we are in agreement that we must reduce the demand for
drugs instead of building more prisons, we should certainly know
what modality of rehabilitation and education works best. It has always been a source of wonderment to me that with the hundreds of
billions of dollars we have spent to combat drug abuse, we still
don't know the best way to treat addicts and addiction or the best
method to teach our children about the peril of drugs.

We have used cold turkey as well as gradual withdrawal; we
have gone from various modes of drug substitution to drug-free
therapeutic communities; we have tried different methods of counseling, psychotherapy, and group therapy, in-house and outpatient
treatment—even acupuncture and hypnosis. But which is best?

Before Nelson Rockefeller embarked on his crusade to enact
awesome penalties for illicit drug use, he thought rehabilitation
would work. In 1966 he formed the Narcotic Addiction Control
Commission, which by 1971 had spent over $1 billion regulating
the compulsory residential treatment of ten thousand addicts in
state facilities and the same number in private programs. The failure of this operation moved him to propose the nation's toughest
drug laws.

But drug treatment has come a long way since 1971. We now
know, according to a just-released study conducted in California,
that one dollar's worth of treatment saves seven dollars in costs that
are incurred by crime, health care, and welfare needs. But we
should be certain, if we are to embark on a concerted effort to
achieve an effective program for drug rehabilitation, that we learn

from past mistakes and take advantage of the knowledge and progress of the past twenty-five years.

And then there is the education of our young people. In a recent survey of college seniors it was disclosed that 45 percent of them had tried illegal drugs at some time in high school or college. Many began in grade school. If we have not been able to reach these educated young people, is there any hope in reaching the unemployed, single-parented, or parentless young person in the inner cities? I don't know—but it is worth a try.

Some small percentage of the billions spent on drug law enforcement should be spent on assembling the most talented educators, ad persons, propagandists, psychologists, and others able to devise a plan which can reach our young people—in and out of school. Our best minds should be able to devise a campaign that will educate them in the most effective way possible about the perils of drug abuse. And we should be prepared to fund the campaign.

I am certain Abe Rosenthal's view will be better received than mine.

If we continue to increase penalties and continue to categorize more offenses as felonies, we will have to build more prisons, and we will continue to believe that the more people in prison, the less crime there is, without distinguishing the violent from the nonviolent offender and without effectively dealing with the drug problem, the real cause of crime.

I read somewhere that when the only tool you have is a hammer, you tend to think of every problem as a nail.

June 9, 1994

Wholesome American values seem to have been spawned in the Midwest. Middle America. The region of the nation that supposedly represents the best of us.

Martin Thomas Lawrence, inmate number 06277029, arrested when he was twenty-five years old for a conspiracy involving one and a half pounds of cocaine and thirty to fifty pounds of pot, was reminiscing about his early youth in Walford, Iowa (population five hundred). He lived there with his parents and older brother and younger sister until he was twelve.

"Five hundred, maybe six hundred acres, and a river ran through it—most of the farm was planted with corn, but we had our own vegetable garden, maybe an acre, where we grew produce for just us. I had my own horse, Apache. God it was beautiful."

Although Marty was quintessential middle America, he and some boys from the neighboring farms were still able to experiment with marijuana when they were ten. When he was twelve, his idyllic life was disrupted by the divorce of his parents. He moved with his mother and two siblings to Cedar Rapids, Iowa.

At first, the twelve-year-old farm boy had difficulty coping with city life. He then fell in with a crowd of young toughs who, impressed by his size and strength, quickly welcomed him as one of the adolescent neighborhood hoodlums. But his nascent criminal career died aborning when he and his companions were arrested for breaking and entering and stealing a bicycle. He was taken from his mother and placed in a boys' home, a reformatory, for eight months.

When he came home, he went to high school and started using drugs. By the time he was fifteen, he was sniffing and shooting cocaine. Everything he earned as a roofer and by sodding lawns went into feeding his drug habit, which by now had become a major addiction. Some weekends he consumed up to three ounces of cocaine. Shortly before he graduated from high school, on March 30, 1981, his son was born to his high school sweetheart. They were married in 1986.

In that same year he came to the realization that drugs had become the centerpiece of his life. He knew that if he did not curb his habit, it would destroy him. When he started having convulsions and required hospitalization, he and his mother sought treatment and rehabilitation for him. They were told that there was a three-to-sixth-month waiting period before he could be accommodated.

So he went back to the streets and continued his destructive habit and criminal activity.

"I'll admit I dealt drugs," he told me, "but I used more than I sold. And the only reason I sold more was to get my hands on more."

Marty Lawrence was an addict. He was not a so-called kingpin or organizer; he was a user who, together with others, sold drugs. He was hospitalized twice for overdoses and was eventually arrested for conspiracy to traffic in controlled substances.

Because he was clearly guilty of the crime, he pled guilty to one count of the indictment. Based on the amount of drugs in his possession, under the guidelines he should have faced a sentence of fifty-one to seventy-eight months. Marty and his lawyer felt that he could endure such a sentence, and so entered into a plea agreement which provided in part that in exchange for his guilty plea, the U.S. attorney "will file no other . . . criminal charges against him based upon information now in our possession or information later provided by him."

His sentence would be about five years—a long time, but he would still be in his early thirties when released. He would still be able to be a father to his six-year-old son. By then he would be free of his addiction, and prepared to start life all over again. He felt a sense of relief. He also felt that a five-year punishment was sufficient for a first-time offender.

The United States attorney from the Northern District of Iowa had other ideas. As the time for sentencing approached, he petitioned the court to amend the presentence report. It seems that Marty himself, while being debriefed by the federal agents after the plea agreement was signed, indicated that the "conspirators" were dealing with larger amounts of cocaine than the government had suspected.

Under the sentencing guidelines, if the defendant is convicted of a conspiracy, the sentence is imposed on the basis of the defendant's conduct "or the conduct of co-conspirators in furtherance of the conspiracy that was known to the defendant or was reasonably foreseeable." And because the government now believed that it had discovered the involvement of a greater quantity of drugs—not in Marty's possession, but in the possession of one of his co-conspirators—they wanted to enhance his sentence.

Marty couldn't understand this. After all, the U.S. attorney had signed a plea agreement in which he had promised no other charges would be filed against Marty based on information now in their possession "or information later provided by him. . . ." How could the judge increase his sentence on the basis of information acquired by the U.S. attorney after he had pled guilty? Because, argued the U.S. attorney, Marty was not being truthful after his arrest when he responded to questions concerning the amount of drugs with which he and his co-conspirators were dealing. The trial judge held a hearing, and agreed with the U.S. attorney.

And so, the plea agreement to the contrary notwithstanding, the court found that over five kilograms of cocaine were involved in the conspiracy, increasing the case under the sentencing guidelines from a level 28 to a base level of 32. Marty was now looking at fifteen years. But the sentencing process under the guidelines was not yet exhausted.

The U.S. attorney moved for a further increase because he considered Marty's inconsistent testimony with respect to drug quantities to be an "obstruction of justice." The penalty for such an obstruction is another two-point enhancement.

Marty's lawyer contended that in order for there to be an "obstruction," the defendant must have the "intent" to deceive. He argued that Marty's brain was too "scrambled" to formulate such an intent. The court agreed but nevertheless added the two-level increase to the sentence. Then, as if for good measure, a point was added for his 1970s juvenile bicycle theft.

The five years Marty had anticipated in exchange for his plea of guilty had suddenly turned into twenty-one years, ten months. Instead of being released in his early thirties, he will be in his late forties. His son will be twenty-eight years old—raised without a father.

Certainly, it is necessary that dealers, even user-dealers like Marty, be punished, severely enough to deter others. But sentencing an addict to spend the better part of his life in prison for a first offense is a perversion of a justice system that is being used not to do justice but to accomplish some other purpose.

That purpose was made clear in today's *Wall Street Journal* in an Op-Ed article written by a Jay Apperson, the federal prosecutor for the Eastern District of Virginia. He rails against the critics of mandatory minimum sentences and urges defeat of any federal crime bill that would diminish their severity. Is it because he feels these defendants deserve such draconian punishment? No. It is because he believes the justice system should be used, as he puts it, as "a common sense 'carrot and stick' approach."

What the critics don't tell you is that mandatory minimums for those assisting in drug distribution are part of a comprehensive scheme which allows the government (e.g. prosecutor) to move to reduce a defendant's sentence below the minimum term if he provides "substantial assistance" in the prosecution of others. In other words, if low-level dealers, drug couriers or "mules" arrested on federal drug offenses, cooperate with prosecutors, identify their sources and higher-ups, testify against them at trial, and help put them out of business, then those low-level defendants can have their own sentence reduced.

Of course, what Mr. Apperson does not tell us is that if the "mule" who carries drugs, or the low-level dealer who sells drugs, is the last to be identified or snitched on, there is no one for them to "substantially assist in prosecuting." I have met dozens of low-level dealers who were "ratted out" by their bosses, already imprisoned, and will be incarcerated for decades.

But this practical, fact-based response to Mr. Apperson's hypothesis is not nearly as important as the perversion of the justice system to which I referred.

As a former judge, I am incensed by the notion that the courts are allowed—indeed encouraged—to be used as an extension of the prosecutor's office. One of the hallmarks of our republic is an independent judiciary, which should function free from the passions of the moment and free from the passions of the crowd.

I am offended by the suggestion of Mr. Apperson, who identifies himself as a "veteran front-line prosecutor," that the sentencing process should be used as a prosecution tool, instead of as a way to accomplish justice.

If this concept is embraced by our lawmakers on the basis of "the end justifies the means," they might just as well reintroduce thumbscrews and the stretching rack. I can assure you that more information can be gleaned by those methods than by extracting information through the guarantee of extraordinarily long sentences. They would also be less expensive as well as less painful.

Maintaining an independent judiciary enabled us, as an American tradition, to fashion the punishment to fit the crime. Yes, this does "make law enforcement more difficult," just as supporters of mandatory-minimum sentences contend. But law enforcement has always been difficult, except in a police state.

June 10, 1994

Tony Accetturo, a leader of the Lucchese crime family who became a government witness, criticized the new mob leaders for being greedy. "All they care about is money," he said, "not honor."

Of course, honor among the crime families includes *omertà*, the Mafia code of silence. *Omertà*, which has been taken to mean "the actions of a man," bound the Italian-American mobsters and their families together. According to the "connected" inmates here, the rat Accetturo should be the last person on earth to talk about honor.

In any event, it appears that the vow of *omertà* is dying, along with the importance of the crime families it once protected. Perhaps the most significant blow to the families was the section of the Organized Crime Control Act of 1970 called the Racketeer Influenced and Corrupt Organization section, RICO.

Before the enactment of RICO, the law defined crimes as acts performed by individuals. With RICO, law enforcement was given a net that could be used to ensnare all of the individuals associated with a racket, a criminal enterprise, provided that the enterprise came within the definition of racketeering (extortion, loan-sharking, fraud, bribery, etc.). In other words, any person knowingly involved in racketeering activities need only be shown to be part of the organization committing the crime to be found guilty.

RICO has been used to stop various types of organized criminal conspiracies, such as the violence directed at abortion clinics by right-to-life groups. But its primary use has been to bring down the mobs. John Gotti, the notorious boss of the Gambino crime family, was one of RICO's main conquests, as was Matty (the Horse) Ianniello. Several of RICO's targets are with me here in Rochester.

Venero Mangano, also known as Benny Eggs, who allegedly became the official underboss of the Genovese crime family on the death of Anthony (Fat Tony) Salerno, who died in prison in 1992, was one of eight defendants ultimately tried in the six-month "windows" trial of 1991, so named because of the alleged involvement of a conspiracy to control New York's window-replacement market. Originally there were twenty-two defendants, many with such colorful names as Anthony (Gas Pipe) Casso, Dominic (Baldy Dom) Canterino, John (Sonny Blue) Morrisey, Vincent (Three Fingers) Ricciardo, Vincent (The Chin) Gigante, and Joseph (Joe Cakes) Marion. Some of the defendants fled, and one was almost assassinated (he lived and thereafter agreed to testify for the government).

All of the defendants were originally tried on RICO charges of participating in a massive twelve-year conspiracy by various alleged members of organized crime. According to the charges in the indictment, four crime families (Colombo, Genovese, Lucchese, and

Gambino), certain officers and members of the Architectural and Ornamental Ironworkers Union, as well as certain officials and employees of various window installation and manufacturing companies conspired to rig bids; through extortion, labor payoffs, and mail fraud they were able to control the awarding of $150 million worth of window-replacement contracts between 1978 and 1989. The principal focus of this conspiracy was the New York City Housing Authority housing projects.

Within the vast array of evidence in this megatrial were taped conversations and testimony of three mob members who had turned government witnesses to save themselves. One, Salvatore (Sammy the Bull) Gravano, who testified during the sentencing phase of the trial, was an underboss of the Gambino family and was ultimately responsible for the conviction of his boss and onetime friend, John Gotti. He testified that Gotti, then the boss of the Gambino family, discussed the "windows" investigation with him and allegedly told him that "the people involved" had come to an agreement to "clean house" (to murder prospective witnesses).

It seems that the destruction of this most lucrative enterprise was being threatened by conversations taped by Peter Savino, a former associate of the Genovese crime family, who agreed to cooperate with the government after being confronted with evidence of his involvement in several murders. Savino wore a wire for one and a half years and recorded hundreds of hours of conversations relating to the corrupt control of the window-replacement industry by the crime families.

One of the defendants, Peter Chiodo, was a Lucchese capo. He testified against the boss of his crime family, Vittorio Amuso, who was convicted of murder. At the Amuso trial, Chiodo testified that in the spring of 1989, his boss instructed him to "take care of" and "clip" Sonny Blue Morrisey, who was another defendant in the "windows" case.

According to Chiodo, Amuso had told him "that we [the Lucchese Family] had to do two guys, Colombo family had to do one, and the Genovese family one." In September 1989, Chiodo and several accomplices murdered Morrisey.

When Chiodo was named as a defendant in the "windows" case, he pled guilty to the RICO charge before trial, specifically acknowledging his role in the labor racketeering, extortion, and bid rigging. After his plea, an attempt was made on his life. He was shot twelve times. That was enough to convince him to continue cooperating with the government and he told of his criminal activities, including the nine murders he had been part of, one of which was the murder of Sonny Blue Morrisey.

The trial had all the trappings of a chapter from Mario Puzo's novel *The Godfather.* One delay occurred when the government uncovered a plot to tamper with the jury allegedly devised by mob associates of Peter Gotti, the brother of John and a "windows" defendant. Not only was there proof of a juror's being contacted, it seems that she in turn had influenced three other jurors. These four jurors were later convicted of jury tampering.

Of the sixty-nine counts charged, three of the defendants were convicted of only one count of extortion and one count of conspiracy to commit extortion. They were acquitted of all other charges. The remaining defendants were acquitted on all counts.

One of the three convicted defendants was my fellow inmate, Venero Mangano, a.k.a. Benny Eggs.

The U.S. attorney for the Eastern District of New York is Zachary W. Carter, a bright young man who inherited the "windows" case. He was once a New York State judge and I knew him when he served in that office. The trial judge on the "windows" case was Ray Dearie, the former U.S. attorney for the Eastern District of New York with whom I established a personal relationship. I spoke at the ceremony when he was sworn in as a federal district judge. But the person to whom I am now closest in proximity and status is Benny Eggs.

"So, Benny," I asked him as we sat together on a bench in the compound, "you must like eggs?"

"Nah," he answered, "my mother had an egg store and I delivered eggs in Little Italy, so all my life I been called Benny Eggs."

"How long will you have to be down?"

"Well, the judge sentenced me to one hundred eighty-eight months and fined me a hundred grand." (I quickly calculated: 188 months is a little over fifteen years.)

Having been acquitted on sixty-seven counts and convicted of only two, Benny faced a sentence of twenty-seven to thirty-three months (approximately two or three years) under the sentencing guidelines. But the guidelines provide for upward adjustments. The court decided that Benny was an "organizer and leader" (add four points), that the "amount demanded" was in excess of $5 million (add seven points), and—inexplicably, because based on hearsay murder allegations for which he was never charged and on which the jury never passed—that Benny was a member of a conspiracy to murder a witness (add two points). These enhancements, which are currently the subject of appeal, added approximately thirteen years to his sentence.

"How old are you, Benny?" I asked.

"I know what you're thinking," he answered. "I'm almost seventy-three—that means I'll get out when I'm almost ninety. But I'm a very sick man, so if my appeals don't work out, I die here. Of course, the feds want me to talk. But I have nothing to say. I really don't—they know everything I know. But I'll tell you something, if I did know something they wanted—and they told me I could get out tomorrow by tellin' them—before I told them, I'd rather finish my sentence in the grave."

So when you hear wiseguys like Tony Accetturo talk about "honor," tell them about Benny Eggs.

Please understand, I believe that uncovering crime and obtaining convictions by using the testimony of co-conspirators, friends, or accomplices is both appropriate and acceptable. Law enforcement should not be deprived of that important device. But I do have a problem with rewarding antisocial predators who destroy someone else to save themselves.

Like Alphonse D'Arco, the head of the Lucchese crime family, who has just started "spilling his guts" about murder and loan-sharking, or Crazy Phil Leonetti, who was made an underboss of a Philadelphia crime family by his uncle Nicodemo (Little Nicky) Scarfo. He repaid his uncle's kindness by testifying against him and sending him away for murder, extortion, and gambling.

Of course, the most notorious of these informers, according to the Gambino family members to whom I spoke, is Salvatore (Sammy the Bull) Gravano. His name comes up often, and is never mentioned without an accompanying sneer. He has one of the most violent records of any mob member: nineteen murders, million-dollar extortions, leg-breaking, loan-sharking, and other brutal crimes that exceed in violence any of the crimes committed by those whom he helped put away.

In 1991 he defected as the underboss of the Gambino crime family after having been indicted with his boss, John Gotti, on murder and racketeering charges. He pled guilty to those charges in exchange for a twenty-year maximum term without parole. But he will never serve anything close to that because he has been setting new records in cooperating with the government.

He has been instrumental in obtaining thirty convictions, mostly against alleged mob leaders. People like Frank Locascio, the consigliere of his own Gambino crime family; and Victor Orena, the acting boss of the Colombo family; and Thomas Gambino, the son of Carlo, for whom the family is named. And, of course, Venero Mangano.

But his most impressive act of cooperating with the government was his helping the government put his former boss, John Gotti, away for life.

I was told of Sammy the Bull's interaction with Gotti in connection with the murder of Gotti's former boss, Paul Castellano. The tale was spun out by a former member of one of the crime families as we walked together around the track in the prison compound. As I listened to the yarn, I was again struck by the incredible turn of fate that placed me in the position of hearing this story from a mob member, not as part of the law enforcement establishment but as a fellow prisoner.

It seems that John Gotti, a member of the Gambino crime family, was taped negotiating a drug contract with a fellow called Fat Ange. These names were thrown at me as if I should have been familiar with them.

Paul Castellano, sometimes referred to as Pauly, the boss of the Gambino family, didn't want any family members dealing in narcotics. Fearful that Castellano would find out about his dealings, Gotti decided he would "whack" Pauly before Pauly "whacked" him.

The narrative continued: "So Gotti gets this group of family members he knew would follow him—The Bull Gravano was one of them—and then, to be sure that the other families would not go crazy because the head of another family was hit, Gotti decided to get the other families [the Gambino, Lucchese, Bonanno, and Colombo families] lined up. He got to them all and they all got word back to him that it was O.K. with them. Look, they didn't want to get in the middle of a war and they knew that, one way or the other, Gotti was going to come out on top."

When Gotti had lined up his forces, he made his move.

I listened to the end of the story, writing down every word when I returned to my cell.

"First, he got four shooters and dressed them all alike—in raincoats, with Russian fur hats. You see, he wanted to confuse any eyewitnesses as to who did what. If an eyewitness saw something, he couldn't tell where the raincoat and fur-hatted guys were because there were four of them—get it? Anyone listening to their story would think they didn't know what they was talking about. And if there was more than one eyewitness, their stories about what the fur-hatted guy was doing would be all confused—because there were four of them.

"Gotti and The Bull, the no-good son-of-a-bitch bastard, were there with walkie-talkies managing the whole thing. Gotti—this was one ballsy guy—was parked right across the street. When Pauly and his bodyguard come pulling up to Sparks Restaurant in Midtown Manhattan, whacko—the four fur hats turned them both to Swiss cheese. There must have been fifty bullets pumped into them. And that's what happened to Big Paul Castellano."

When it comes time for Sammy the Bull to be sentenced, his prosecutor will reward him for his cooperation by presenting him with a 5k1.1 letter; "5k1.1" means that he cooperated with the prosecutor. This letter will be given to the sentencing judge, who will be enabled thereby to depart from the sentencing guidelines. There is no question that there will be such a departure, and that Gravano will not serve his twenty years. In fact, the bets around here are that he will be sentenced to time served and will be released very soon. Or, to put it as it was put to me, "He'll be out before you will be, judge."

That is probably true, but when I get out I will not be in a witness-protection program spending most of my time looking over my shoulder.

In addition to getting alleged members of the crime families to "roll over," the government has ways of uncovering mob activity and subjecting it to the bite of RICO. One of the major New York crime families, not involved in the "windows" case, was the Bonanno family. The way in which the government disrupted its operations is the stuff legends are made of. Listening to pieces of the tale, told by some of my fellow inmates, sounds like imaginative fiction. Maybe some of it is—but the story is fascinating.

Donnie Brasco was a burglar who grew up in the tough Italian neighborhoods of New Jersey. He was personable and well liked by the "wiseguys," those who belonged to mob families, who considered him "good people." What they didn't know then, but know

now, was that Donnie was really Joe Pistone, an F.B.I. agent. I don't mean a small-time hoodlum working for the F.B.I.; I mean a real live agent who had been working undercover as a mole since 1976.

He did well enough to become a part of the Bonanno crew in Brooklyn. Well enough to be told of the in-fighting which was developing for control of the family while its boss, Philip (Rusty) Rastelli, was in prison. Sonny Black, a captain under Rastelli, supported his imprisoned boss. But Anthony (Sonny Red) Indelicato, Dominick (Big Trin) Trinchera, and Philip (Philly Lucky) Giaccone, three other Bonanno captains, together with Indelicato's son, Anthony Bruno Indelicato, were on the other side.

One of Sonny Black's soldiers was Benjamin (Lefty Guns) Ruggiero. Rastelli and Black were fortunate to have Lefty Guns on their team. He was a tough and supposedly ruthless gunman, raised in New York's Little Italy.

Pistone became friendly with Lefty Guns and was told by him that he and Sonny Black had taken care of things. "Everything is going good," he said. "We'll be all right. We're on top."

One of Lefty Guns's apparent accomplishments was to get the "two-ups" lined up with Sonny Black. The two-ups were young Sicilians who had entered this country illegally. They took low-level jobs, mostly in restaurants, but their real function was to kill whomever the family bosses wanted out of the way.

Another of Ruggiero and Black's goals was to get rid of the three Bonanno captains who were lined up against Rastelli: Indelicato, Giaccone, and Trinchera. They accomplished this by inviting the three to a "peace meeting."

"We should work this out between us at a sitdown," they told the three. When the three came to the meeting they were killed with "multiple gunshot wounds," according to the crime report.

Everything was going smoothly for the Black-Ruggiero takeover. Except, of course, for the fact that an F.B.I. agent had become a part of their operation. He, along with an assistant U.S. attorney for the Eastern District, Richard Guay, by means of wiretaps authorized under RICO and dozens of sleepless nights, was able to break the Bonanno crime family. Lefty Guns will be in prison perhaps for the rest of his life. Sonny Black was not as fortunate. Eighteen months after his indictment on the RICO racketeering charges, his body washed up on Staten Island. Although it was badly decomposed, it was apparent that both his hands had been cut off. This is supposedly the Mafia's way of demonstrating its disappointment in an individual's performance.

Richard Guay, the U.S. attorney credited with initiating the downfall of the crime families through the use of RICO, is a partner in the law practice of my son-in-law, Paul Montclare. Guay was the best man at my daughter Lauren's wedding, which I performed. And now I spend much time with the remnants of the families he helped bring down.

Because Rochester houses the federal medical center many convicted members of these crime families who become ill will be serving their time—some, their lives—here. I've watched others come and go: Don Giuseppe, allegedly involved with the worldwide narcotics ring called the "Pizza Connection"; Joseph Caval; Joseph (Joey Butch) Corrao, a restaurant owner allegedly in charge of gambling in Little Italy and a reputed capo of the Gambino family; the Alfano brothers; and Luciano Paolone from Illinois; Bracco, Zipolini, and Salerno, alleged capos of the Genovese family; the capos of "the Outfit" from Chicago—Dominick Cortina, Donal (Angel) Angelini, and Nick Maliozzo. A veritable *Who's Who* of alleged organized crime.

Supposedly one of the most notorious of these was a young man, only in his twenties, named Louis Ruggiero. Otto Obermaier, the U.S. attorney for the Southern District of New York, described him as the head of the "new Murder Incorporated." He was a cellmate of Michael Goland's, one of my present cellmates, when they were both new arrivals at Rochester. Michael describes him as "smart, cold, calculating, considerate, and generous," an interesting mix of vices and virtues. A person who showed little emotion except when he was sleeping. It seems he would sit bolt upright during night-mares and call out the name of his aunt.

The other inmates generally stand apart from "the Italians," as they are called, and the Italians also keep to themselves. It took me a long time to establish a relationship with these men. When I finally started to meet with them on the walking track, or near the bocci or handball courts, they told me the reason they keep their distance.

"I wouldn't walk on the same side of the street with these bums on the outside. Why should I have anything to do with them here?" one told me.

Sensing that I might consider myself insulted, he added: "Now wit' you it's different, you're a class guy, you're a judge, for God's sake. We figure you may not want to be seen talkin' to us—so we leave it up to you."

The Italians even eat by themselves, if not in the dining room at their own table, then in the medical unit where most are housed. They take turns making various sauces, almost in competition with one another. For the last three nights, samples of their culinary art have been sent over for me to taste. My only worry is that they will ask me to decide which is best.

June 12, 1994

Today they did. I was walking the track with a friend, Bill Kampiles, when I was stopped by some of those who had been making me sauce.

"So which one is best?" asked a reputed Gambino soldier who was recuperating at Rochester from a surgical procedure while serving a sentence for murder.

He wasn't smiling, but there was no anger in his voice.

"Very hard to say," I answered in a tone as serious as the one used by my questioner. "But, you know, the sauces are like my children—they are all different but I love them all equally."

The answer seemed to satisfy him. My many years in politics had served me well.

June 13, 1994

One of the features of life at Rochester, for which the unit manager, Roger Gabel, claimed credit as part of his Gabelizing process, was "controlled movement." That means the inmates can move to and from work assignments, medical visits, meals, recreation, etc. only during ten-minute intervals at specified times. At all other times the steel doors to the units are locked.

I can remember waiting behind those locked doors like a caged animal waiting for the ten-minute time span to begin. When the "movement" did begin and the doors opened, I and the other inmates spilled out onto the compound, doing our best to make it to our destination before they locked those doors.

Of course, this was far better than the method of movement imposed on prisoners several generations ago. Back in the thirties, prisoners were marched in groups, in lockstep and in single file, compelled to do the "convict shuffle," a sort of foot-dragging quick march. Now we are permitted to walk how and with whom we please, under the watchful eyes of guards with walkie-talkies, so long as we do not take too long.

As I said, we had ten minutes to leave one building and arrive at the other. "Controlled movement" did not permit tarrying. I was about five minutes into my walk ("*Walk!* If I catch you running I'll put your ass in the hole") when I was approached by a five-foot-two-inch older-looking man who introduced himself as Mickey Feinberg.

"My lawyer tells me that you were a brilliant judge who could have beaten Cuomo and been governor of New York," he said in one breath.

"And who are you?" I asked, still walking quickly to reach my unit before my ten minutes expired.

"I'll catch you tomorrow in the yard," he responded as he turned to walk to the medical unit.

June 14, 1994

True to his word, Mickey approached me the next day in the compound and began his conversation as if we hadn't been interrupted by yesterday's time constraint.

"For a little guy, I was one of the biggest in the pornography business," he said. "Now I'm here, in need of a heart transplant, looking at a minimum of thirty years in prison."

Herbert (Mickey) Feinberg, sixty-three years old and from Los Angeles, was an associate of the so-called king of porn, Reuben Sturman. Mickey was convicted of conspiracy, attempted extorting, using an explosive device, and other charges stemming from a 1992 plot to blow up two Chicago adult bookstores.

It seems that Sturman had increased the rental fees he charged the two bookstores for his "Wild Man Films" peep show. He supposedly increased the fees by $1.37 million, and the bookstore owners refused to pay. Sturman did not feel it was an increase. It seems the Internal Revenue Service had put a lien on the funds that the peep-show owners were paying to Sturman, so that Sturman saw no part of the rental paid by the porn houses. Sturman was not interested in *why* he never saw the money that the I.R.S. sequestered— all he knew was that he didn't receive it. Enter Mickey. He was going to help Sturman out as he had done in the past.

On a previous occasion, in 1991, when Sturman was having a similar problem with a porn shop in Phoenix that refused to pay up, he sought Mickey's help. Mickey hired a group of California bikers to "teach a lesson" to the offending store owner. They were supposed to "mess things up a little." As Mickey put it, "They were supposed to go in there with a hammer—you know, to break a few things." Instead they went in with baseball bats and demolished the establishment. They even broke up Sturman's peep-show machines.

When Sturman asked Mickey to "take care of" the Chicago stores, he told him to "take it easy this time." But Mickey made the mistake of going back to the same California bikers. They apparently didn't know how to "take it easy." They botched this job far worse than they had the one in Phoenix.

The bikers decided to use pipe bombs. They figured that doing the destruction in that fashion would be more complete and less risky for them. Two of them traveled in one car, planted a bomb, and took off. The bomb missed the target bookstore and blew up the wrong building. Two others, in another car, were even less fortunate. The bomb blew up in the car en route to the target, killing one of the "bombers," a twenty-eight-year-old biker who should have stayed in California. The three other bikers were sentenced to seven and a half to twelve years.

The defense attorney representing Mickey contended that while Mickey did hire the men at Sturman's request, he was unaware they would try to bomb the Chicago stores. The jury demonstrated its disbelief of this defense by staying out just over an hour before finding Mickey guilty.

Mickey waits here in Rochester to be sentenced. He waits with his severely debilitated heart. He knows that his sentence will be over thirty years—far longer than his heart will hold out. He tells me his heart will give him an "early parole."

Summer has come to Minnesota, and with it memories of that summer when my life began to disintegrate—the summer of 1990.

One day that summer while I was walking my left leg collapsed under me and I fell to the ground. When I attempted to walk, I noticed that my left foot seemed to flap. When I lifted my leg, my foot no longer responded but instead dropped.

Some months before, my constant and severe headaches had brought me to Long Island Jewish Hospital for an examination. At that time a "shadow" had been seen on a C.A.T. scan, which was diagnosed as a "right ethnoid sinusitis." Despite this diagnosis, the continued severe right-side headaches, together with the left-foot drop, convinced me that I was suffering from a brain tumor. So hypochondriacal were the beginnings of my depression that I was positive that the right-side "shadow" and severe headaches were a product of this tumor.

Initially, I discussed this malady and my suspicions with no one. Instead I spent sleepless nights and anxious days going deeper and deeper into my depressed state. I saw my life as a healthy person who had never spent a single night in a hospital coming to an end. I had visions of a deteriorating and debilitating affliction crippling and eventually killing me.

I considered my suspicions confirmed when I attended a meeting of the Decision Making Regarding Life Sustaining Medical Treatment (LSMT) Project. I was vice chair of this council, which was funded by the State Justice Institute and the Conference of Chief Justices. The goal of the project was to prepare a monograph to be used by trial judges faced with the difficult task of determining if and when life support systems should be withdrawn.

The project consultant was the distinguished neurologist Dr. Ronald Cranford, who was associated with the Hennepin County Medical Center in Minnesota. At the time of my sentencing, Dr. Cranford was asked to recall my discussions with him. He noted:

> In the fall of 1990, Judge Wachtler contacted me for medical advice about a hypothetical "friend" who had a brain tumor, presumably a low grade infiltrative astrocytoma.
>
> On subsequent occasions when we interacted personally and professionally at meetings, he and I would usually discuss his hypothetical friend and he would usually have questions for me concerning the diagnosis and treatment of this type of brain tumor. After my initial discussion with him on this matter, I sent him medical literature concerning the controversial nature of treatment of his brain tumor.
>
> I also made some recommendations concerning specific physicians in the United States who I thought were experts in this field.

Since this was a highly confidential matter, probably involving one of his close friends, colleagues, relatives, or possibly the judge himself, I never discussed our conversations with anyone except my personal secretary who types my correspondence.

In the fall of 1990 I discussed my hypothetical friend's brain tumor with other leading physicians and neurologists, all of whom told me that it would be difficult and inappropriate to make any diagnosis without an examination of the patient and an MRI. But they did say—as had Dr. Cranford—that the symptoms described were consistent with those caused by a "low grade infiltrative astrocytoma."

It was during this time that I increased my use of drugs to overcome my depression. But the fear of the tumor and the unrest it brought my troubled mind could not be eclipsed.

Added to my personal concerns were those involving my official duties. New York State's fiscal crisis strained the cordial relationship that Governor Cuomo and I had shared for so many years. He felt it was necessary to cut the court budget as part of the state's overall belt-tightening policies. I felt that because of the crack cocaine epidemic and the resultant enormous increase in crime and caseloads generally, it was necessary that the resources available to the judicial branch be increased.

Our exchanges became unfriendly and at times even hostile. The governor took advantage of the public's propensity to blame all of society's ills on the courts and attributed the judiciary's budget woes to our own profligacy. I, on the other hand, blamed the governor for having no sense of priorities: devoting vast and unwarranted sums for prison construction and showing insufficient concern for crime prevention, rehabilitation, and the justice system.

At one point the governor likened me to a "fishmonger" in the village square, asking for much and settling for whatever he could get.

But after the court budget was passed by the legislature, the governor called and apologized for his part in accelerating the rhetoric. "You and I shouldn't quarrel," he said. And I believe he meant it. He went on to be reelected for his third term and, true to his pledge to retrench the cost of government, said that there would be no formal swearing-in ceremony and the incidental inaugural festivities.

To demonstrate my continued affection for him, I suggested that he and his wife, Matilda—whom I greatly admired—together with other members of his family, come to the Court of Appeals Hall for a swearing-in ceremony on January 1, 1991. He accepted my offer.

June 17, 1994 (the day after O. J. Simpson's arrest)

The universe of a prisoner is made up of a series of small worlds, each independent of one another but still part of the same universe.

There is the world of confinement, which each of us must deal with in his own, very personal way. It is not possible for me to tell you what it is like. Just the knowledge that you cannot go into town, or visit a friend, or be with someone you love—the haunting vision of the razor wire and the ever-present locks holding metal doors shut—these things conspire to make this world the most frightening of all.

And then there is the world of loneliness. There is an old adage that you come into prison alone, and you leave alone. This is not the place to make lasting friendships. You tend to think of yourself and are made to feel a lowly creature, someone who has done wrong, and hurt someone else—usually someone close to you. Not necessarily the victim of your crime, but the friends, family, and loved ones who are so profoundly affected when you are incarcerated. You think no more of your fellow inmate than you think of yourself.

Although new inmates arrive and others leave, your circle of associates remains relatively constant. The people you work for and with are the same, day after day. Your human contacts are as circumscribed as your environment. Your world is a small one.

I know of the difficulty President Clinton is having with his health-care plan, the conflict in Bosnia-Serbia, the instability in Haiti, and the unrest in Yemen and the Middle East, but those places and the news of them are remote. They are of another world, another universe. Outside news does not interest us—or so we thought until O. J. Simpson was charged with a double murder.

We all know O.J., "The Juice"—at least we think we know him. He was everything an American hero should be, and we Americans, who so desperately need heroes, love him. When the evidence and the media started pointing to a blood-stained glove, and we were told of the brutality of the crimes and the indicia of O.J.'s guilt, we were numbed with a sense of disbelief.

I am told that some 75 percent of Americans watched prime time television last night, watched while a fleet of police cars followed O.J.'s vehicle, when he failed to turn himself in voluntarily. Watched while he held a gun to his head, watched while hundreds of onlookers cheered him on as if he were running through a broken field of tacklers, ready to sprint across the goal line.

I thought that the staring inmates, so engrossed in this real-life TV drama, were visiting the outside world. A short visit, but a visit nonetheless. And then I realized that they hadn't gone anywhere at all. They were not visiting another universe, they were watching a fallen hero enter theirs.

When the TV voice said that O.J. had a gun to his head, the viewing inmates urged him to use it:

"Man, keep out of court," one said.

"Do it, man, or else you going to die the way they want you to die," said another.

One started to rap: "You're O.K. man, O.J. jus' don' end up in Pelican Bay." He was referring to a maximum-security penitentiary in California.

Written on the day O.J.'s grand jury was disbanded

News and talk of O. J. Simpson dominate the chow hall, the yard, and compound. This morning the grand jury hearing the case was

disbanded because of the excessive publicity regarding his prior assault on his wife. The judge was concerned that the grand jury
might not be fair if it was exposed to this sort of information, which
had no business being a part of the proceedings.

I have always had very strong thoughts about the grand jury.

Soon after I was appointed Chief Judge, in 1985, I was interviewed by some New York *Daily News* reporters and their editorial
board. Marcia Kramer, who was later able to elicit the confession
from candidate Bill Clinton that he smoked marijuana (but did not
inhale), asked me my opinion of the grand jury system, a system that
is secretive, excludes the defendant and his lawyer, is conducted by
prosecutors using leading questions, and relies primarily on hearsay.
This system is used in all of the federal courts, and many of the state
courts, to determine whether a defendant should be tried for the offense charged.

I told Marcia Kramer that I felt the historical purpose of the
grand jury had been so contorted as to render it meaningless. That
it no longer provided protection for the presumed innocent, but instead worked as a handmaiden to the prosecutor.

To illustrate the point I noted that "any prosecutor who wanted
to, could indict a ham sandwich." The quote made the headline of
the *Daily News* and found its way into publications and novels,
some without attribution, and others that gave appropriate credit,
like Tom Wolfe in *Bonfire of the Vanities*.

One rabbi took it and, undoubtedly for reasons of Kashrath,
changed the "ham sandwich" to a "bowl of Jell-O." One television
script made it a "bologna sandwich," and still another just a plain
"sandwich." It seemed somewhat perverse that after my having had
some twelve hundred opinions and over one hundred articles published, part of my legal legacy would relate to a ham sandwich.

Actually, the remark was not intended to amuse.

Consider how today's grand jury functions. Information comes to
a prosecutor concerning the commission of a crime. Witnesses are
interviewed and evidence is gathered. The prosecutor concludes

that sufficient proof exists to charge an individual with a crime. Now, with mind made up, the prosecutor goes to the grand jury to obtain an indictment—the stamp of approval. The same witnesses, already interviewed, and the same evidence, already gathered, will now be presented to the grand jury. This selfsame prosecutor will be the legal adviser to the grand jury and the only lawyer in the grand jury room. The prosecutor alone will decide what they will hear. Although the defendant can testify, the defense has no right to present its case, or cross-examine, or have counsel present. It is, by design, a one-sided affair.

In the law, as elsewhere, practices often remain long after the need for them has diminished and disappeared. History teaches us that the original grand jury was convened by England's Henry II (1133–1189) to wrest power from the church and the barons. Under Charles II (1630–1685) the institution evolved into a body that protected the Earl of Shaftesbury from the awesome accusatorial power of the Crown. Seventy-five years ago, when the English realized that the purpose had evolved as one to prosecute instead of protect, it was eliminated.

Under many state constitutions, including New York's, felony charges can be instituted only on indictment of a grand jury, unless a defendant consents. An institution originally established in England in the twelfth century to protect against the arbitrary power of the throne, still survives in a nation that has never known a throne. An institution established to provide both a sword and a shield now for the most part provides neither. Abuses that were real enough at the time are corrected by rules. Rules ripen into tradition, and tradition persists, even in the face of change. It is called the law of inertia. Things in place have a tendency to remain in place.

Investigative grand juries, such as those dealing with organized crime, still serve a valuable purpose. Cases involving rape or child molestation, where there is a need to test the ability of a victim to testify in a nonconfrontational setting, are ideal for grand jury presentment. But in the vast majority of cases, grand juries are a waste of time and money.

The grand jury is provided for in the Fifth Amendment to the United States Constitution, so it cannot be eliminated from our federal courts. But the Supreme Court held in 1884 that the grand jury can be eliminated by the states, and most states have done so. Every state should do so.

But grand jury indictments have an aura of legitimacy. If a prosecutor stands before the public and announces a charge made against an individual, it is looked upon as just that—a charge. The presumption of innocence remains. But the announcement of a grand jury indictment clothes a prosecutor's charge with the dignified trappings of citizen endorsement. The presumption of innocence gives way to "Where there's smoke there's fire." Publicity noting "indictment by a grand jury" has the ring and almost the stigma of proven guilt.

In light of this, those of us who know the grand jury system were pleased to see the Simpson case gravitate to a "preliminary hearing" allowed in California in lieu of a grand jury. There will be a rational presentation of so much of the prosecutor's evidence as will be necessary to convince a judge that there is probable cause to believe Simpson committed the crime. And Simpson and his attorneys will be given an opportunity to examine the evidence and cross-examine the witnesses.

The justice system works better when it works in public view— "sunlight is the best disinfectant." If Simpson is bound over for trial, the trial will be held with everyone knowing the facts and evidence that led to his being charged and tried. We will not have to guess about what some group of citizens may have been shown or told by a prosecutor seeking an indictment in the veiled secrecy of a grand jury room.

In my case, the prosecutor charged me with a violation of the Travel Act, a law passed by Congress designed to combat interstate racketeering. He alleged that in conspiring with others, I embarked on a criminal enterprise that ranged from threats to kidnap to extortion. The penalties for the crimes alleged were sixteen years in prison and fines totaling $250,000.

Months before the grand jury was asked to vote on an indictment in my case, the prosecutor held several press conferences outlining the charges that were to be brought. The prosecution was especially forthcoming with the journalist Lucinda Franks—the wife of Manhattan District Attorney Robert Morgenthau—for an article she was writing for *The New Yorker* magazine. The article, entitled "To Catch a Judge," was so replete with quotes of conversations of Chertoff and F.B.I. agents that *The New Jersey Law Journal* cited it in an editorial decrying "circus" prosecutions, saying, "The leaks were so detailed that *The New Yorker* was able to publish a fascinating blow-by-blow description" of the events leading up to my arrest. Television rights to *The New Yorker* article were subsequently sold by Franks to ABC for $200,000.

Someone who tries to tell you that the grand jury process protects an accused by preserving the secrecy of evidence; or that the F.B.I. files are sacrosanct and not subject to press leaks or pretrial disclosure, lest a prospective trial jury be biased against a defendant, may also try to convince you that water is not wet.

If anyone should try to convince you that the grand jury is not a device used by prosecutors to garner publicity at the expense of someone still presumed innocent, watch out! The deed to the Brooklyn Bridge is probably in his back pocket.

June 20, 1994

The telephone is one of the few lifelines a prisoner has to the outside world. Each unit has one or two phone booths on each floor. Before you can use one of the phones, you must acquire a telephone code number, deposit funds in an account, and have each number you intend to call approved by the unit manager. This approval process usually takes two weeks.

You cannot call a number unless it has been previously approved, and if there are insufficient funds in your telephone account, you cannot place a call. No collect calls are permitted, and there is no such thing in prison as charge cards. And, oh yes, all of your calls are monitored.

One of the inmates told me a story about receiving a letter from his wife asking whether she should plant potatoes that particular year. He called her on the phone and told her, "It's O.K. to plant them—but for God's sake don't plant them in the backyard. That's where I buried the money from the bank robbery." The F.B.I. appeared at his home the next day and turned over every inch of soil in his backyard.

When his wife called that evening to tell him of the "plowing" he said, "Good, now it should be easy to plant the potatoes."

I'm not certain I believe the story, but I'd like to believe it.

June 30, 1994

Michael Goland left today. He has served his time and is on his way to a halfway house in Los Angeles. Because he refused to eat in the chow hall, eschewing the meals that he considered unkosher, he is painfully thin. He claims to have lost close to one hundred pounds. He avoided barbers as he avoided meals and left with a twelve-month growth of unkempt beard, looking like someone who spent most of his days living in a large cardboard box. In fact, as he left, one of the inmates shouted after him, "Hurry up, Michael. You may still be able to get a park bench to set up housekeeping."

Given the crowded conditions of our prisons, it was no surprise that Michael's bed didn't even lose its warmth before our new cellmate moved in.

His name is Spyridos Manasses. He was born forty-six years ago in Corinth, Greece. He became a United States citizen when he was sixteen years old and by his eighteenth birthday was starting to live the American dream as many Greek immigrants lived it. He worked twelve-hour days, pushing a hot-dog cart through the south side of Chicago.

Because he was unlicensed, the only way he could maintain his operation and preserve choice locations was to bribe members of the Chicago Police Department. He recalls on occasion not having sufficient paper money to give them so they had to content themselves with bags of coins. His ability to get along with members of the police force was to stand him in good stead in the years to come.

When he was twenty-one, he was able to trade in his pushcart for a pizza parlor; later he graduated to a twenty-four-hour-a-day diner.

His industry was further rewarded by his accumulation of enough money by 1977 to buy one of Chicago's largest nightclubs, the Nickel Bag. Spyridos, now more properly called Spiro, prospered. He and his wife moved into a large home, complete with swimming pool, in the Chicago suburbs.

His nightclub did well—but he looked for ways for it to do better. He was anxious to fill the five hundred parking spaces and seven hundred seating capacity the Nickel Bag provided. He hit on an idea that had proved successful as far back as the days of Babylon: He decided that the barmaids should wear very suggestive see-through lingerie tops.

The idea was an instant success, and Spiro's business and fortune increased dramatically. And then, through unfortunate happenstance, disaster struck.

One of the barmaids sent by an employment agency was seventeen instead of the required eighteen or over. Spiro had no way of knowing, but the liquor authority did, and for this infraction it suspended his liquor license.

He tried to keep the club in business, but his kind of operation without a liquor license was like a politician without a campaign promise: The atmosphere may be nice, but without the intoxicant there's no sale. With extensive redecorating and remodeling, he tried to make his failing nightclub into a successful restaurant. But the rent of $10,000 per month and his inability to serve alcohol were too much for him to overcome. After six months he was forced to sell out and salvage whatever he could from the ruins of his American dream.

In 1980 he bought a small delicatessen, and he and his wife worked seven days a week, twelve hours a day to rebuild their lives. It was during this struggle that Spiro, now called Sam, read an article in *Time* magazine about a shortcut to wealth: cocaine. He read of the enormous profits that could be made. There was some risk, but so what? He had taken risks all his life.

In fact, he remembered, when he was a teenager pushing his hot-dog cart in the mean streets of Chicago there was also a risk. One day he was hit accidentally by a car; another day someone hit him with a crowbar in order to rob him. Another time he was robbed at gunpoint. Life had its risks, but nowhere were the rewards greater than they were in dealing drugs.

Through contacts that he had made during his nightclub days, he was able to communicate with a Cuban from Miami who assured him of an ample supply. The margin of profit was staggering. His first transaction was for one ounce, for which he paid $1,500. After cutting it ("stepping on it") he was able to sell it for $3,000, a 100 percent profit.

As his cocaine enterprise prospered, his personal life deteriorated. In 1986 he was divorced and in the property settlement gave his wife the delicatessen, together with all of his other legitimate assets. He had found a new way to an easier, more lucrative life. He became a womanizer and an alcoholic. He had a child out of wedlock, and gained more money in two years than he had earned in his entire law-abiding life. When Sam Manasses traveled, first class was not good enough. He chartered jets.

His main clientele?

Members of the Chicago Police Department. Some of the same officers to whom Sam had given small bags of coins as bribes were now paying him well for bags of cocaine. So profitable was this market that a rival seller attempted to gun Sam down on the street in broad daylight, to take these customers from him.

He prospered in his new enterprise. He recalls making up to $50,000 in a single day, and dealing up to seventy kilos of cocaine in a single transaction.

One day in 1988, he received an order for five kilos, delivery to be made in Detroit, Michigan.

Unfortunately (but, given what happened in Detroit I should say "fortunately") Sam had to fill another order and so had only two kilos to bring with him to Detroit. Of course, he would not take the risk of traveling to another state with two kilos of cocaine if he weren't delivering it to someone he knew. Someone who owed him $170,000 from another drug transaction.

When he arrived in Detroit, he called Frank, his customer cum friend cum debtor: "Frank? Sam. I'm here. I'll meet you at the Star Restaurant in a half an hour."

"Good," said Frank. "Are you ready?"

"Yes," said Sam.

Sam was ready with the two kilos and ready to be paid for the cocaine and some part of the $170,000. When Frank arrived at the restaurant, he and Sam had a few drinks and Sam apologized for not having the five kilos that Frank had ordered.

"But, Sam, two kees is not five. I've got my responsibilities too. Where are the two?"

"In my car."

"Can I see it?" Frank asked.

"Sure," said Sam, "here are my keys. My car is in front."

Frank went to the trunk of Sam's car, cut open one of the kilo bags, and removed a small amount of cocaine. He took the sample back to the restaurant, went to the men's room, and came out.

"Good stuff, Sam. Here are your keys. How about driving it over to my house. I'll meet you there in a few minutes."

Sam felt uneasy. He decided to wait awhile, to look around. Was he being set up? Why did Frank leave in such a hurry? Why didn't they exchange the "kees" for cash and both be on their way? And why had Frank tested the product? In his three years of dealing with Frank, he had always been a trusting customer.

Sam looked around for anything suspicious. All seemed normal. No one seemed to be watching him. He left the restaurant and walked slowly across the street to a 7-Eleven convenience store. He used his peripheral vision, looked over his shoulder, stopped to hear any approaching footsteps. Nothing. He purchased a newspaper at the store and while appearing to read scanned the area. Nothing.

Satisfied that all was well, Sam walked slowly back to his car, got behind the steering wheel, and suddenly became the target of a swarm of D.E.A. agents. He had been set up by his friend Frank, and caught red-handed with two kilos of cocaine. Had he been able to provide Frank with his five-kilogram order, he would have been facing thirteen years in prison. As it was, the two-kilogram possession carried only five years. Had he been in possession of amounts as high as he had carried in the past, he would have been faced with a life sentence.

Sam was taken back to Chicago. After having his bond reduced from $300,000 to $100,000, he went back to the street. There he stayed for three weeks, not preparing himself to go to jail, but rather planning his escape to Greece. His father resided in Athens, and because Sam retained his Greek citizenship, he thought entry into that country would be relatively easy.

It took him three weeks to get his affairs in order and have a "temporary replacement" for his Greek passport fabricated under a fictitious name. Two days later he was disembarking a KLM jet in Athens. The Greek immigration officer looked at his replacement passport, smiled, and said, "Eh patrida, Eh hases to tha-va-tirio soo, eh?" ("Hey countryman, lost your passport, huh?") He winked.

Sam responded in his unaccented Greek, "Neh." ("Yes.") He smiled back and was waved through customs.

After a year in Greece, and after his father's death, Sam longed to see his daughter. He also missed his adopted home, Chicago. Although he was safe from extradition in Greece and had taken up the life of an idler—*nepenthe* ("without care")—he found himself preparing to return to Chicago for a short visit. He now had a legitimate Greek passport and a round-trip ticket to Toronto.

He took the precaution of choosing Toronto instead of Chicago as his destination, traveling with a friend from Toronto to Chicago, rather than renting a car. He monitored his every move and association while in Chicago. But sometimes, as most prisoners will tell you, no matter how careful you are, you make the mistake of trusting a friend.

That's what happened to Sam. A few days before returning to Toronto on his journey back to Greece, Sam met his longtime friend Keith for dinner. Shortly after their arrival, Keith borrowed twenty-five cents from Sam to make a phone call. With that phone call Keith summoned the police.

When he returned to the table, Keith and Sam began to drink. In retrospect, Sam remembers being somewhat suspicious of Keith's repeated insistence of "C'mon, one more round." But after seven tequilas, with beer chasers, his suspicions turned to bonhomie. As they left the restaurant they heard "Put your hands up, Sam, you're under arrest," and what appeared to be a dozen guns, all pointed at him, came out of the darkness.

Sam pled guilty and was sentenced to two five-year terms, to be served concurrently. He's been "down" for three years so he has two years to go. He'll be the first to tell you he was lucky. He believes his punishment fits his crime, and I agree.

But not all punishments do. As I have already noted, the perversity of the sentencing guidelines becomes obvious when you look beyond their hypothetical rationales, and examine actual cases.

Danny Reynolds, a thirty-two-year-old black man, occupies the cell across from mine. He's scheduled to be released in forty years, when he is seventy-two years old.

Danny was the youngest of eight children, raised with his two brothers and five sisters in a small apartment in the projects on Chicago's West Side. He held dozens of part-time jobs as he worked his way through high school and one year of college at the University of Illinois. He spent all of his free time, what little there was, at the local skating rink. Skating was and still is his passion. During recreation hours, anyone who wants to find Danny need look no further than the tarmac track. He'll be there skating.

It was at the skating rink that Danny and James Johnson became friends. In early 1992 James moved to Houston. He invited Danny to come down to that city for the Fourth of July holidays to attend a Luke Skywalker concert. Danny went. After a few days, James was scheduled to return to Chicago with Danny.

Because James had a few last-minute matters to attend to, he had his cousin take Danny and the luggage to the train station. James would be along shortly. Enter the F.B.I. They stopped Danny and James's cousin. They answered a few questions, and Danny denied that he owned the pieces of luggage, which he claimed belonged to James. Then the agents opened the bags. Danny's bags contained nothing illegal, but the others contained over thirty kilograms of cocaine and some $14,000 in cash—"more money," Danny was to tell me later, "than I had ever seen before."

Danny was charged with interstate trafficking in cocaine. He stood fast by his story, but could not identify the address of James Johnson. ("I don't know anything about Houston. How'm I going to tell them where somebody lives?") A jury found him guilty—and I have no quarrel with this finding. But his sentence bordered on the uncivilized.

Although it was his first offense, the amount of cocaine was substantial. The quantity of drugs involved placed him at an extremely high level for sentencing guideline purposes. His sentence was "enhanced" because he didn't cooperate with the prosecutor in naming names and identifying sources. ("But how could I? That wasn't my stuff. How did I know who and where it came from?") And because he didn't show remorse ("Why should I show remorse for something I didn't do?") and obstructed justice by forcing the prosecutor to prove his guilt at trial ("They punished me for pleading 'not guilty'") he received no amelioration. What he did receive was a forty-year sentence.

A person is presumed innocent until proven guilty. Inasmuch as Danny was found guilty, it must be presumed that he did indeed traffic in cocaine. I believe he should be punished for this transgression, and even though it was his first offense, his criminal conduct should not be condoned. The justice system cannot provide even a modicum of deterrent if it doesn't punish.

But how can we justify a forty-year sentence? We go beyond deterrence and into the constitutionally prohibited area of "cruel and unusual" punishment when we sentence a first-time offender of a nonviolent crime to what is virtually a life sentence without parole.

I apologize for being repetitious, but a sentence of far fewer years, properly administered, together with education and rehabilitation would have been all that Danny would need to turn his life around. And the close to $2 million that will be spent on his protracted incarceration could be better spent on rehabilitating other addicts and educating children as to the perils of illicit drug use.

July 1994

July 4, 1994

It is not only illicit drug abuse that can be destructive. During the summer of 1991 I continued my slide into what was to become a major depression, exacerbated by my abuse of drugs—legally obtained, but abused nonetheless.

I'm writing this entry while lying on my bunk, tied to a hot-water bottle, smelling like Ben-Gay, and in great pain.

I went to the physician's assistant Friday. He said, "I don't think the ribs are broken or cracked. We'll have to wait until Tuesday to find out."

"But today's Friday," I protested weakly. "Tuesday's almost a week away."

"Hey, it's the Fourth of July weekend. Whaddya expect?" he shot back.

"Do you have any painkiller?" I asked. "This thing really hurts. I don't think I'll be able to sleep tonight."

"Tuesday."

"What if a rib is broken, can it wait until Tuesday?"

"The only thing we could do for it is strap it, and we can do that—"

"I know," I interrupted. "On Tuesday."

Today is July Fourth; tomorrow is Tuesday. Thank God. The pain was so bad last night that I threw up twice.

How did it happen?

Friday, as the start of the July Fourth weekend, they had a sprint race. Given the fact that the average age here is twenty-nine years, you have to be pretty fast to compete.

"Hey, judge," one of my younger friends called to me, "how about entering the fifty-yard dash competition?"

I thought he was poking fun at me.

"When I was your age, I would have, but at sixty-four, I think I'll pass."

"C'mon, judge, you can race with the sixty-plus crowd—most of them are in the medical unit. They're sick old men. You could win. It would make our unit look good."

Why not? Since coming here I've been working out. I'm ten pounds lighter, and haven't been in such good condition since my army days.

But then my mind played the same trick it had been playing with ever greater frequency: I started to remember another time when my athletic prowess was challenged. A time when, like that Friday, I tried to convince myself that I was capable of doing something that was within my ambition but beyond my physical abilities.

I was twelve years old when my father traded in his itinerate auctioneer's life for that of a retail jeweler. It was 1942, and he thought it time that his family settle and put down roots. He chose St. Petersburg, then a small city on Florida's west coast, and there he opened up a jewelry store on Central Avenue, the main street.

My parents actually bought a home. I can remember how excited I was at the prospect of living in a place I could call my "hometown." We joined a temple, and I started a crash course in Hebrew so that I could be Bar Mitzvahed on my thirteenth birthday.

I started to do all the things a normal twelve-year-old does, things I had never done, like having friends and attending the same school for more than a semester at a time.

My mother and father both worked long hours. They came home for dinner, which was always served at six P.M. sharp, and then went back to the store until nine P.M. This routine was followed six days a week. Morty, then starting high school, also went to work at the store. He was expected to—he was going to be part of the business one day.

But not me. Because my schoolwork was above average, my parents started thinking of me as the member of the family who was going to go into a profession. And because I expressed an interest in the law, I was thought of as "the future lawyer in the family." My destiny was a certainty in everyone's mind, including my own.

Since those days I have often thought of Morty's ready acceptance of our respective roles. After school he would go right to the store, there to work until dinner. I, on the other hand, would go with my friends to the beach, or fishing, or just to a friend's house to hang out.

On Saturdays, while I was at play Morty was at work. We both knew what was expected of us. Morty had to prove himself capable of one day taking over the business and I had to wait for my turn to become the world's most gifted attorney.

But by the time I was fourteen, the seams in my patchwork education started to show, and by the time I started high school, it became important that I organize at least to the extent of figuring out exactly what grade I should be in. As I said, when I was in the North, I was left back a grade, and when in the South, I was advanced a grade.

My father's sister Lucy lived in New York and told my parents of a boarding school in Milford, Connecticut, that she felt would be able to prepare me for college. So when I was fifteen I left the one permanent home I had ever had—at least, it had been permanent for four years.

Before I left St. Petersburg, the small high school I was attending had decided it would start a basketball team. Although I was then, as I am now, a terrible athlete, I was nevertheless popular with my classmates. When the prospective members of the basketball team in formation had its first meeting, they elected me captain of the team.

That explains why, when I arrived at Milford on a bitter-cold day in January 1945, my high school transfer record noted the fact that I was "captain, varsity basketball." That also explains why Jerry Pepper, the coach of the Milford basketball team, was awaiting my arrival with breathless anticipation.

The year before, Milford had just missed winning the Eastern Preparatory School Association championship. Although the team was made up of World War II veterans, there to finish high school on the G.I. Bill of Rights, there was always room on the squad for the captain of another high school's team. They could hardly believe their good fortune—I might just provide the one additional element necessary to capture the association championship.

No sooner had I arrived at the dorm than I was greeted by Coach Pepper and the Milford team captain. They gave me a uniform and told me to report to the gym to "shoot a few baskets."

I liked the uniform. It fit as though it had been tailored for me. It was maroon with white trim and bore the number 19. My three roommates, whom I had not yet met, looked at me with awe. Here I was, not ten minutes at Milford, and I had already made the varsity.

I put my overcoat on over my uniform to protect myself from the cold night air. After ascertaining where the gym was, I left the dorm for what was to be my most embarrassing experience since appearing at the Blowing Rock Elementary School with shoes on.

The gym, having been closed since dinner hour, was cold. The lights were turned on to illumine my debut. Coach Pepper, the team captain, and the team manager were waiting for me at mid-court. They were all smiles.

For some strange reason, I thought that I would not disappoint them. Although I knew that I had no talent or ability, I believed that somehow, in some way, I would meet the challenge. Maybe I would get lucky—or maybe I would prove to be a natural. Or maybe, just maybe, through some magical or celestial intervention, I would astonish even myself with a performance worthy of their expectations.

The coach threw me the basketball. It bounced off my hands. "I know," he said, "it's cold in here," and he threw it to me again. This time I caught it.

"O.K., now," he said, "take the ball up court, throw a three-pointer, hook a two-pointer, take it down court, and take two free throws from the foul line."

I didn't know what he was talking about, but I proceeded toward one of the baskets.

"Dribble!" he shouted.

I knew that meant to bounce the ball, which I promptly did. But I found it impossible to "dribble" and run at the same time.

"Shoot!" he shouted.

I shot, but the ball went under the backboard. It hit the back of the gym and bounced back to me.

"Hook it!" he shouted.

I quickly looked around to find a hook. Seeing none, I made the fatal mistake of saying, "There is no hook."

At first this inane observation was greeted by silence. Then:

"Turn in your uniform and lock up," said the coach, and without another word, he and his two companions turned and left the gym, throwing the light switches off as they walked out into the freezing darkness.

And there stood number 19, alone in a dark, cold gym in a strange school. I had not only failed, I had made a fool of myself. Why hadn't I come clean and declared my incompetence from the start?

I pondered that question as I walked back to my dorm at Milford, and I pondered it again as I lay in my prison cell once again having my meager physical abilities challenged. My desire to prove myself had overcome my reason.

"O.K.," I had told the young inquiring inmate, "I'll be right out to sign up."

Only problem was they had no sixty-plus category. They had nineteen to twenty-nine, twenty-nine to thirty-nine, thirty-nine to forty-nine, and fifty-plus.

"Good," I said, realizing that I was a winner by default. "I won. Where's my prize?"

"We're really sorry, but if you want to race, you'll have to go with the fifty-plus sprinters."

I started to leave, and then I thought: Although I'm a terrible athlete because of my poor hand-eye coordination, and although I never was able to play basketball, I was on the track team at Milford Academy. I wasn't very good, but I did manage to win a varsity letter doing the 440 and 880. I should be able to beat these over-fifty arsonists, murderers, and drug dealers. If they were so fast, how come they were caught?

I signed up for the fifty-yard dash.

There was only one opponent up for the event. His name, according to the roster, was Champagne. I really felt I could win. The first prize was six cans of soda. If I didn't win, I was assured of the second prize: three cans of soda.

But the real prize would be in terms of the approval of the general population. What could be better, in a prison environment, than to be perceived as a successful athlete? A real man among men. Because of my occupation "on the street," I was already considered smart—but now I had another chance to prove myself as an athlete. I could win the fifty-yard dash in my age class and be the champ of Rochester. The best in the whole prison. And then I met Champagne.

He is six feet, five inches tall, mostly legs. If Central Casting were asked to provide a fifty-plus Native American who looked like he could run like the wind, they would have come up with Champagne. With his flowing silver mane tied in a neat pony tail and his magnificent, well-proportioned physique, there was no question who would win the race.

A silence was falling over the compound. Hundreds of inmates were gathering to see the race. I could hear the shouts of encouragement: "Get him, chief"—directed at Champagne. "You can beat him, judge"—directed at his runty opponent.

I thought it would do well to meet him before he beat me.

"Hi," I said, extending my hand.

He accepted neither my hand nor my greeting.

"Champagne sounds French," I continued, undaunted. "Where are you from?"

"North Dakota," he answered, more to shut me up than to educate me. "Turtle Mountain Reservation."

"Sioux?" I asked.

He stared at me, his eyes narrowing. Oh Lord, I thought, they don't tolerate being called Sioux. They are of the Lakota tribe. Sioux is the name given them by the French.

"I'm sorry," I quickly corrected myself, "I mean Lakota."

He continued to stare.

"I didn't mean Sioux. I'm sorry. I mean Lakota."

He continued to stare. Finally he spoke through clenched teeth: "Chippewa. And I'm fifty-one. And no more talk."

Now, was this fair? He's thirteen years younger, six and a half inches taller, and when my grandfather was in Austria candling and carting eggs, his grandfather was in North Dakota running down buffalo in his bare feet. In addition to everything else, I had just offended him by referring to him as a member of a tribe that warred for a century with the Chippewa.

And now he was taking off his sneakers. Like his grandfather, he was barefoot.

"On your mark. Get set. Go!"

The large assemblage of spectators started to cheer. I heard them shouting encouragement to the "chief," a title I had enjoyed during my last eight years as a jurist. For a moment I forgot who the real chief was—I thought they were rooting for me. I was wrong.

I made a good start, but his long legs put him ahead of me by a couple of yards. And then I noticed he was loping with an uneven gait. I was in an even stride, and he was bouncing. I caught him and started to pass him. I thought for a minute that I was going to win.

And then my foot went into a gopher hole. I flew forward, hit the ground with my ribcage, bounced up six inches, and then hit again. And now I'm waiting for Tuesday.

July 5, 1994

Tuesday morning has finally come. I have not slept for three nights. I have a persistent cough because I still haven't quite gotten rid of a bronchitis that has been with me for three weeks. And every time I cough or move, my ribcage hurts terribly. But I'm finally going to see the physician's assistant.

The comedian Henny Youngman tells the story of a fellow who goes to the doctor complaining of a pain in his leg.

"What should I do, doc?" he asks after the examination.

"Limp," replies the doctor.

"Let me see your I.D. card," said the nurse, somewhat officiously.

Fortunately, I had remembered to bring it with me. Without it I would have been denied medical assistance.

"What's the trouble, Ashtler?" she asked.

"The name's Washtler," I said, mispronouncing my own name so as not to add more confusion.

"Look at this card. Do you see a W in front of your name, Ashtler?" she asked.

"No, ma'am," I answered, "the W was cut off when they printed my card. But you can see the W in my signature."

She studied the card, looked at the picture of my forlorn face, taken that first day at Butner (it seems so long ago), looked back at me, stared for a few moments, and then said, "O.K., Washtler, what's your problem?"

I detail this encounter because I believe it was the first time since being in the custody of the Bureau of Prisons that I was able to convince any member of the staff that I, a prisoner, was on the right side of the argument. I only wish that the focus of my victory had been something more dramatic and significant than the pronunciation of my own name.

"What were you doing running sprints, across a grassy field with gopher holes?" she asked.

"Because that's where they told me to run," I answered, realizing how stupid I sounded. I may have bested her in the spelling argument, but she certainly had me on this one.

"Go outside and wait to be called for X-ray," she said.

I walked to the small waiting alcove, just outside the nurse's station. It was a windowless room with two dozen or so chairs facing the wall. Actually, the chairs were facing a small wooden cabinet against the wall, its doors held closed by a large locked padlock. I was told by one of the nurses that in the eight months I have been here, that cabinet door has only been opened twice: once when the judges visited, and once when the director of the Bureau of Prisons, Kathleen Hawk, visited.

The small cabinet housed a television set. Because the TV was used just twice, I must assume that it was there solely to deceive visiting dignitaries and not for the use and enjoyment of the inmates, who were compelled to sit and wait—often for hours—while staring at the small wooden cabinet and blank wall.

I recall being in that same alcove last winter. There was no ventilation and the room was overheated. I, along with some forty other inmates, went there every night for medication, a routine that, thankfully, is no longer required of me. Forty of us in this stifling room, half of us standing, the other half seated, all facing the wall. Wheelchairs, crutches, and claustrophobia. Inevitably, the seated inmates would turn their chairs around to face the room in which they were seated. Just as inevitably, a guard would come over and order them to turn the chairs back to the wall.

I was thinking of this strange ritual while seated, facing the wall, waiting to be called to X-ray.

"Ashtler?"

"Washtler!"

"Whatever. Go down the hall to X-ray."

After the pictures of my ribcage were taken, I went back to my chair facing the wall. And waited. And waited. I finally looked over my shoulder to find that no one else was in the waiting area. I asked a nurse when I would be able to see the physician's assistant.

"Why?" she asked.

"To see if my ribs are broken. I just had an X-ray taken," I answered.

"Those X-rays won't be ready for a few days," she said. "Check back."

"But the pain, the sleepless nights. What do I do for it?"

I was expecting her to give me Henny Youngman's response: "Limp." Instead she assisted me in having a P.A. prescribe Motrin, an anti-inflammatory, and apologized for her inability to prescribe a painkiller or sleeping aid. But that was all right. The most therapeutic part of "sick call" is getting it over with.

I limped back to my unit, and now I'm going to try again to sleep on my three-and-a-half-inch-thick oilcloth-covered mattress, on this stifling hot night. All because of a gopher hole.

I wondered whether Champagne was savoring his victory. I was also wondering if my fall was really an accident, or if Chippewa can talk to gophers.

An X-ray taken after my release from prison indicated that I had broken four ribs. The doctor who took the X-ray said, "The pain must have been excruciating." It was.

July 15–16, 1994

In order to be certain that each prisoner is present and accounted for, the Bureau of Prisons mandates that "counts" be taken at a certain time during the day and through the night. The most important is the four P.M. count, which I have already mentioned—the time when each prisoner stands by his bunk waiting to be seen and counted. When the count is completed, an announcement is made on the loudspeaker: "Count check." You are then permitted to leave your cell to attend mail call.

Although I usually receive a good deal of mail, today there was only one letter—more of a package, actually. It came in a Federal Express envelope. At first I thought it was from Joe Bellacosa, who has been so diligent in sending me opinions of the court and other reading material to keep my mind from atrophying.

When I returned to my cell, I opened the envelope. It was not from Joe. It was from a book publisher and it was a book. The title: *Double Life*. On the jacket was a picture of me and Joy separated by a judge's gavel, and the subtitle: "The Shattering Affair Between Chief Judge Sol Wachtler and Socialite Joy Silverman." The author: Linda Wolfe.

I read the book in one gulp. I had finished it by the nine P.M. count. I have not been able to sleep, and so I find myself writing this journal entry immediately after the three A.M., July 16, count (yes, counts continue through the night).

I knew the book was being written. Joan and I had met with the author and had been interviewed. But that seemed so long ago. So long ago that I had almost forgotten the details of my aberrational conduct. The book brought it all back.

How could I have written those detestable letters? How could I, in playing my mindless "mind games" with Joy, have been so insensitive, so indifferent to the pain I was inflicting on so many people, not to mention my court and my profession? How could my judgment have been so skewed as to blind me to the ruin I was bringing to a career, a profession, and a marriage, all of which I had nurtured for over forty years?

If Sandy Solomon, the psychiatrist who treated me after my arrest, were here, he would answer those questions by saying, "You were sick."

After speaking to Sandy and no less than half a dozen other psychiatrists—including the president of the American Psychiatric Association; Dr. Robert Spitzer, the author of the psychiatric diagnostic manual and perhaps the country's leading diagnostic psychiatrist; and Dr. Donald Klein, one of the nation's most prominent psychopharmacologists—I know that I was indeed sick. And I need no psychiatrist to tell me how manic I was when I did what I did—but I still have difficulty fathoming the mystery of how a human mind, my mind, could become so bereft of reason.

One of the blurbs on the dustjacket of *Double Life* was "Lust, discovered late, destroyed Wachtler, but the woman who tempted and taunted him may be more guilty."

I do not believe that Joy is guilty of anything. It was I who violated my marriage vows and acted so bizarrely, I who was the guilty one.

I knew exactly who and what Joy was when I became involved with her. Although I may have been, as Chertoff's psychiatrist contends, "sexually naive," I was not a child. I was an adult who had lived an unsheltered life—someone who should have known better.

July 20, 1994

Sixteen years ago today, July 20, 1978, William Kampiles spent his last day as a free person.

Bill is now forty years old and he is serving a forty-year sentence for his misdeed. Although it was a major news story sixteen years ago, few people remember the tale of this young man who was determined to become America's premier double agent.

The odyssey that destroyed Bill's youth began when he was just twenty, a senior at Indiana University. He had always wanted to be a C.I.A. agent working in clandestine services—spying—and so was excited to meet a C.I.A. recruiter on his campus. He was even more excited a year later, when he received notice that a job with the

C.I.A. was available to him. It was not with clandestine services, as he had hoped—he was not to be a spy. Rather, he was assigned to the Watch Office in the C.I.A. Operations Center in Langley, Virginia.

He was quick to accept the Watch Office position, and took leave of his widowed mother and mentally impaired older brother to begin to fulfill his lifelong ambition of working for the C.I.A. After three weeks' training, he reported to the Operations Center to begin his duties on the night desk. His responsibilities consisted of reviewing, categorizing, and logging in cables that came into the office from posts all over the world.

After only a few months on the job, Kampiles saw a copy of the *KH-11 System Technical Manual*. This was a manual kept in the Watch Office that described the capabilities of the KH-11 spy satellite, which orbited the Soviet Union sending photographs to C.I.A. intelligence-gathering sources.

According to testimony at the Kampiles trial, the manual was not locked up and was available to any of the sixty-five watch officers on duty at the Operations Center. Its normal resting spot was on a shelf alongside a copy of an almanac, in an unlocked cabinet beneath a standard copying machine. The particular manual in question was Copy 155 of a total of 350 in print.

In the late summer of 1977, William Kampiles put the *KH-11 System Technical Manual* under his jacket and walked out of the C.I.A. Operations Building. Shortly thereafter, convinced that his ambition of becoming a spy for the C.I.A. was not progressing and might never be realized, he seized on a dramatic scheme. In true James Bond fashion, he would infiltrate the Soviet intelligence system, thereby proving his ability in counterintelligence. If he could pull off such an exploit, the C.I.A. clandestine service would have to invite him into its sanctum—or so he thought.

His first act was to resign his Watch Office job. His next move was to put his infiltration plan into operation in Athens, Greece. Being fluent in the Greek language, he thought he would achieve instant credibility with the Soviet embassy in that country.

Without having had any prior contact with the Soviets, Kampiles went to their embassy in Athens. When he arrived, he found there was some sort of a celebration taking place—he was to find out later that they were celebrating Russian Armed Forces Day. He told the person who greeted him at the door that he wanted to speak to someone in Soviet intelligence—that he had some important information that the Soviet Union would find of interest.

His plan was working. A meeting was arranged at dusk on February 23, 1978, at the Tomb of the Unknown Soldier in Athens. There, William Kampiles, age twenty-three, handed over the first pages of the KH-11 manual to a man whom he knew only as Michael.

The Soviet intelligence agent, Michael Zavali, satisfied as to the authenticity of these pages of the technical manual, met with Kampiles again on March 2, 1978. At this meeting, near the Greek National Stadium, Zavali gave Kampiles an envelope containing $3,000 in U.S. currency and Kampiles gave the balance of the manual to the Soviet agent. Kampiles felt he had accomplished the first part of his self-managed mission.

The next month he set himself to the task of convincing the C.I.A. that he had established the necessary contact to become a disinformation agent for the agency, to feed misleading information to the Soviets.

In April 1978 he went to the C.I.A. headquarters in Langley to speak to George Joannides, a veteran C.I.A. officer who had counseled him while he was at the agency. He told Joannides of his activity in Athens and tried to convince him that the total secrecy of his operation—secret from even the C.I.A. hierarchy—would make him an ideal candidate for a clandestine role in counterintelligence.

Joannides, not being familiar with Soviet matters, telephoned an officer in the Soviet Section, who suggested that Kampiles detail his experience in a letter. As was found by the trial judge, Kampiles sent such a letter to Joannides in May or June of 1978 stating his willingness to "discuss his experience in full detail."

Joannides inadvertently failed to forward the Kampiles letter to the appropriate C.I.A. employees until July 1978, and it took until the latter part of that month for an officer of the C.I.A. Soviet Section to arrange a meeting with Kampiles in Washington. Not until after this meeting did the C.I.A. even suspect that Copy 155 of the KH-11 manual was missing. After ransacking the Watch Office, it was established that the manual was indeed missing and that Kampiles' story of his sale of the manual to the Soviets must be true. Instead of being rewarded for his ingenuity he was arrested for his self-confessed crime.

Kampiles' deed was not motivated by evil intent but by the opposite. He naively thought that his contrived plot would lead to the enhancement of his ability to serve his country as well as to the improvement of C.I.A. operations. He was terribly wrong and his poor judgment and criminal act resulted in his being tried and convicted on a six-count indictment that charged him with unauthorized possession, delivery, and sale of Copy No. 155 of a 1976 *KH-11 System Technical Manual* to a representative of the Soviet Union in violation of Paragraph 18 United States Code, Sections 641 and 794, Subsections (a) and (e).

For the government to prove its case it was necessary for it to convince a jury that Kampiles' treasonous act alone was responsible for the compromise of the KH-11 manual. At the trial the government stated with certainty: that there was no possibility "that the Soviet Union gained its knowledge from a source other than [Kampiles]." But by the end of the trial the government had conceded that seventeen other copies of the KH-11 manual were missing.

It was also proved that another and earlier possible date for compromise of the information in the KH-11 manual arose from information revealed in a 1977 espionage case in Los Angeles involving two Californians, Christopher Boyce and Daulton Lee (known as the Falcon and the Snowman). It appears that Lee confessed in that proceeding to having met with Soviet agents in Vienna in early 1976, some months prior to the launching of the KH-11 satellite.

The defense in the Kampiles trial made a motion to develop information connecting Lee with the KH-11 information leak. It was found that Lee had alluded to passing to the Soviets information relating to a "communications satellite, the type that flies daily over Russia taking photographs." The only satellite system capable of such performance was the KH-11. The motion to admit this into evidence was denied by the judge presiding over the Kampiles trial.

The defense raised other questions regarding the "probable harm" done by Kampiles, and indeed the intrinsic importance of the KH-11 manual when it was turned over by Kampiles to the Soviets in 1978. If the manual was so important, why was it kept so casually in an unlocked spot? Why was a new employee like Kampiles, only three weeks with the C.I.A., allowed complete access to it? Why wasn't the manual missed? Kampiles removed Copy 155 of the manual months before he told the C.I.A. that he had taken it. Indeed, if Kampiles himself had not gone to Joannides and the C.I.A., the fact that the manual was missing might never have been discovered. During the trial it came out that no record had been kept as to who in the Watch Office had signed out Copy 155 of the manual.

From these facts and others in the trial record, it is difficult to determine that there was any "probable harm" caused by the Soviets' receiving Copy 155 of the KH-11 manual. Indeed, facts recently made available as a result of our new and amicable relations with Russia confirm that the wrongful act of William Kampiles caused little harm. A motion is now pending before the court that sentenced Bill to reconsider his punishment.

Whenever I am asked to cite an example of disproportionate sentencing, the case of William Kampiles comes to mind. William Kampiles delivered one document in return for $3,000 in a misguided attempt to become a double agent for the United States. It is instructive to look at sentences meted out to other "spies."

For several years during Bill Kampiles' incarceration in the federal prison in Rochester, the cell next to his was occupied by

Richard W. Miller. Miller, you may remember, was the former F.B.I. agent who sold secrets to the Soviets, asking at first for $2 million. He ultimately received little more than a personal relationship with a female émigré who claimed to be a major in the K.G.B. After his first trial, Miller received a sentence of two life terms plus fifty years. After a retrial and reconviction he was resentenced to twenty years. Shortly after I met him here in Rochester, and after he had served a total of twelve years, his sentence was reduced to the time he had already served and he was freed.

Then there was the case of Clayton Longtree, a Marine guard in the U.S. embassy in Moscow who maintained a longtime relationship with the K.G.B. He was originally sentenced to twenty-five years, but in 1993 his sentence was reduced to qualify him for immediate parole eligibility.

Lieutenant Colonel William Henry Whalen worked as armed forces chief of staff and was convicted of spying for the Soviets at the highest intelligence levels. Colonel Whalen was sentenced to fifteen years and paroled after six years of incarceration.

Aldrich Ames received millions for repeated deliveries of classified information, which reputedly led to the death of thirty-five C.I.A. undercover agents. C.I.A. agent David Henry was recruited by the Soviets in 1976 and was paid $92,000 over his three years of work with the Soviets. William Kampiles' youthfully misguided single act for which he received $3,000 (turned over to the government), and which was discovered only when he told his story to the C.I.A., has already resulted in sixteen years in prison.

If William Kampiles is unsuccessful in having his sentence reduced, given his age and the length of time he still must serve, it is conceivable that he will spend more years in prison than any other spy in this nation's history—even the most notorious.

In the meanwhile he has the most important supervisory job given an inmate at the Rochester UNISAT operation, which assembles electronic components for the United States Department of Defense.

July 27, 1994

The more meals I eat at Rochester, the better those at Butner seem in retrospect. At Butner, often at lunch the soda fountain machine was operating, giving the inmates a choice of different beverages. At Butner they offered such menu variations as fish baskets (various sizes and shapes of deep-fried nameless fish and fish sticks of the same species), and a broad spectrum of ethnic and traditional American fare. The food wasn't good—it was greasy and caloric—but it wasn't bad. The same was true of Rochester when I first arrived.

But that was then. Since then, the food and its quality has deteriorated. It has gotten so bad that I seldom take my meals in the chow hall and instead use the unit microwave to cook my own meals. I should say that Bill Kampiles, who makes superb pasta dishes, cooks meals for the two of us in the unit microwave.

Because I am able to spend $150 a month and Bill has a decent paying job, we can afford to buy pasta, garlic, grated Parmesan cheese, tomatoes, and canned chicken at the overpriced prison store, we eat well. But not all the inmates are as fortunate. Last night, for instance, while Bill and I were eating pasta al dente with a light piquant sauce, most of our fellow inmates were eating barbecue beef "sloppy Joes" in the mainline. "Barbecue beef" is a nondescript melange of meat that has been put through a strainer to disguise prior body parts. This strained meat is then soaked in a spicy red sauce, put on a hamburger bun and, voilà, a sloppy Joe.

Prisoners do not have the right to act in concert to protest a grievance. No picket lines, no petitions, and no strikes are allowed. An individual can file a "cop out," a written form to register a complaint, but organized protest or conspiring with others for the purpose of protesting will get you in the hole or worse. The five inmates knew that. They also knew that if something weren't done about the quality of the food soon, there could be mass starvation—all right, not mass starvation, but a lot of hungry and unhappy inmates.

And so the five of them attempted to engineer a food strike without "conspiring" to do so. They passed the word to all the inmates to boycott the chow hall and they chose tonight as the night for the strike, because the menu called for liver and onions. Liver and onions is an easy meal to pass up. They can't afford to fail: If they are found out, reprisals will be severe. To be punished for a failed enterprise is not a novel experience for most of us.

In addition to the whisper campaign ("Psst—July twenty-seventh—supper—boycott—pass it on" behind cupped hands), flyers were posted in the bathrooms:

FOOD BOYCOTT

LET THEM KNOW THAT WE WON'T EAT GARBAGE

PASS UP SUPPER ON JULY 27TH

All they needed was a courageous leader. Someone who would not be afraid to bang his tin cup on the cell door.

Word reached the warden and the staff very soon after the boycott was planned. It was the kind of infraction that could not be tolerated. An inmate demonstration, an organized protest, smuggling, possession of contraband, an escape attempt—none of these could be allowed to happen. Any such violation would not only speak poorly of the discipline within the institution, it would be an indelible blemish on the record of the warden and anyone else in the chain of command, one that would be a permanent part of his career record within the Bureau of Prisons.

Yesterday, in a show of force, the warden and some high-ranking members of the staff toured the units. Before the clearing of the four o'clock count, the warden went into some of the cells. "Everything all right, men?" he asked with a benign smile.

"Everything's fine," "Yes sir," "Fine," "Yes sir," chirped the inmates, all with smiles.

If Pat O'Brien were the warden, he would have said, "All right, you scum suckers, which one of you is planning the boycott? If you don't step forward, you'll all be locked down until I can find the bastard."

And Jimmy Cagney, as the ring leader, would answer, smiling at his fellow inmates: "We'd rather do the rest of our time locked down than rat out any one of us. Instead of coming around here botherin' us, why don't you go to the kitchen and taste some of that swill they're feeding us?"

And the other inmates would say in chorus, "Yeah, yeah, yeah, yeah." Every cell would join in. "Yeah, yeah, yeah, yeah." The warden would look around, his face pained by the din, point to Cagney, and say, "Throw that bum in the hole and lock them all down." He would then retreat with the "Yeah, yeah, yeah" following him through the corridors.

I guess they just don't make prisoners like they used to.

After the warden left, some two dozen inmates were brought to the lieutenant's office to be interrogated. And just before chow, the five inmate leaders were put in the hole.

When the mainline was called the number of inmates in the dining hall seemed about normal. In fact, I'm told that more liver and onions was consumed tonight at dinner than ever before.

July 25, 1994

The heat is unbearable. The temperature hit 100° and there is no relief in the forecast. A slowly oscillating fan brings little relief as it moves the hot air from one corner to the other of our twelve-by-fourteen-foot cell. We are reminded that it is a cell and not a room by the fact that the window does not open except for four inches at the top.

Our living space seems to have shrunk with the heat. The cell is far too small for four adult males, two double bunks, two desks, a wardrobe closet, four lockers, three chairs, and a wheezing and useless fan.

The mattress seems to generate heat of its own. If it weren't for the protection of a sheet, its unyielding, impenetrable covering would be soaking wet from perspiration. As it is, the sheets are always damp.

I lie on my bunk thinking about the book of Job, of all things. Of how the faith of that good and devout man was tested, and of his great strength under adversity. I don't mean to make a comparison between his great travail and my far lesser punishment, but I do envy his constancy. What I don't envy is the reward God gave him for his suffering: six thousand camels, fourteen thousand sheep, and an assortment of donkeys and oxen. I don't know where I would put them—although we do have one empty bunk in the cell.

My daydreaming was interrupted by the arrival of our new cellmate, Jeff Wiley. It seems that as soon as you get to know, understand, and appreciate one of your cellmates, he is transferred or moves on or—in rare instances—is released.

Jeff looked familiar to me. He reminded me that he was the bathroom orderly assigned to the mental health unit when I was housed there. He had just returned from his daily job of cleaning toilets and sinks and was preparing to move into his new, very warm, cell.

"Glad to have you, Jeff," I said.

"Is it always so hot in here?" he asked.

"Wait until the six thousand camels arrive," I said.

"What camels?" he asked with a quizzical look.

"Never mind," I said.

Jeff is another of the inmates here for selling marijuana. He has a college degree and is an expert mechanic; he operated Jeff Wiley Enterprises, which in turn operated machine shops, hauled cars for dealers, and manufactured motor parts. His specialty was repairing motorcycles, which he did out of a shop in a small town in Iowa.

One day one of the bikers he knew convinced him that marijuana, which was so much a part of the biker culture, should become a part of Jeff's inventory. Soon, along with the spark plugs and generators, Jeff Wiley Enterprises also stocked some pot. It was a small, almost insignificant, part of his inventory. But it was illegal, and Jeff knew that it was—but he didn't know how illegal until he was arrested in 1988.

As is the case with so many arrests of this sort, he was turned in—snitched on. The great irony is that Jeff's Judas was the very biker who convinced him to go into the marijuana business in the first place. As is also invariably the case, this erstwhile customer gave Jeff up so that Jeff, and not he, would end up in jail.

Jeff was convicted of possessing twenty-one pounds of marijuana. After spending $300,000 on lawyers and having $700,000 worth of properties and two businesses seized, he was fined $82,000 and sentenced to sixteen years in prison. His long sentence, like so many others, is attributable to the sentencing guidelines enhancements. Because he was alone in his enterprise, such as it was, he was considered a "leader and organizer." Because he pled not guilty and had no one to snitch on, he was enhanced for "obstructing justice." The person who delivered the pot to Jeff was the only one Jeff could have "ratted out," and he was already known to the prosecutor. Indeed, he was given immunity for ratting out Jeff!

My new cellmate, arrested at the age of forty-one for possession of twenty-one pounds of marijuana with intent to sell—with no prior convictions or trouble with the law—will not be free until he is in his late fifties. He will return to his community with no property, money, or assets of any sort.

Even his skill as a mechanic will be diminished, because the Bureau of Prisons does not assign jobs on the basis of skills—in fact, it does just the opposite. It makes a conscious effort to keep you from doing anything you're able to do well. Why? Because if you do a job that you enjoy, and you do it well, you might start thinking of yourself as a person instead of a prisoner.

August 2, 1994

Tonight I was listening once again with my earphones to a radio talk show. Tonight the talk was about the Crime Bill currently being debated in Congress. As usual, the host and his caller were exchanging shibboleths, this time about prison life. Also as usual, neither knew what he was talking about, but the fact that they agreed with each other seemed to reassure them both of how insightful and smart they both were.

They were discussing the "easy" life that prisoners enjoy—complete with pay-per-view movies.

"You'd think," said the host, "that the bleeding-heart liberals in Congress could think of something better to do with taxpayer's money than show movies to the criminals." And, of course, the caller-listener practically shouted his agreement.

Let me tell you about the movies and who pays for them. Here in Rochester and other prisons there are prisoner clubs or organizations that the inmates join. There is the Sportsman's Club, once a part of the Jaycees (Junior Chambers of Commerce); the G.A.D.A. (Growth Awareness Development Association), predominantly African American; the International Club, once the Hispanic Club; and the Veteran's Club.

Each club is granted permission by the prison authorities to raise funds by some unique method. The Sportsman's Club has the camera concession: for $2.50, an inmate can have a photo taken (two prints of each photo). The International Club collects aluminum cans, which are sold for recycling. G.A.D.A. receives a percentage of the revenue from the video games in the visitors' room, and the Veteran's Club sells greeting cards to the other inmates.

The money made by each of these enterprises is spent by the various clubs for pay-per-view movies, which approximately fifty inmates per TV set are able to watch. Of course, the money spent by the inmates to buy photos and greeting cards is money earned by them on prison jobs. Given the fact that the wages range from $15 to $60 per month and that the pay-per-view rate for a movie piped into the several units is over $400, the money spent for a movie can qualify as "hard-earned dollars."

In other words, the prisoners spend their own hard-earned dollars to see these movies, usually two a month, without the assistance of "bleeding-heart liberals in Congress."

The movies to be seen are selected by the officers of the various clubs, subject to the approval of the prison officials. At their last meeting, G.A.D.A. selected *Sugar Hill*, a movie about Harlem drug kingpins, the Veteran's Club selected *Philadelphia*, and the one we saw last night, *On Deadly Ground*, was sponsored by the International Club.

The Sportsman's Club selected the film *The Piano*, but this selection was vetoed by the warden. Reason? Because it showed "frontal nudity." Now it couldn't have been rejected because of female frontal nudity, because that seems to be endemic to the movies of today. So it must be the male frontal nudity that offended the warden. If that is the case, the warden should continue to spend his time in his office and avoid walking about in the units.

It is ironic that *The Piano* is banned, but we are permitted to see last night's *On Deadly Ground*. In that film, which details the struggle of Alaskan Eskimos to protect their environment from a ruthless oil baron, we saw people turned into human torches, decapitation, shotguns blowing apart stomachs and exploding chests—but there is no frontal nudity.

There was a tradition in our television room for inmates to reserve certain chairs for a scheduled movie. They placed their mark on the chair, usually a towel, much as an animal marks territory with his peculiar scent. For the eight months I have been here the system has worked. It was one of those systems devised by the inmates to avoid conflict by avoiding disputes.

The reason a "first come, first seated" basis does not work is because there are inmates who, because of work shifts, cannot arrive early. Conversely, there are others who practically live in the TV rooms. If the reservation system were abolished, there would be some inmates who would never see the movie. But the most important thing is that for whatever reason, the reservation system works.

At least it did work until certain guards decided that they were smarter than the inmates—which is rarely true. They decided that the towels and other markings should be removed, that no one should be able to reserve a seat. One evening, after the inmates retired, their reservations for the next show were canceled. The guards removed the markings and invited chaos.

As I was dozing off last night, a guard named Vogel who has the blond hair, demeanor, and insensitivity of a storm trooper woke me and my cellmates up and asked to see our hands.

"Excuse me?" I said, half awake.

"Your hands—show me your hands," he ordered. I held my hands out to him, palms up.

"Not your hands—your hands," he said, making no sense at all. "The other side!" he demanded.

I turned my hands over. He inspected them and then left.

"What was that all about?" I asked one of my cellmates. "Must have been a fight," he answered. "They're trying to find the participants by looking for bruised knuckles."

He was right. It seems that several moviegoers had a dispute over whose towel had been where before the midnight removal. The score was settled after the movie was over, in the shower room.

Now the big question is: Will they allow the inmates to go back to the system that has worked for years? Or will they continue to invite disorder and fights for seating privileges? Chances are they will resolve the problem as they do most problems here in prison: They will cancel the movies.

Shortly after I left prison, Congress outlawed pay-per-view movies. The clubs have also been disbanded. Some of the inmates believe that it is only a matter of time until there will be an elimination of all television sets in the units. The purchase of exercise equipment for the use of prisoners has also been stopped.

August 4, 1994

Perhaps it is the heat, or maybe it is the anxiety I feel knowing my release date is approaching. Whatever the cause, I can't seem to fall asleep. Every sound, every breath taken by my three cellmates, seems magnified. My mattress and sheet are soaked with sweat, and the suffocation with which my antagonist claustrophobia smothers me causes me to gasp for air.

And now my mind replays past scenes. They are so vivid.

It was the fall of 1991. I had met Joy for lunch and been told by her that she had become involved with another man. His name was David Samson and she described him as young, handsome, wealthy, and very successful. With this news I returned to Albany, suffering the persistence of my depression and the seemingly endless problems and pressures of my work.

The governor was again threatening to gut the state court system budget that I had submitted to the legislature. I could not allow his proposed court budget cuts to adversely effect the operation of the courts, particularly the family court. These courts, responsible for the shattered lives of children, were always improperly funded. To retrench their operations even further would be unthinkable. We could not allow budget constraints to cause delays in this court's process. One day in the life of an abused child is like ten years in the life of an adult.

Nor could I permit a slowdown in the operations of the criminal courts. Rikers Island, with its population of over sixteen thousand prisoners, as well as county and city jails all over New York State, were well beyond capacity. If we did not keep the criminal parts functioning at their optimum level, New York would suffer the same fate as most other large states. Overcrowding would lead to the premature release of prisoners and the inability to comply with the constitutional mandate of a speedy trial.

The criminal courts had to keep in full operation for another reason. Almost all cases in state courts are resolved by plea negotiations—plea bargaining. If a defendant knows that there aren't the personnel or courts to try his case, the prosecutor is put to the disadvantage of not being able to even threaten a trial in exchange for a more meaningful plea.

Because of this need to continue full operations of the family and criminal courts, we had to close down many of the civil court operations, responsible for everything from the enforcement of contracts to the trying of negligence cases. New York State, at the center of the world's commerce, found itself with a crippled commercial court system.

Our only recourse was to constantly monitor our resources to balance competing interests, while at the same time trying to convince the public, the legislature, and the governor that endangering the operations of the courts through the imposition of fiscal constraints was a perilous pursuit capable of undermining our governmental and commercial superstructures.

But even more horrendous for me and my already troubled spirit was the prospect of firing some five hundred nonjudicial employees in order to keep the court system from bankruptcy.

Because of civil service laws and contractual obligations, laying off a particular court employee did not mean that the employee in question left. Under the mandated "bumping" system, if the employee had seniority over another employee in the same title, the senior employee did not leave. He or she simply took a reduction in grade, and the employee on the next lower rung was bumped down another grade. This continued until the employee with the least seniority had no one else to bump. That junior employee was the one who was fired.

One of the primary objectives Matt Crosson and I sought to achieve in improving the justice system of New York State was to increase the number of women and minorities working for the judicial branch. In order to accomplish this, in 1990 we instituted a workforce diversity program, which had a dramatic effect on the personnel complement.

A hiring freeze imposed by the governor kept us from filling some fourteen hundred job vacancies that could have been used to further diversify our workforce and at the same time improve the functioning of our overburdened courts.

But even more traumatic than the hiring freeze was the emerging necessity of firing five hundred employees. Because of the bumping system, the bumped employees would be those most recently hired, young men and women, many of them Hispanic and African American.

The necessity to fire these newly hired employees affected me in a strange way. I kept thinking of their recent marriages, home purchases, family planning, and new lives of promise—their time of hope. And then I thought of how they would feel to be plunged into the despair of unemployment.

Under normal circumstances cutting these young people from the workforce would have distressed and saddened me. Depressed as I was anyway, I found myself sobbing when I was alone at night.

But there was something more constructive I could do: I could sue the governor.

I was convinced that under the New York State Constitution, the governor had no authority to reduce or in any way tamper with the budget submitted by the judiciary. His only prerogative was to send the court budget to the legislature "without revision." If the court budget was to be cut, it was up to the legislature and not the governor to do so.

Instead of following this constitutional mandate, the governor sought to treat the budget submitted by the judiciary as if it were a budget submitted by one of his departments, as if it were an agency of the executive branch.

Matt Crosson and I felt that the only way to assert the independence of the judicial branch, vindicate the constitutional integrity of the judiciary, and preserve the fiscal integrity of the court system was to sue the governor. Before doing so, however, we thought it prudent to consult with members of the legal profession who would be profoundly affected by so dramatic a confrontation.

I convened a meeting of the presidents of many of our state bar associations, to be held at the Association of the Bar of the City of New York, to discuss the possible gains and pitfalls of the proposed litigation. During the meeting, a message was sent to me by the governor telling me that he would see to it the court budget was cut and that there would be "no further negotiations." The gauntlet had been thrown down.

The summons and complaint in *Wachtler v. Cuomo* was served on the governor on the same day that I sent the five hundred discharge notices to the court employees.

Cuomo began to claim, both publicly and privately, that I had begun the lawsuit as a matter of "personal promotion." Nothing could have been further from the truth. The idea of the lawsuit was anathema to me. This unprecedented constitutional confrontation between the executive and judicial branches could bring nothing but embarrassment to the governor and the Chief Judge.

In addition, this "clash of the Titans," as *Newsweek* magazine was to call it, was to me a horrendous personal rent. Mario Cuomo, my friend and, in a real sense, my benefactor, whom I respected and admired, was holding a series of press conferences criticizing the judicial branch and its Chief Judge for "refusing to share the burden of the state's fiscal crisis." He went on to note that I wanted money for the courts, "no matter what poor people, sick people or children are denied."

The pettiness of our squabble was apparent in my response suggesting that the governor should "spend more time governing, more time finding ways to properly fund the courts, and spend less time holding press conferences." The governor and I were caricatured by editorial writers as "schoolyard gladiators."

I went so far as to submit a detailed schedule of increased filing fees and other revenue devices that I proposed be levied by the courts to raise the funds needed for our budget and that needed legislative approval. In other words, we informed the governor that we did not require additional revenue from the state's general fund. We were willing to raise our own money with the cooperation of the legislature.

"If you can raise more money through the courts," countered the governor, "the state can use it for better purposes than buying ermine robes for the judges."

Not to be outdone, the governor filed a countersuit against me in the federal court relying on a Civil War–era civil rights provision to argue that elected officials' budget-making decisions could not be overridden by unelected officials. Jack Weinstein, the federal judge who had the case, admonished "the two Titans of New York to avoid an unseemly conflict by negotiating a resolution." He recommended former Secretary of State Cyrus Vance as a mediator. I agreed to participate in a mediation, but the governor refused, holding fast by saying that "the state's fiscal condition was not amenable to negotiation."

Despite the governor's personal involvement in the federal suit (he told reporters that he "was up late every night researching the law"), the suit was dismissed, with costs. The suit that I brought persisted until January 16, 1992. At four-thirty that afternoon the governor and I spoke on the phone and arranged a settlement.

After four months of suits and countersuits as well as trading personal insults the case was settled. The governor agreed not to interfere with our receiving the needed increases, indeed he would not object to our receiving an additional $19 million for an unforeseen contingency.

In the short term we were able to reopen all the courts that had been temporarily closed. And we were able to rehire the five hundred employees who had been laid off, which took place at a mass swearing-in ceremony, attended by their spouses and children as well as by a young governor from Arkansas named Bill Clinton who happened to be in town at the time. In the longer term, I feel we reasserted the independence of the judicial branch of government. The governor has never since interfered with the constitutionally mandated budget.

I believe we won a great victory for the court system, but on a personal level my self-confidence weakened as I grappled with my depression and the "brain tumor." The lawsuit drained me further, and my despair grew. Some people noticed but were ready to buy my excuses: "The limp? Oh, yes. I'm having a terrible time with my back." "I seem down? Well, the lawsuit and the sadness of dismantling a court system which had been doing so well was distressing."

August 5, 1994

This will be another sleepless night, not only from the heat, but from the distress that a newspaper story causes me. In writing of my forthcoming release a reporter tells the world that my stabbing at Butner was self-inflicted. The article notes that this was the conclusion of an F.B.I. investigation.

The F.B.I. never came to that conclusion. Indeed, the location of the stab wounds demonstrates that self-infliction would have been impossible. In fact, if the F.B.I. had come to the conclusion that I filed a false report of an assault and "possessed a sharpened instrument," I would have been guilty of a Code 108 violation under Section 541.13 of prison regulations ("Prohibited Acts and Disciplinary Severity Scale") and would be subject to the same "greatest category" punishment as the offense of killing. Or, if they wanted to be kind, they would simply have found me guilty of the lesser Code 405 offense of self-mutilation.

And if they had come to that conclusion, why in the world would they have put me in solitary confinement "for my protection"? Obviously, if I had stabbed myself, I would not be protected by the solitary confinement because the perpetrator would have been housed with the victim. This never occurred to the members of the reporting press.

Nevertheless, the "self-inflicted wound" story will take on a life of its own and, because it was reported in the press, it will assume an aura of legitimacy.

After my arrest the press had a feeding frenzy in reporting not only what I did—which was bad enough—but also a series of misdeeds that I never did. Of course, retractions were printed, but long after the event and at a time and place where they were never read.

Strange, isn't it? When you read something inaccurately reported about yourself in the press, you realize how irresponsible that medium can be. And yet, when the report concerns someone else, you assume it is correct and accurate.

And here is another irony: After the 1964 landmark case of *Sullivan v. The New York Times* (which concerned the issue of press freedom as opposed to individuals' right to privacy) was decided by the United States Supreme Court, that same court left it to the state courts to determine the standard of responsibility for the press in reporting matters concerning "public figures," in other words, the distance the press had to stray from the truth before it could be held liable for defamation.

In the decision of *Chapadeau v. Utica Press*, New York State gave the press the greatest latitude of any state in the union. That decision set the standard for other states, holding that even if a journalist was negligent in gathering and reporting news, there would be no liability so long as that negligence was not gross or wilful. So even if the reporter who falsely reported the story about my stabbing was negligent, he cannot be held liable. I know, because I wrote *Chapadeau v. Utica Press*.

Of course, in my case the question would really be academic. With me there could not have been a question of defamation: You see, felons are defamation-proof. Even if you prove the wilful publication of a falsehood, the damages would be measured by my loss of reputation, and you cannot damage something that does not exist. At one time my reputation was my life and favorable press reports nurtured and seemed to sustain me. A person seldom seeks service in either of the three branches of government for financial gain. Fifteen years ago, when I was still an associate judge on the New York Court of Appeals, I turned down an offer to head the litigation department of a major New York City law firm. I was offered an annual salary of $1 million. At the time the state was paying me less than $100,000.

Some seek government office for the power it gives them over the lives of others. These people are a danger. They are usually discovered and undone by their own overreaching, corruption, and greed.

Then there are the others, the vast majority of office holders. Ask such a person why he or she chose a political career and the inevitable answer will be that the motivation was "public service," or to "make a better life for generations yet unborn," or "to pay society back for all the advantages I have received," or to discharge "an obligation to serve this great nation/state/city/town and its citizens," or "the intellectual challenge to make things better."

I don't mean to disparage these lofty sentiments. Some of them might even be genuine; at one time or another I felt and expressed every one of them. But now I realize that my motives were not nearly so noble. I also believe that the catalyst for my ambition was the same as the compelling force behind most politicians: ego.

Maybe narcissism. Whatever label is applied, the truth is that vainglory—leaving a legacy of extolled virtue, reading glowing press notices, wanting to be smiled on by an adoring public—these are the things that make most people run for public office. And if they tell you otherwise, they are being dishonest with you or with themselves.

I can now face the fact that this vanity is what brought me into a life of public service.

The process of building a good reputation and a positive image in politics is a painstaking one. If your mission were to sell a product, you could promote the product's qualities by its job performance. If you seek recognition as a leader in business or industry, you show your balance sheet. But when you are running for office for the first time, you can only be measured by the intangibles of your prior service to your family, community, and country.

You start off at a disadvantage because the public is skeptical of a newcomer seeking public office. So what if you are a good father, what are you going to do about taxes? You were a Boy Scout commissioner and chairman of the United Community Fund? Big deal—what are you going to do about the neighborhood crime problem? You served in the army? Wonderful—but what solution do you have for repairing my sidewalk? The first obstacle is to prove your worthiness, to convince them that you are good enough to merit their confidence.

You make promises, and if you're just starting out you want to be certain they are promises you can keep. You will be expected to work hard at your job. The public demands that during the weekdays their elected officials always be around, available and productive. On weekends they are expected to show up at public and political picnics and sporting events. At night they should be in evidence at charity balls and community gatherings. All this they do for the recognition—the vanity.

The day after I took office as town supervisor of the town of North Hempstead, I held an all-night meeting with the four members of my town board. We devised a comprehensive plan addressing many of the town's problems and developed concepts for the growth of our municipality, everything from comprehensive rezoning to the building of parks and the creation of two major urban renewal projects with low- and moderate-income housing. I spent the next three years working ten-hour days to implement those plans. No promise went unfulfilled. I was enormously popular. Although I would not admit it at the time, not even to myself, the popularity meant more to me than the accomplishments.

My popularity was undiminished during my years of public service. My vanity was nurtured by an adoring press. Before I became a judge, reporters and editorial writers were convinced not only that I would be governor but that I would be a great governor. These predictions persisted after I became a judge, but now my virtues as a politician were coupled with accolades concerning my wisdom in general and my judicial wisdom in particular.

When I went into a place where the public gathered, the smiles and nods of approbation; the greetings and salutations—"Your Honor," "If it please the Court," "The Honorable," "Mr. Justice," "Chief Judge," and, best of all, "Judge"—the donning of black robes; everyone rising on command when you enter a courtroom; it all meant so much to me. I wallowed in my vanity.

Because public approbation meant so much to me, the loss of it—so sudden, so swift—was that much more painful.

The press inflicted the most pain of all by printing any number of stories that were sensational and many of which were untrue. I am certain that these stories caused my once adoring public to ask whether the awards and accolades they had bestowed on me were any more of an indication of who I was than my conviction and imprisonment? The stories certainly convinced me of the evanescence of homage. The lifetime I spent accumulating public admiration would have been better spent in pursuit of more lofty or meaningful goals.

August 7, 1994

When Joan's grandfather died, he left a legacy as one of New York's most significant philanthropists. He gained his wealth by being astute enough, while selling glass from a pushcart in Brooklyn, to recognize the potential value in salvaging glass. This was one hundred years ago, and the salvaged glass was from the buildings being torn down to make room for the Brooklyn Bridge.

If we were to search for a Midwest parallel to this unique and innovative story of how millions can be made through a man's imagination, it would be the story of Dale Vogt. He was a farmer living in Atkins, Iowa. One day, responding to a train accident near his farm, it occurred to him that the grain dumped in the wreck could be salvaged and resold. From a family business utilizing shovels, wheelbarrows, and a pickup truck, he and his five sons created the West Side Unlimited Corporation in Cedar Rapids, Iowa.

West Side evolved into a multimillion-dollar corporation involved in coast-to-coast trucking, nationwide salvage operations, worldwide ship discharge services, and distribution and rental of pneumatic conveyors.

Thomas Dean Vogt was the third of the five sons. He was born in 1956. His mother died when he was nine years old, and he worked the farm with his father and brothers while attending school. On graduation from high school he became a mechanic for the Rock Island Railroad. When the family business, West Side Unlimited, started to burgeon, Tom, at the age of twenty, went to work full time for his father helping to turn the family grain salvaging and transferring company into a forty-eight-state service that grossed $40 million in revenue last year.

Tom became an expert in cleaning and transferring grain, using a unique screening device that he designed and constructed in the family shop. He traveled to ports throughout the Third World, bringing badly needed grain to these countries. As the company and Tom's responsibilities grew, so too did his income. He was vice president of the corporation, responsible for overseeing its worldwide operations, and in addition to his six-figure salary was the beneficiary of many corporate perquisites.

This unsophisticated Iowa farm boy found himself being driven in a Lincoln Continental limousine, driving a 560-SL Mercedes convertible, playing aboard his twenty-eight-foot day cruiser, and living in a magnificent twelve-room home in an exclusive neighborhood in Cedar Rapids.

He was a handsome, wealthy bachelor. He was also an alcoholic and drug addict who began using cocaine in 1987. He was arrested in 1988 in Cedar Rapids for cocaine use. A year later, he was admitted to a psychiatric ward and, up to the date of his trial in October 1989, was in and out of hospital treatment every month of the year.

In a speech he made as president of this prison's chapter of Alcoholics Anonymous on December 7, 1991, he described his addiction:

> If there ever was a classic story of an addict that refused to accept the fact of his addiction, it was mine. I've depended on and have been beholden to alcohol for as long as I would care to remember, and when cocaine came on board, wow, it was just that much better and easier to get by. Today would turn into tomorrow and yesterday never really was. Procrastination and acceleration became as one. . . . I had it all. . . . I had alcohol and cocaine. . . .

He had been arrested not for selling cocaine or any other controlled substance but for using it regularly. The government conceded that Tom's involvement with cocaine was on a purely social and not-for-profit basis. He was charged with "conspiring to distribute cocaine, making his house available for cocaine use, and possession with intent to distribute."

The sole predicate for the charges was the fact, not denied by Tom, that he shared cocaine with friends, mostly at parties. His one-month jury trial consisted almost entirely of testimony from his friends, for the government, that they had used cocaine with him in social settings.

The position taken by Tom's lawyers was this: The harsh penalties provided for by the sentencing guidelines were intended to inflict severe punishment on those who trafficked in drugs for profit; the commission on sentencing guidelines never contemplated that these severe penalties would be imposed where the activity did not involve any potential economic gain to the participants. His lawyers might be correct. Indeed, I have never read a reported case where the government has ever successfully prosecuted a not-for-profit conspiracy to distribute drugs.

In order to determine the amount of drugs involved in the conspiracy, the court engaged in a fascinating speculative exercise. For example, on two occasions, Tom bought cocaine from a Keith McVary, a supplier and unindicted co-conspirator. McVary had, or said he had, 283.5 grams of cocaine when he made the two small sales to Tom.

The court made no finding whatsoever that McVary possessed the 283.5 grams in furtherance of the alleged conspiracy. Rather, the court attributed all of McVary's cocaine to Tom on the sole ground "that it was not unreasonable for [Vogt] to foresee that McVary—a drug dealer—would have such a large quantity of drugs on hand."

The court attributed another 250 grams of cocaine as a result of his purchases from another supplier, one Tim Johnson. The court provided no explanation for its determination. It simply picked a number halfway between the amounts that Tom and the government contended Johnson possessed.

Although the guidelines permit the sentencing court to estimate the amount of unseized drugs attributable to a defendant, common sense and case law dictate that there must be some evidence in the record to support the court's estimate. This was not the approach of the judge who sentenced Tom; he ultimately concluded that 861.45 grams of cocaine should be attributed to the "conspiracy."

Consequently, Thomas Dean Vogt, who never sold or attempted to sell cocaine but who illegally gave cocaine to his friends to use while partying, was convicted of "trafficking." As part of his sentence, his vehicles, boat, home, and cars were forfeited to the government. More painful was his prison sentence: 110 months, more than nine years. He was thirty-three years old when he went to trial and will be forty-three when he is released. Too high a price to pay for an addicted user's first offense.

There is another price he will pay, one that he and I can understand. His one sin will forever dim the luster of a family name that the ingenuity and hard work of his father took a lifetime to establish.

August 27, 1994

I'm getting "short" and every inmate here envies me. Being "short" means "they're ready to cut you loose." You have served your time, and you're about to go home.

I have many of the same feelings now as I did when I was serving my last few weeks in the army: the feeling of impending freedom. I rejoice in the knowledge that soon I will be able to embrace my children and grandchildren, be free of fences, jangling keys, barked orders, and humiliation.

Soon I will have privacy, and be able to seek out quiet places. I will do all the things that free people do, like close a bathroom door, or turn on whatever television station I want to watch. I will be able to go to a store to buy whatever I need — or even things I don't need. I'll be able to carry a wallet in my back pocket and use paper money, something I have not seen or touched in over a year. I will even be able to pick up the telephone and call whomever I please whenever

I want, and there will be no one monitoring the call. No one will open my mail but me. And I will be able to drive a car—something else I haven't been able to do for more than a year—and eat wherever, whenever, and whatever I desire.

These simple pleasures and choices are more precious than anyone who has never been without them can imagine.

When I was about to be discharged from the army, I felt optimistic about the future that I was about to begin. Now I have a sense of foreboding about what will happen and how I will be treated when I am back "out on the street."

Thankfully, my seven grandchildren are too young to know where I've been. I dread the day when they find out. How will they deal with the fact that their grandfather was a prisoner? And what about my friends? Many were extraordinary in their support of me before I went to prison. Was that an act of forced compassion that, when I am out and an ex-con, will evaporate? And how will I face the public, the people who in the past elected me to office, only to realize that the man in whom they reposed their faith was imprisoned for the commission of a crime?

And what will I do for employment? I have spent my entire life in public service, but my conduct and imprisonment have placed me beyond consideration for that service. My discipline and training have been in the law, but I am no longer able to practice law.

Teach? I know I could do it well. I have taught many classes and have always felt comfortable in the classroom. I know I could teach the law; the casebooks are filled with decisions I have written and few people know more about appellate advocacy than I. But will any law school have the courage to allow me the privilege of teaching?

When I am freed from prison I will begin another sort of punishment: a form of banishment. When the designers of the sentencing guidelines were calculating their levels and degrees of discipline, they never factored in this harshest of all penalties. God did when He sought to punish Adam and Eve for their transgression. He chose exile. That is what I fear—a form of exile, or shunning, that will disable me for the rest of my life.

And when God punished Cain, he did so by sending him into the world with a mark so that everyone would know of his shame. A mark that must have been very much like a red snake. Very much like the red snake that I saw that first day in Butner.

August 29, 1994

Today I leave prison. My orders from the Bureau of Prisons are explicit. I will be awakened at 4:00 A.M.—which of course will not be necessary. I'm certain that this night will be as sleepless as so many others. At 5:00 A.M. I will be met at the prison gate by my attorney, my son-in-law Paul Montclare, and at 6:10 A.M. I will leave Rochester Airport. After changing planes at Minneapolis, I will continue on to La Guardia, scheduled to arrive at 11:11 A.M.

From La Guardia I am to proceed directly to the Brooklyn House Community Corrections Center, located on Myrtle Avenue in Bedford-Stuyvesant. "MUST AR CCC NO LATER THAN 1:15 PM ON 8-29-94"—so reads my furlough order. "And don't even think about going near your home or family," instructs my unit leader.

I will be free, but not free. After my two months in the Brooklyn House Community Corrections Center, sometimes referred to as a halfway house, I will be able to go home. But I still will not be free. For two years after that, until October 1996, I will be serving a term of "supervised release," a kind of parole, where I will have to report to and be under the supervision of a federal probation officer. And after that? There are all different kinds of freedom—you can be free of chains and bars and still not be free.

Bill Kampiles comes to my room to help me with my few belongings, mostly papers.

He walks me to the receiving room, where I first arrived. I remember arriving in chains and in physical and mental pain. How long ago? I don't remember. But "a lifetime" seems the right answer.

A guard gives me a pair of blue denim pants, a white shirt, socks and underpants, and a pair of brown suedelike Hushpuppy shoes. I'm locked in a very small cell, furnished with only a wooden bench, and told to shed my khakis and get dressed in my newly issued civilian clothes. After a short wait—just long enough to feel again the pain of claustrophobia—a guard escorts me through several barred doors, past a paymaster who puts my accrued wages and unspent commissary funds in my hand, to the gate, where Paul meets me, as planned. We get into the waiting taxi—toward freedom.

When I arrive in New York, Philip is at the gate. Joan stays in the car to avoid the press. Philip embraces me and we both weep, oblivious to the many cameras and shouts from the press. Intelligent newsworthy questions are posed, like "Joy Silverman says she still fears you. Do you intend to see her soon?" And "How does it feel to be moving into a halfway house across the street from a low-income housing project in Bed-Sty? Would you rather be in prison?" And "Why did you stab yourself?" But the best of all was "How was Club Fed?" The myth of my having been in a prison camp, instead of a secure prison, had apparently taken root.

Epilogue

"With my background, I can do one of two things: teach law, or become mayor of Washington, D.C."

"Thank you for telling me how good I look. Your compliment reminds me of the story of John Wesley Hardin. After a lifetime of inflicting physical violence as an outlaw he was gunned down by a longtime sworn enemy. The next day's territorial newspaper carried his obituary, quoting the coroner, who said, 'If it weren't for the fact that Mr. Hardin was dead, he would be in excellent physical condition.' "

"Icebreakers," they are called. Those are the opening lines of the speeches I was prepared to deliver. It would be a lighthearted way of acknowledging my imprisonment and letting my audience know that I am aware of my demise.

The only trouble is, I have received very few invitations to speak.

A few years ago, a taped recording of a speech I delivered before an audience of over five thousand persons at the Chautauqua Institution sold more copies than any other of their presentations that summer. There was a time when I was invited to speak before bar associations and other groups all over the country. Once I delivered twelve addresses in one week in four different states. Over a four-year span, the United States Information Agency sent me to seven European countries as a speaker.

Now, no one is interested in hearing me, although I believe I have more to say than I did then.

I was always told that I was a good teacher. The dean of a law school where I had delivered a commencement address and several discourses once told me that I was one of the most talented lecturers he had ever heard. He went so far as to tell me that if I ever wanted to teach, I would always be welcome at his law school. Of course, when he extended that invitation he had no way of knowing that he was speaking to a soon-to-be convict. I tried twice to reach him by phone after my release from prison. He returned neither call.

I wanted so much to become a part of academia, not only because I thought I would do well teaching law, but also because I thought it a wonderful way to redeem myself.

For a while I thought that redemption was at hand. When I was in prison, Jay C. Carlisle, a law professor at Pace Law School, wrote to me on a regular basis. His letters were addressed to "Chief Judge Wachtler" and were welcome reminders of the world I had left behind. We had met and corresponded when I was still a judge. I was familiar with his legal writings and excellent reputation as a scholar, but we had no association beyond that.

In a series of letters shortly before my release, he urged me to consider teaching law at Pace. He told me that those responsible for making faculty appointments were pleased with the prospect. The idea excited me. I had been associated with the law school at Pace since its inception, had launched its law review, and was the recipient of one of its honorary doctoral degrees. I was the law school commencement speaker in 1992 and Professor Carlisle's invitation brought back memories of a congenial faculty and a bright, receptive student body.

Permission was given for me to leave the halfway house for an afternoon so that I could deliver a lecture to one of Professor Carlisle's classes. I considered it a sort of an audition. The experience was exhilarating. Professor Carlisle wrote me telling of the enthusiasm of the class and that he felt he "learned more than the students."

The newly installed dean of the law school indicated that Pace would be pleased to have me teach, but that because of timing, it would be impossible for my position to be included in the budget for the current year. I told him that I was not interested in being paid. Being given the opportunity to return to the law—to teach the law I had helped write—would be compensation enough.

My assignment was to teach alternate classes in New York Practice with Professor Carlisle. "Team teaching" it is called. It was to be, as the professor wrote me, "the best New York Practice course in the history of the Empire State!"

And it started off that way. The class was well attended, its complement of close to one hundred senior law students attentive, excited, and exciting. Because I had written many of the opinions in the text and had been on the Court of Appeals when almost all of the others were written, I was able to share with the members of the class elements and insights of the court's reasoning not readily apparent from merely reading of the court's decision.

Perhaps there could be a life for me after all; the redemption I hoped for might be at hand.

And then, after some six weeks, Professor Carlisle told me that he had been advised that my services were no longer wanted, that complaints had been received, not about my teaching—which he assured me was "fantastic"—but because there was fear of "criticism" if I were permitted to continue. He asked me to return one more time to say good-bye to the students. I did, telling the students that the only person to be blamed for my unacceptability was me. That I had, by my conduct, forfeited the right to be judged with fairness.

I received many letters from students who were in my classes expressing their gratitude and regret; one even told me, hyperbole I am sure, that he had learned more in that class than he had "during the rest of his law school career." But I never heard from the dean.

I will always be grateful to Professor Carlisle for his concern and assistance. There were so many other law school deans and professors who called on me often and for whom I was always available during my quarter of a century on the bench. I have heard from very few.

My fear of being shunned by the academic community has been realized. I regret that very much, not only because of my personal situation, but because law schools should be among the first to realize that after punishment there should be a degree of forgiveness, mercy, and the opportunity for rehabilitative redemption.

Rosemary Kelly, the daughter of a friend of mine, the late Judge Paul Kelly, headed a large voluntary public service organization, the Educational Assistance Corporation. When I was released from the halfway house, I was able to volunteer my services to work with the various recipients of services from E.A.C.: welfare mothers just released from prison, in need of education and encouragement; teenagers who had disciplinary problems and were considered unsuited for the public school classroom and in need of special education; drug addicts seeking a treatment alternative to imprisonment; and imprisoned AIDS patients in need of hospice care so that they could die free and with dignity.

I performed the five hundred hours of the community service component of my sentence with E.A.C., and my commitment and service to that organization continues.

My desire to speak about what I have learned to be the malfunctioning of the criminal justice system also continues. I have been given a greater insight to the workings of this system than I ever anticipated—or wanted. It enabled me to look into the darker corners and to see what very few people with my background ever see.

It has also brought me wisdom from unexpected sources. For example, various public officials are taking credit for the reduction of violent crime in the cities; however, I believe the major cause is reflected in the analysis of one of my erstwhile companions. He predicted this would happen because of the substituted street use of heroin ("which puts you on the nod") for crack cocaine ("which makes you act crazy and break heads"). His other prediction is that methamphetamine, or speed—another drug of violence—will soon replace heroin. I hope he is wrong in that prediction.

Recently the National Criminal Justice Commission, a project of the National Center on Institutions and Alternatives, issued its report on the criminal justice system in America. The report discusses familiar issues from a fresh perspective and presents statistics that support many of the anecdotal impressions I formed in prison. To name but one: There are over eleven million admissions to prison or jail in the course of a year in this country. Less than 3 percent of these relate to a violent crime.

The report confirms that drug treatment works, and that it is far less expensive than putting addicts in prison. It also demonstrates that mandatory minimum sentences are counterproductive and that the justice system itself with its blunt instrument of imprisonment appears to be destabilizing our American society. The nation rails at men who abandon children—and then locks them up for ten-year mandatory sentences; demands that they find work—and then saddles them with criminal records no employer will come near; extols education—and then transfers the budget from schools to the prisons.

In 1996 the Rand Corporation released a comprehensive study that compares the cost of protracted prevention programs with that of more politically popular, mandated lengthy sentences. The study demonstrates conclusively that prevention programs deter crime more effectively and in a less costly manner than long-term imprisonment.

I would love to talk about these things. Unfortunately, there are very few people interested in hearing them.

• • •

My mental health has improved. I am still being treated by my psychiatrist, Dr. Solomon, and still take medication. My depression, which Dr. Miller first suspected and later convinced me was a matter of genetics and biochemistry, has responded well to medicine and treatment. I have not experienced any recent bouts with mania, and am able to be engaged in a constructive enterprise.

In the spring of 1991, in an address at the Harvard Law School, I made an appeal for the increased use of alternative forms of dispute resolution, the resolution of conflict between individuals and corporations by arbitration or mediation instead of the courtroom. I felt then, as I feel now, that our courts, and the taxpayers who support them, can no longer bear the financial burden of private litigation.

Now, with the advice and assistance of such good friends as R. Preston Tisch, Fred Wilpon, and John Rosenwald, I have started a business: Comprehensive Alternative Dispute Resolution Enterprise, Inc. (CADRE), which has a roster of distinguished mediators, arbitrators, and retired jurists available to settle disputes through mediation or binding arbitration. The mission of CADRE is to provide a quicker, less costly forum for the resolution of civil disputes outside our crowded courtrooms. I do not draw a salary, and all profits are donated to legal services for the poor.

When I was in prison, one of my fellow inmates, a former F.B.I. agent, asked me the rhetorical question, "Whoever thought we would end up like this?" If I were able to answer him today, I would say, "I'm not ending up—just beginning again."

I begin by knowing more about a world I had dealt with all my adult life but never saw; more about mortal weakness and the frailty of the human spirit and how little we understand about those we condemn. I have learned a great deal more about myself.

I have also learned the importance of friends and family, those who are unflinching in their devotion and attention. Every person who is in a position of significance should fall from grace just long enough to sort the wheat of true friendship from the chaff of opportunistic association. These friends and my family have encouraged and have convinced me that I am capable of living a good and productive life. A new beginning.

Index

A

Abscam trials, 89
Accetturo, Tony, 274–75, 278
Admissions and Orientation, 220,
    244–45
Adultery, 185–86
AIDS, 80–82, 246
Aiuppa, Joey (Doves), 164–66
Alexander, Fritz, 251
Alfano brothers, 283
Altimari, Angela, 142–43, 146
Altimari, Frank, 142–43, 144–46
American Bar Association, 195
American College of Physicians and Sur-
    geons, 246
American Law Institute, 92, 114
American Zionist movement, 111
Ames, Aldrich (C.I.A. agent), 237, 320
Amnesty, 111
Amuso, Vittorio , 276–77
Anderson, Alexander (Butner inmate),
    41
Angelini, Donal (Angel), 283
Angell, Arlen, 178, 195
Apperson, Jay, 273–74

Arrest of Wachtler
    and bail, 36, 105
    charges in, 100, 101, 294–95
    by F.B.I., 18, 97–104, 197
    and hospitalization, 5–7, 19, 105–10,
        130, 234
    and media, 335, 338–39
    and tests and diagnosis of illness, 5–7,
        71, 105–10, 130, 315
Asche, Sidney, 264
Atlanta prison (Georgia), Marielitos at,
    226
Attica prison (New York state), 92, 212,
    218, 223–24
Auburn prison (New York state), 222
Austin & Dupont, 144

B

Baker, Mark, 138, 139
Bank fraud, sentencing guidelines for,
    193–94
Barnes, Leroy (Nicky), 253, 256
"Beating the man," 238–40, 242
Beetlejuice, attempted suicide of, 113

Bellacosa, Joseph, 133, 134–35, 140, 249, 263, 267, 314
Ben Sorek, Esor, 204
Bill of Rights, U.S., 61–62, 190. *See also* *specific amendment*
Bipolar disorder
  drugs as factor in, 4, 10, 13, 289, 304
  and family history, 6, 352
  and sentencing of Wachtler, 115–16
  symptoms of, 12–14, 19
  tests and diagnosis for, 5–7, 71, 105–10, 130, 287–88, 315
  treatment for, 19, 352
  See also Depression; Mania episodes
Black box, 149
Black, Sonny, 282–83
Blackmun, Harry, 181–83
Blacks, and drug crimes, 265
Blood tests, 172
Blowing Rock, North Carolina, Wachtler's childhood in, 43–51
Blumberg, Stephen, 199–200
Bolle, Stan, 23, 205
Bonfire of the Vanities (Tom Wolfe), 292
Book thievery, 199–200
Boyce, Christopher, 318–19
Brain tumor
  and imaginary illness of Wachtler, 4, 9, 10, 142, 163, 230, 288–89, 334
  of Lake, 163
Brasco, Donnie , 281–82
Braunstein, Alison (daughter), 25, 102, 107, 108, 109–10, 134, 147, 232
Braunstein, Barry (son-in-law), 134, 232
Broken ribs, of Wachtler, 304–5, 311–13
Brooklyn House Community Corrections Center. *See* Halfway house
Brooklyn, New York, Wachtler's childhood in, 83–87
Brown, Lee, 251
Brown v. Board of Education (1954), 62
"Bucking," 223
Burden, Amanda, 252
Burger, Warren, 181
Bush, George
  attempted assassination of, 57–58
  and drug war, 265–66
  and Horton issue, 191–92
  Weinberger pardon by, 111
Butner prison (North Carolina)
  Admissions and Orientation at, 244–45
  Bureau of Prisons' decision to place Wachtler in, 27
  escapes from, 75
  family visits at, 79–80, 82
  as federal correctional institution, 78
  general population at, 38–42, 58–59, 69
  jobs at, 57, 243–44
  Mental Health Division at, 34–35, 52–58, 68–70, 77–78
  physical conditions at, 42, 153
  prisoners' attitudes toward Wachtler at, 58–59, 77–78
  protection for Wachtler at, 59
  Rochester compared with, 153, 231–32, 321
  safety of Wachtler at, 39, 41, 74, 124, 125, 335
  stabbing of Wachtler at, 118–22, 124–29, 130–32, 334–35
  tests and diagnosis of Wachtler at, 71, 124–25, 141–42
  visitors for Wachtler at, 76–77, 79–80, 82, 131, 132, 134, 142–43, 145–46
  Wachtler in solitary confinement at, 30–38, 42, 52, 112, 119–22, 124–29, 130–33, 140–42, 146–47, 335
  Wachtler's anxiety about going to, 24–26
  Wachtler's first day at, 27–30
  See also specific person

C

Cabey, Darryl, 135–36, 137
California
  death penalty in, 160
  drug treatment in, 268
Campbell, Dr. (Rochester prison doctor), 183, 184
Capital cases
  costs of, 160
  See also Death penalty
Carlisle, Jay C., 348–50

Carlyle, Thomas, 169
Carter, Zachary W., 277
Castellano, Paul, 279–81
Castillo, Miguel, 246
Castro, Bernadette, 157
Caval, Joseph, 283
Central Intelligence Agency (C.I.A.),
    209, 315–20
Chambers, Whittaker, 59–60
Champagne (Rochester inmate),
    309–11, 313
Chapadeau v. Utica Press, 336
Chekhov, Anton Pavlovich, 240
Chertoff, Michael
    and arrest of Wachtler, 103, 104,
        105–6, 107, 109, 196
    and charges against Wachtler, 295
    and house arrest of Wachtler, 36, 130
    and media, 105–6, 130, 195, 295
    and mental illness of Wachtler, 6,
        130, 154, 315
    and nurturing of Wachtler criminal
        behavior, 19–20, 196
    and Wachtler case as high-profile
        case, 195, 196–97
Chesterton, G. K., 70
Chicago Police Department, 297, 298–99
Chief Justice
    appointment of Wachtler as, 63–65,
        292
    perquisites of, 234–35
    resignation of Wachtler as, 129
    responsibilities of, 37–38
Chiodo, Peter, 276–77
Choi, Chet, 166–68
Christmas holidays, 154–55
Clinton, Bill, 111, 112, 292, 334
Coal mine violations, 162–64
Cocaine
    and Johnson (James) case, 301–3
    and Lawrence case, 270, 271
    and Manasses case, 298–301
    and Reynolds case, 301–3
    and Vogt case, 340–42
    See also Crack cocaine
Codeine, 9
Committee on Codes (New York State
    Assembly), 224

Community courts, 251–52
Community service, of Wachtler, 350
Commutation, 111
"Compassionate release," 245–47
Competency, 113–15
Comprehensive Alternative Dispute Res-
    olution Enterprise, Inc. (CADRE),
    352
Comprehensive Crime Control Act
    (1984), 115
Conference of Chief Justices, 288
Confessions
    and *Miranda*, 169–72
    and Putnam case, 187
Congregate system, 222
Conjugal visits. *See* Family visits
Conspiracy
    and drug crimes, 253–54, 341–42
    and Lawrence case, 270–73
    not-for-profit, 341–42
Constitution, U.S.
    and Cubans, 226
    differing interpretations of, 62–63
    as ideal reflection of aspirations,
        61–62
    and *Miranda*, 169–70
    and presidential powers, 111
    and punishment, 30
    See also Bill of Rights, U.S.; *specific
        amendment*
"Controlled movement," 181, 285–86
Cooperation
    and conspiracy laws, 253–54
    and drug crimes, 253–54, 273,
        302–3
    and racketeering, 278–84
    and sentencing, 281, 325
    See also Snitches
Corporal punishment, 223. *See also*
    Death penalty
Corrao, Joseph (Joey Butch), 283
Cortina, Dominick, 283
Counterfeiters. *See* Jim
Counts, 117–18, 221, 313–14
Court Facilities Law (New York, 1987),
    250
Courthouses, infrastructure of New York
    state, 249–50

Courts
   as extension of prosecutors' offices,
      274
   overwhelming number of cases in,
      265
Crack cocaine, 264, 266, 289, 351
Cranford, Ronald, 288–89
Crime
   drugs as cause of, 269
   and prevention programs, 351
   punishment as means for disappear-
      ance of, 222
   See also Nonviolent crimes; Violent
      crimes
Crime Bill, 92, 176, 326
Crime families, 164–66, 274–84
Criminal justice system, report about
   American, 351
Criminal predisposition, 89, 90
Crosson, Matt, 247, 249, 251, 331, 332
"Cruel and unusual" punishment,
   30–32, 303
Cuban prisoners, 225–28
Cuomo, Mario
   and court system budget, 16, 289–90,
      330–34
   and death penalty, 159, 160
   swearing-in of, 156–57, 290
   Wachtler sues, 332–34
   Wachtler's relationship with, 63–65,
      289

D

D'Arco, Alphonse, 279
Darrow, Clarence, 70
Dearie, Ray, 277
Death penalty, 159–61
Decision Making Regarding Life Sus-
   taining Medical Treatment (LSMT)
   Project, 288
Declaration of Independence, 61–62
Deer, Dan, 23, 95–97
Defendants' rights, 191. See also
   Miranda v. Arizona
Depression
   of Choi, 167
   of Jack, 72–73

   of Lorenzo, 225
   symptoms of, 4, 7, 9, 10, 16, 72,
      287–89
   See also Bipolar disorder
Depression of Wachtler
   after release from prison, 352
   at Butner, 70, 142
   and court budget fight, 331, 334
   following arrest, 130
   Joan Wachtler's concerns about, 7, 8
   medications for, 4, 9–10, 13, 16,
      72–73, 97–98, 142, 289, 304, 352
   and memories of Wachtler, 64
   onset of, 3–5, 287–89
   at Rochester, 154, 207
   and Silverman relationship, 5, 9,
      329
   See also Bipolar disorder; Imaginary
      illness
Dershowitz, Alan, 58
"Diminished capacity," 116, 168
Dinkins, David, 251
Dispute resolution, 352
Double Life (Linda Wolfe), 314, 315
Dred Scott decision (1857), 62
Drug crimes
   and blacks, 265
   and conspiracy, 253–54, 341
   and cooperation, 253–54, 273, 302–3
   and crime families, 280–81
   and interdiction, 266
   and "kingpins," 253, 254, 273
   and law enforcement, 265–66, 269
   nonviolent, 220
   and police corruption, 256, 297,
      298–99
   sentencing for, 177, 178, 194, 220,
      237, 255, 263–64, 265–66, 267,
      269, 271–73, 302–3, 325, 341–42
   and violence, 266
   Wachtler's proposals concerning,
      266–69
   See also Drug dealers
Drug dealers
   and Jim as counterfeiter, 76
   sentencing for, 265, 273, 302–3, 325
Drug Enforcement Administration, 76,
   174, 300

Drugs
  Bush administration war on, 265–66
  education about, 268, 269, 303
  government involvement with, 208–9
  increase in use of, 191
  percentage of crimes related to, 265
  and police corruption, 297, 298–99
  smuggling of, 208–9
  treatment for, 267–69, 271, 303, 351
  and violent crimes, 264
  See also Drug crimes; Drug dealers;
    Medications; *specific drug*
Due process of law, 190

E

Eagan, Marjorie (daughter), 25, 102,
    107, 108, 109–10, 134, 147
Eagleton, Thomas, 9
Education, about drugs, 268, 269, 303
Educational Assistance Corporation, 350
Elbow injury of Wachtler, 140, 142, 146,
    150
Elections of 1964, 145
Elections of 1988, 191–92
Electric chair, 159–60
England
  grand juries in, 293
  prisons in, 222
Entrapment, 88–90
Espionage
  and Ames case, 237
  and Kampiles case, 315–20
  and Miller case, 235–36, 237
  and Pollard case, 110–12
  sentencing for, 319–20
Eto, Ken, 165
Evaluation of Wachtler. *See* Psychiatric
    evaluations of Wachtler
Exclusionary rule, 206–7

F

Family visits, 79–83
Federal Bureau of Investigation (FBI)
  and Aiuppa, 164
  arrest of Wachtler by, 18, 97–104, 105,
    109, 197, 295
  and Barnes-Johnson (Reggie) case, 256
  and Blumberg book case, 200
  and Bolle case, 206, 207
  and entrapment, 89–90
  and Johnson (James) case, 302
  and media, 295
  and Miller (Richard) case, 235–36,
    237, 320
  and monitoring of inmate telephone
    calls, 296
  in movies, 65–66
  and organized crime, 164, 282–83
  and Pepe's bank robberies, 168
  and Putnam case, 184–87
  and search and seizures, 206, 207
  and stabbing of Wachtler, 121, 125,
    126, 128, 334–35
  statistics about marijuana by, 177
  surveillance of Wachtler by, 18, 19,
    77, 104, 197
  and Tony's bank robberies, 73–74
  undercover agents for, 282
Federal correctional institutions, 78–79
Federal Medical Center (F.M.C.). *See*
    Rochester prison (Minnesota)
Federal penitentiaries, 79, 221, 246
Federal prison camps, 27, 78
Federal Prison Industries, Inc., 243–44
Feinberg, Herbert (Mickey), 285–87
Feinblatt, John, 252
Ferguson, Colin, 159, 161
Fernandez (Marielito), 226–28
Fifth Amendment
  and due process, 190
  and grand juries, 294
  and Marijuana Stamp Act, 172
  and *Miranda*, 169–72
Fink, Stanley, 224
First Amendment
  and freedom of speech, 63
  and KKK members as guards, 213–18
First-time offenders, sentencing for,
    263–64, 265, 267, 303
5k1.1 letter, 281
Flaubert, Gustave, 199
Florida
  Wachtler family in, 123, 143, 305–7
  Wachtler's trip with mother to, 7–8

Food service
    and "beating the man," 238–39
    boycott at Rochester about, 322–23
    and dehumanization of prisoners,
        260–61
    and Italian prisoners, 284–85
    for Jews in prison, 201–4, 296
    prisoner complaints about, 321–23
    quality of, 321–23
    and ritualistic qualities of mealtime,
        94, 240–42
    and shakedown after meals, 241–42
Four o'clock counts, 117–18, 221, 314
Fourth Amendment, and search and
    seizure, 62–63, 206–7
Fox, Jim, 103
Frankl, Viktor, 91
Franks, Lucinda, 295
Fratianno, Aladena (Jimmy the Weasel),
    165
Freedom of association, and KKK mem-
    bers as guards, 213–18
Frosch, William, 5–7
Fund for the City of New York, 252

G

Gabel, Roger, 23, 244–47, 285
Garcia (Rochester inmate), 158
Giacone, Philip (Philly Lucky), 282
Giuliani, Rudolph, 157
Giuseppe, Don, 283
Goetz, Bernhard, 135–39
Goland, Michael, 201–2, 203–4, 244,
    283–84, 296
"Good cop, bad cop" routine, 121, 125
Gotti, John , 275, 276, 277, 279–81
Gotti, Peter, 277
Gould, David, 247–48
Government, U.S., and drug smuggling,
    208–9
Grand juries, 291–94, 295
Gravano, Salvatore (Sammy the Bull),
    165, 276, 279–80, 281
Guards
    and helplessness of prisoners, 218–20
    and judges' visits to prisons, 225
    Ku Klux Klan members as, 213–18

and movie-seats matter, 328–29
and transfer of Wachtler from Butner
    to Rochester, 149
treatment of prisoners by, 41–42,
    210–20, 239–40, 260–61, 267, 325
and visitors, 231–32
Guay, Richard, 282–83

H

Halcion, 4, 9, 10, 13
Haldol, 113
Halfway house
    Goland released to, 296
    Wachtler denied release to, 237–38
    Wachtler released to, 20, 344–45
Hanover, Donna, 157
Harassment cases, 198
Harrison, Mr. (Rochester inmate),
    157–58
Harvard Law School, Wachtler address
    at, 352
Hawk, Kathleen, 312
Heffner, Richard, 247
Helicopter pilot (Rochester inmate),
    231–32
Hell's Angels, 127
Henry, David, 320
The Hermit, 174–77
Heroin, 253, 264, 266, 351
Hinkley, John W., Jr., 115
Hoffmann, Ted, 144–45
Honor, among crime families, 274–75,
    278
Horton, Willie, 191–92
House arrest, of Wachtler, 19, 25, 36,
    129–30
"How Prisons Save Lives" (Rosenthal),
    263, 264
Hughes (threats against president),
    158–59

I

Ianiello, Matty the Horse, 275
Imaginary illness, brain tumor as
    Wachtler's, 4, 9, 10, 142, 163, 230,
    289, 334

Indelicato, Anthony Bruno, 282
Indelicato, Anthony (Sonny Red), 282
Individual rights, in prison, 28
Informers. See Cooperation; Snitches
Insanity/sanity plea, 113–16, 200
Interdiction, 266
Internal Revenue Service (IRS), and
    Feinberg case, 286

J

Jack (Butner inmate), 71–73
Jails, 221
Jamal ("beating the man"), 241–42
Jamison, Kay Redfield, 19
Jews
    law and tradition of, 111–12
    in North Carolina, 43–45, 49–50
    and Pollard case, 111–12
    in prison, 201–4, 296
    and Wachtler's childhood, 43–45,
        49–50
Joannides, George, 317–18, 319
Jobs
    at Butner prison, 57, 243–44
    at Rochester prison, 325
    See also UNICOR; UNISAT
Johnson, James, 302
Johnson, Reggie, 23, 256
Johnson, Sally, 128, 141
Jonas, Milton, 224
Jones, Elisha, 252–53
Journal of Wachtler
    case histories in, 22–23
    reasons for, 20, 21
    and stabbing of Wachtler, 120, 126
Judges
    conservative appointments of, 192
    and effects of decisions, 30–31
    and exclusionary rule, 206–7
    and interpretations of Constitution,
        62–63
    need for independence of, 274, 332
    public opinion as influence on, 191,
        237
    responsibilities of, 30–31, 61–62, 63
    sentencing discretion of, 192–95,
        196–98, 263, 267

visits to prisons by, 91–92, 220–21,
    223–24, 312
See also Courts
"Judicial notice," 216–17
"Justification statue," 137–39
Juveniles, in prison, 53–55

K

Kafka, Franz, 99
Kampiles, William (Bill) (Rochester
    inmate), 284, 315–20, 344–45
Kaye, Judith, 134
Keating, Bob, 251
Kelly, Mike, 23, 192–93
Kelly, Paul, 350
Kelly, Rosemary, 350
"Kingpins," 253, 254–56, 273. See also
    specific person
Kipling, Rudyard, 260
Klein, Donald F., 10, 315
Koch, Edward, 156
Kramer, Marcia, 292
Ku Klux Klan, 213–18
Kuby, Ronald L., 197–98
Kunstler, William M., 197–98

L

LaFarge, Jack, 23, 43–45, 48
Lake, Arvil, 161–64, 166
Lanman, Geraldine, 108–9
Law enforcement
    arbitrariness of, 189–98
    and cooperation, 278–84
    and drug crimes, 269
    and independence of judiciary, 274
    and war on drugs, 265–66
"Law-and-order" issues, 190–92
Lawrence, Martin Thomas, 270–73
Leavenworth prison (Kansas), Marielitos
    at, 226
Lee, Daulton, 318–19
Legal knowledge/assistance, of prisoners,
    40–41, 89–90, 127, 205–7, 219
Leonetti, Crazy Phil, 279
Life support systems, withdrawal of, 288
Lithium, 19, 207

Locascio, Frank, 279
Lonardo, Angelo, 165
Long Island Jewish Hospital, 105–10,
    287–88
Longtree, Clayton, 320
Love
    and absence, 80
    importance to inmates of, 134
    and sex, 83–87
LSD, 166–67

M

McCrory, Jim, 23, 56, 59, 117
McGuire, John, 182
McHugh, Betty, 23, 46–48, 49, 50, 86
McHugh, Claude, 49–51
McIntyre, John S., 12
McNaughton rule, 114, 115
McVary, Keith, 341
Magnuson, Paul A., 178, 195
Mail, for Wachtler, 82–83, 232, 314
Mainline, 240, 323
Maliozzo, Nick, 283
Manasses, Spyridos (Sam), 296–301
Mangano, Venero (Benny Eggs), 275,
    277–78, 279
Mania episodes
    characteristics of, 11–12
    and Silverman relationship, 17, 315
    of Wachtler, 10–12, 16, 17, 98, 207,
        315, 352
    See also Bipolar disorder
Manic-depressive disorder. See Bipolar
    disorder
Margolick, David, 196
Marielitos, 225–28
Marijuana, 173–78, 208–9, 264, 270,
    292, 324–25
Marshall, Thurgood, 181
Martin, Harold, 154
Matter of Curly v. Benjamin Ward, Com-
    missioner, 213–18
Max (lawyer inmate), 23, 58
Mayo Clinic, 163, 183
Media
    and appointment of Wachtler as Chief
        Judge, 292

and arrest of Wachtler, 6, 105–6, 295,
    335, 338–39
and drug crimes, 255
F.B.I. leaks to, 295
and grand jury indictments, 294
and house arrest of Wachtler, 130
and Miller and Ames espionage cases,
    237
and press standard of responsibility,
    335–36
and prosecutors, 295
and public service, 338
and release of Wachtler, 345
and stabbing of Wachtler, 121,
    127–29, 334–35, 336
and Wachtler's first day in prison, 27
    See also specific newspaper or reporter
Medications
    for bipolar disorder, 19, 207, 352
    for broken ribs of Wachtler, 304–5,
        313
    as contributor to Wachtler's illness, 4,
        10, 13, 289, 304
    for depression, 4, 9–10, 13, 16, 72–73,
        97–98, 142, 289, 304, 352
    and stabbing of Wachtler, 119, 128
    for Wachtler after release, 352
    for Wachtler at Butner, 69, 142
    for Wachtler at Rochester, 207, 304–5,
        312, 313
    Wachtler's withdrawal from, 19
    See also Drugs
Meko, Mr. (Butner prison official),
    128–29
Memorial Day, 257–61
Methamphetamines, 351
Midtown Community Court (New York
    City), 251–52
Milford Academy (Milford, Connecti-
    cut), 306–9
Military service, of Wachtler, 44, 97,
    123–24, 143, 171, 197, 233–34,
    343
Miller, Frank T., 5–7, 13, 17, 352
Miller, Richard W. (FBI inmate),
    235–36, 237, 320
Miranda v. Arizona, 169–72, 191
Model Penal Code, 92, 114

Mollen, Milton, 256

Montaigne, Michel, 195

Montclare, Lauren (daughter)
    and arrest of Wachtler, 102, 103–4,
        107, 108, 109–10
    birth/birthdays of, 124, 233
    Butner visits by, 79–80, 82, 134
    childhood of, 233–34
    marriage of, 283
    Rochester visits by, 233
    and stabbing of Wachtler, 128, 129
    and Wachtler's preparation for going
        to prison, 25

Montclare, Paul (son-in-law)
    and arrest of Wachtler, 103–4, 105,
        107
    Butner visits by, 76–77, 134
    law firm of, 283
    and release of Wachtler, 344, 345
    Rochester visits of, 233
    and stabbing of Wachtler, 128, 129

Mood swings, 10–12. See also Bipolar
    disorder

Morrisey, John (Sonny Blue), 275, 276,
    277

Movies, in prisons, 326–29

Moyers, Bill, 209

Murderers
    juveniles as, 53–54
    and Putnam case, 184–87
    and Tony's case, 53–55
    and Ziggy's case, 57, 93

Murdoch, Laurie, 248

N

Narcotic Addiction Control Commis-
    sion, 268

Nassau County, New York
    Republican politics in, 145
    Wachtler as official in, 60, 70, 171,
        259–60, 338
    Wachtler's friendships in, 232
    Wachtler's legal practice in, 144–45

National Center on Institutions and Al-
    ternatives, 351

National Criminal Justice Commission,
    351

National Depressive and Manic-Depres-
    sive Association, 10

Native Americans
    as prisoners, 203–4
    See also Champagne

The New Jersey Law Journal, 295

New World newspaper, 159

New York Daily News, 127–28, 292

New York Hospital—Cornell Medical
    Center. See Payne Whitney Psychi-
    atric Clinic

New York state
    corporal punishment in, 223
    courthouse infrastructure in, 249–50
    See also specific agency or court

New York State Bar Association, 61, 97,
    234

New York State Court of Appeals
    and Matter of Curly v. Benjamin
        Ward, Commissioner, 213–18
    procedures in, 214–16
    resignation of Wachtler from, 129
    and sentencing issues, 263–64
    Wachtler's career with, 60–65
    Wachtler's responsibilities on, 38
    and Wilkinson v. Skinner, 30–32

New York State Office of Court Adminis-
    tration
    budget for, 16, 289–90, 330–34
    laying off of personnel in, 332–2
    Wachtler's reforms while at, 249–52
    Wachtler's responsibilities for, 38

New York State Supreme Court,
    Wachtler appointed to, 60

The New York Times
    and death penalty, 159
    Pollard article in, 110, 111
    Rosenthal's column in, 262–63
    sentencing guidelines article in, 196
    and Wachtler's arrest, 106

The New Yorker magazine, 295

Newsweek magazine, 333

Nickerson, Eugene, 60

Nixon, Richard M., 174, 190–91

Nonviolent crimes
    and purpose of prisons, 22, 266–67
    sentencing for, 220, 264, 267, 269
    See also Drug crimes

O

Oakdale prison (Louisiana), Marielitos at, 226
Obermaier, Otto, 103, 283
Obstruction of justice, 271, 303, 325
O'Connor, Theresa (aka Wachtler), 15–16, 17
Omertá (Mafia code of silence), 274–75
Orena, Victor, 279
Organized Crime Control Act (1970), 275

P

Pace Law School, 348–50
Pamelor, 4, 9
Paolone, Luciano, 283
Pardons, 111
Payne Whitney Psychiatric Clinic (New York City), 6, 129, 130
Pepper, Jerry, 307, 308
Percogesic, 9
Personal items, of prisoners, 33–34, 243
Peters, Anthony J. (Tony), 255–56
Peters, Larry, 255
Pistone, Dave, 23, 59, 117, 127
Pistone, Joe (undercover F.B.I. agent), 282
Plea bargaining, 271–72, 330
Plessy v. Ferguson (1896), 62
Police corruption, 256, 297, 298–99
Political contributions, 201
Pollard, Jonathan, 110–12, 116–17
Powell, Lewis, 181
Precedents, 138–39
Predisposition, criminal, 89, 90
Preliminary hearings, 294
President, U.S.
  powers of, 111
  See also *specific person*
Presumption of innocence, 36, 294, 303
Prevention programs, 351
Priestley, J. B., 180
Prison gangs, 55
Prison officials
  and "beating the man," 238–40
  and food boycott at Rochester, 322–23
  and movie censorship, 327
  prisoners talking with, 180–81, 238
  See also Guards; *specific person*
Prisoners
  aging of, 246–47
  attitudes toward Wachtler of, 58–59, 77–78, 227–28
  and "beating the man," 238–40
  brotherhood among, 238–42
  and choosing attitudes about prisons, 91
  clubs and organizations for, 326–27
  and compassionate release, 245–47
  complaints about law enforcement by, 188–95
  Cubans as, 225–28
  defamation of character of, 336
  dehumanization of/respect for, 41–42, 126, 179–80, 210–20, 227–28, 239–40, 260–61, 267, 325
  family attachments of, 80–82
  helplessness of, 218–20
  Italians as, 284–85
  Jews as, 201–4, 296
  and legal knowledge/assistance, 40–41, 89–90, 127, 205–7, 219
  narrow world of, 290–91
  Native Americans as, 203–4
  petitions by, 236–38
  prison officials talking with, 180–81, 238
  public indifference to lot of, 218–19
  reform of, 219–20
  released, 80
  rights of, 28
  rules of, 328–29
  and snitches, 238, 253
  suicide/attempted suicide by, 69, 79, 113, 225
  veterans as, 257–59, 260
  wages of, 243–44, 327
  See also Rehabilitation; *specific person*
Prisons
  categories of, 78–79, 221
  devil in, 87–88
  in England, 222
  increase of population in, 191, 194–95
  inmate rights in, 28
  jobs in, 57, 243–44, 325

judges' visits to, 91–92, 220–21, 223–25, 312
juveniles in, 53–55
as miniature versions of world, 69–70
movies in, 326–29
mythology about life in, 20–22, 224, 225, 326, 327
and public safety, 22, 92, 259, 264, 266–67
purpose of, 22, 92, 219, 222, 259, 264, 266–67
and rehabilitation, 22, 178, 219, 222, 259, 266–67
synonyms for, 92
who should be in, 92–97, 263–69
See also specific prison
Prosecutors
abuse of powers by, 190–91, 195
and conspiracy laws, 254
courts as extension of offices of, 274
and drug crimes, 271
and grand juries, 292–93, 294, 295
and media, 295
and sentencing, 195, 196–98, 271, 273, 274
See also Chertoff, Michael
Prozac, 72–73, 142, 207
Psychiatric evaluation of Wachtler
and arrest, 5–7, 71, 105–10, 130
at Butner, 71, 124–25, 141–42
at Rochester, 153–54, 172
Psychiatrists
stigma of seeing, 4, 8, 9
See also specific person
Public figures, and press standard of responsibility, 335–36
Public safety, and purpose of prisons, 22, 92, 259, 264, 266–67
Public service, 336–39
Punishment
alternative, 267
banishment as form of, 343–44
corporal, 223
"cruel and unusual," 30–32, 303
and disappearance of crime, 222
and purpose of prisons, 266–67
types of, 223
See also Death penalty; Sentencing

Purdy, David (aka Wachtler), 6, 7, 13–18
Putnam, Mark, 184–87

R

Racism, and KKK members as guards, 213–18
Racketeer Influenced and Corrupt Organization law (RICO), 189–90, 275–77, 281, 282–83
Racketeering
and crime families, 274–84
and Travel Act, 294–95
See also Racketeer Influenced and Corrupt Organization law (RICO); *specific person*
Ramseur, James, 135–36
Rand Corporation, 351
Rapists, 94–97. *See also* Deer, Dan
Rastelli, Philip (Rusty), 282
Reagan, Ronald, 115, 143
Recreation
at Butner prison, 37, 65–66
at Rochester prison, 309–11, 326–29
Redemption
of Wachtler, 348, 349, 350
See also Rehabilitation
Rehabilitation
and administration of prisons, 219
and Auburn system, 222
and drug crimes, 267–69, 271, 303
and guards' abuses and brutality, 220
and nonviolent offenders, 22, 266–67
prisons as deterrent to, 178, 219, 259
and purpose of prisons, 22, 219, 222, 266–67
and Putnam case, 187
of young offenders, 54
Release of Wachtler
anxiety about, 342–44
supervised, 344
and trip to halfway house, 344–45
See also Halfway house
Religiosity, of Pepe, 168–69
Reynolds, Danny, 301–3
Rhodes, Kenneth, 200
"Richard Cory" (poem), 8
Roberts, Burton, 194–95

Rochester prison (Minnesota)
  Admissions and Orientation at, 220,
    244, 245
  attitudes of prisoners toward Wachtler
    at, 227–28
  Butner compared with, 153, 231–32,
    321
  cellmates of Wachtler at, 161–64,
    166–67, 201–2, 296–301, 324–25
  judges' visits to, 220–21, 223, 224–25,
    312
  medical treatment for Wachtler at,
    183–84, 311–13
  physical conditions at, 20–21, 153,
    154, 224, 323–24
  psychiatric diagnosis of Wachtler at,
    153–54, 172
  recreation at, 309–11, 326–29
  visitors for Wachtler at, 164, 181–83,
    228, 231, 232, 233, 247–48
  Wachtler assigned to Mental Health
    Unit at, 161
  Wachtler transferred to, 142, 147–50
  Wachtler's job at, 235
  work cadre at, 172–73, 244
Rockefeller, Nelson, 60, 266, 268
Roselli, Johnny, 165
Rosenblatt, Albert, 249
Rosenthal, A. M. (Abe), 262–63, 264,
    265, 269
Rosenwald, John, 352
Ruggiero, Benjamin (Lefty Guns),
    282–83
Ruggiero, Louis, 283–84
Russell, Judy G., 197–98
Ryan, Ray, 165

S

Safety
  of Wachtler at Butner prison, 39, 41,
    74, 124, 125, 335
  See also Public safety
Salerno, Anthony (Fat Tony), 275, 283
Samson, David, 13–14, 16, 329
Sanders, Paul (Butner inmate), 40
Savino, Peter (organized crime), 276
Scarfo, Nicodemo (Little Nicky), 279

Schloth, Neil (security officer), 108, 180
Schoolteachers, and urine testing, 66–67
Search and seizures, 206–7
Seclusion. See Solitary confinement
Self-incrimination, 169–72
Self-surrender, 197, 198
Sentencing
  and aging of prisoners, 246–47
  and community courts, 252
  and cooperation, 281, 325
  for drug crimes, 177, 178, 194, 220,
    237, 255, 263–64, 265–66, 267,
    269, 271–73, 302–3, 325, 341–42
  and espionage cases, 319–20
  for first-time offenders, 263–64, 265,
    267, 303
  goal of, 92
  guidelines for, 192–95, 196–98, 255,
    263, 271–72, 278, 301, 341
  and judicial discretion, 192–95,
    196–98, 263, 267
  mandatory, 92, 194–95, 196–98, 220,
    263, 267, 273, 274, 351
  for nonviolent crimes, 220, 264, 267,
    269
  and presidential powers, 111
  and prosecutors, 195, 196–98, 271,
    273, 274
  and racketeering, 278
  reconsideration of, 237
  reduction in, 319–20
  and violent crimes, 264, 265, 269
  of Wachtler, 115–16, 172, 350
  and who should be in prisons, 263
Sex, and love, 83–87
Sex offenders, 93–97
Shapiro, Elsie (mother-in-law), 16, 122,
    123
Shaw, George Bernard, 77
Sheraw, Don, 64
Silverman, Joy
  breakup between Wachtler and, 5, 9,
    329
  extortion of, 18, 100, 101
  and F.B.I. surveillance of Wachtler,
    14–15, 18, 104
  letters from Wachtler to, 5, 13–16, 18,
    196

and "O'Connor plan," 15–16, 17
and "Purdy plan," 6, 7, 13–18
and Samson relationship, 13–14, 16, 329
Wachtler as trustee of trust for, 3
Wachtler's relationship with, 3, 6
Wachtler's reflections about, 77, 101–2, 315
Wise's letter about, 83
and Wolfe's *Double Life* book, 314
Simon (Rochester inmate), 158
Simpson, O. J., 291–92, 294
Slotnick, Barry, 138
Snitches
as acceptable behavior, 79
and Blumberg case, 200
and entrapment, 88
and food boycott at Rochester, 323
"kingpins" as, 273
prisoners' views about, 238, 253
and Wiley case, 325
See also Cooperation
Solitary confinement
and Auburn system, 222
and confessions, 170
as "cruel and unusual" punishment, 30–32
Dominic in, 79
and food boycott at Rochester, 323
Goland in, 202
Jamal in, 241–42
Pollard in, 112
Simon in, 158
Tony in, 74
visitors for people in, 131
Wachtler in Butner, 30–38, 42, 52, 112, 119–22, 124–29, 130–33, 140–42, 146–47, 335
Wachtler in Rochester, 150
young offenders in, 55
Solomon, Sanford, 108–9, 314–15, 352
Speaking engagements, of Wachtler, 347–48, 350–51, 352
Spitzer, Robert, 315
Stabbing of Wachtler, 118–22, 124–29, 130–32, 140, 141–42, 146, 150, 334–35, 336

State Justice Institute, 288
State prisons, 221, 246
Stewart, Potter, 181
Strickland (inmate), 241
Strip searches
at Butner prison, 28–29, 32, 82, 140
and individual rights, 28
at Rochester prison, 166
Wachtler's opinions about, 67
Sturman, Reuben, 286–87
Styron, William, 4
"Substantial capacity," 114–15
Suicide/attempted suicide, by prisoners, 69, 79, 113, 225
Sullivan v. The New York Times (1964), 335
Sulzburger, Arthur O. "Punch," 262
Sunday blue laws, 31, 61
Swearing-in ceremonies, 156, 290, 334

T

Talk-radio, 20–21, 326
Teaching, of Wachtler, 343, 348–50
Telephone calls, for prisoners, 295–96
Tenuate, 4, 9, 10, 13, 97–98
Terpac, Carl, 257–59, 260
Thanksgiving dinners, 129, 130–31
Thompson, Angela, 263–64, 267
Thompson, Anne, 26
Tigar, Michael, 247
Tisch, R. Preston, 352
Tocqueville, Alexis de, 221
"Tommy" (Kipling poem), 260
Touched by Fire (Jamison), 19
Trainor, Mike, 234
Travel Act, 294–95
Treatment facilities, 267–68
Trinchera, Dominick (Big Trin), 282
Tuberculosis, 246

U

UNICOR, 243–44
UNISAT, 244, 320
Unisom, 9, 13
United States Sentencing Commission, 178, 192

United States Supreme Court
   and defendants' rights, 191
   and grand juries, 294
   and press standard of responsibility,
      335–36
Urban vigilantism, 135–39
Urine testing, 66–68

V

Vance, Cyrus, 333
Veterans, as prisoners, 257–59, 260
Victims of crime, 191
Villanell, Frankie (executive assistant),
   108, 180
Violence, and reform of prisoners,
   219–20
Violent crimes
   decrease in, 350–51
   drug-related, 264, 266, 351
   increase in, 191
   and purpose of prisons, 22, 266–67
   sentencing for, 264, 265, 269
Vogt, Thomas Dean, 339–42

W

Wachtler, Faye (mother), 7, 8, 102,
   229–30, 305–7
Wachtler, Joan (wife), 130, 140, 147, 57,
   181, 233–34, 243
   and arrest of Wachtler, 102, 107,
      108
   Butner visits by, 79–80, 82, 131, 132,
      134
   education of, 123
   letter to Judge Thompson from, 26
   marriage of, 122–23
   and release of Wachtler, 345
   Rochester visits by, 154–55, 164, 166,
      231
   and stabbing of Wachtler, 121–22,
      127–28
   support for Wachtler by, 26, 107, 108,
      109
   and Wachtler's appointment as Chief
      Judge, 64, 65
   and Wachtler's depression, 7, 8

and Wachtler's preparation for going
   to prison, 25
and Wolfe's Double Life book, 314
Wachtler, Kimberly (granddaughter),
   231, 232
Wachtler, Morty (brother)
   and arrest of Wachtler, 102, 107
   Butner visits by, 134
   childhood/youth of, 85, 87, 306
   marriage of, 122
   Rochester visits by, 228
   Wachtler's relationship with, 85,
      228–30
Wachtler, Philip (son)
   and arrest of Wachtler, 102, 107, 108,
      109–10
   Butner visits by, 131, 134
   and release of Wachtler, 345
   Rochester visits by, 154–55, 164, 231
   and strength of Wachtler in prison, 91
   and Wachtler's preparation for going
      to prison, 25
Wachtler, Robin (daughter-in-law), 147,
   231
Wachtler, Sol
   as athlete, 305, 306–11, 312
   birthdays of, 231–32
   childhood/youth of, 42–51, 83–84,
      228–30, 305–11
   education of, 306–7
   future of, 352–53
   legal career of, 60–65, 143–45
   marriage of, 122–23
   military service of, 44, 97, 123–24,
      143, 171, 197, 233–34, 343
   reasons for seeking public service of,
      336–39
Wachtler v. Cuomo, 332–34
Wages, of prisoners, 243–44, 327
Wall Street Journal, 273
Ward, Benjamin, 213–18
Wardens. See Prison officials
Warren, Earl, 191
Weeks v. United States, 206
Weinberger, Caspar, 111
Weinstein, Jack, 333
West Side Unlimited Corporation,
   339–40

Westrick, Ruth, 150, 181, 182
Whalen, William Henry, 320
Wiley, Jeff, 324–25
Wilkinson v. Skinner, 30–32
Wilpon, Fred, 231, 352
"Windows" trial (1991), 275–76, 277
Wiretaps
    and organized crime, 276, 282–83
    on telephone calls of prisoners, 296
    on Wachtler, 14–15, 18, 104
Wise, Max, 83

Witness (Chambers), 59–60
Wolfe, Linda, 314, 315
Wolfe, Tom, 59, 292

Y

Yoke, 223

Z

Zavali, Michael, 317

About the Author

SOL WACHTLER began his government career in 1963, when he was elected a councilman of the town of North Hempstead. He was appointed to the New York State Supreme Court in 1968 and elected to the Court of Appeals, New York's highest court, in 1972. In 1985, he was appointed Chief Judge of the State of New York and the Court of Appeals. He lives in Manhasset, New York, with his wife, Joan. They have four children and seven grandchildren.

About the Type

This book was set in Electra, a typeface designed for Linotype by W. A. Dwiggins, the renowned type designer (1880–1956). Electra is a fluid typeface, avoiding the contrasts of thick and thin strokes that are prevalent in most modern typefaces.